ACA Ethical Standards Casebook

Sixth Edition

Barbara Herlihy
University of New Orleans

Gerald Corey
California State University, Fullerton

AMERICAN COUNSELING ASSOCIATION
5999 Stevenson Avenue
Alexandria, VA 22304
www.counseling.org

ACA
Ethical Standards Casebook

Sixth Edition

10 9 8 7 6

American Counseling Association
5999 Stevenson Avenue
Alexandria, VA 22304

Director of Publications
Carolyn C. Baker

Production Manager
Bonny E. Gaston

Copyeditor
Kay Mikel

Cover and text design by Bonny E. Gaston.

Library of Congress Cataloging-in-Publication Data
Herlihy, Barbara.
ACA ethical standards casebook/Barbara Herlihy, Gerald Corey.—6th ed.
p. cm.
Includes bibliographical references.
ISBN 1-55620-255-5 (alk. paper)
ISBN13: 978-1-55620-255-1
1. American Counseling Association. 2. Counseling—Moral and ethical aspects—United States. 3. Counselors—Professional ethics—United States. 4. Counseling—Moral and ethical aspects—United States—Case studies. 5. Counselors—Professional ethics—United States—Case studies. I. Corey, Gerald. II. Title.

BF637.C6A37 2006
174´.91583—dc22 2005025160

Dedication

To ZEW, whose compass is true.

—BH

To Heidi Jo and Cindy, stalwart skippers in all kinds of weather.

—JC

And to our student readers—the next generation of counseling professionals who will guide us through some uncharted waters.

—BH & JC

Contents

Acknowledgments

This sixth edition of the casebook is truly the product of the collaborative efforts of many people over time.

Many individuals contributed to the development of the 2005 *ACA Code of Ethics.* The ACA Ethics Code Revision Taskforce worked from 2002 until mid-2005 to develop proposed revisions to the 1995 *Code of Ethics and Standards of Practice.* The taskforce was chaired by Michael M. Kocet, and members were John W. Bloom, R. Rocco Cottone, Harriet L. Glosoff, Barbara Herlihy, Courtland C. Lee, Judith G. Miranti, and E. Christine Moll. Student note-takers Anna Harpster and Michael Hartley assisted throughout the process. Many ACA members also gave helpful input during the comment period for the draft of the *Code.* Although we cannot thank them all by name, this is their book too.

We thank the following doctoral students at the University of New Orleans who contributed some of the illustrative vignettes that appear in Part III: Jamison Davis, Stephanie Hall, Bianca Puglia, and Daniel Stroud.

It has been a joy to work with the capable and conscientious publications staff at ACA. Carolyn Baker's prompt and careful attention throughout the production process is greatly appreciated, as always. We also appreciate the talents of Kay Mikel who copyedited this book.

About the Authors

Barbara Herlihy, PhD, NCC, LPC, is a professor of counselor education at the University of New Orleans. She has served on the ACA Ethics Committee as chair (1987–1989) and as a member (1986–1987, 1993–1994), and as a member of the Ethics Code Revision Taskforce (2002–2005). She is the coauthor of five previous books on ethical issues in counseling: *Ethical, Legal, and Professional Issues in Counseling,* 2nd edition (2005), with Ted Remley; *Boundary Issues in Counseling* (1997, 2006), the *ACA Ethical Standards Casebook,* 5th edition (1996), and *Dual Relationships in Counseling* (1992), all with Gerald Corey; and the *ACA Ethical Standards Casebook,* 4th edition (1990), with Larry Golden. She is also the author or coauthor of more than 65 journal articles and book chapters on ethics, multicultural counseling, feminist therapy, supervision, and other topics. She is a frequent presenter of seminars and workshops on ethics across the United States and internationally.

Gerald Corey, EdD, ABPP, NCC, is a professor emeritus of human services and counseling at California State University at Fullerton, and an adjunct professor of counseling and family sciences at Loma Linda University. He is a Diplomate in Counseling Psychology; a licensed psychologist; and a Fellow of the American Counseling Association, the Association for Specialists in Group Work, and the American Psychological Association. He has authored or coauthored 15 textbooks in counseling that are currently in print, and approximately 58 journal articles and book chapters. Among his coauthored books are *Issues and Ethics in the Helping Professions,* with Marianne Schneider Corey and Patrick Callanan. In the past 25 years the Coreys have conducted workshops for mental health professionals and students at many universities in the United States as well as in Mexico, Canada, Ireland, Germany, Belgium, Scotland, China, and Korea.

About the Contributors

Adriane G. Bennett, MA, is a doctoral candidate in the Department of Psychology at the University of Akron.

Walter Breaux III, PhD, is an assistant professor of counseling at Columbus State University.

Karen Daboval, MEd, NCC, is a doctoral candidate in the Counselor Education Program at the University of New Orleans.

Beth A. Durodoye, EdD, is an associate professor of counseling and guidance at the University of Texas at San Antonio, and was a member of the ACA Ethics Committee 1993–1996.

Holly Forester-Miller, PhD, is president of Wellness Consultants International, PLLC, and was cochair of the ACA Ethics Committee 1995–1997.

Jorge Garcia, PhD, is a professor of counseling at George Washington University, and was cochair of the ACA Ethics Committee 1993–1995.

Harriet L. Glosoff, PhD, is an associate professor and director of the Counselor Education Program at the University of Virginia, and cochair of the ACA Ethics Committee from 2003–2006.

Larry Golden, PhD, is an associate professor of counseling and guidance at the University of Texas at San Antonio, and was a member of the ACA Ethics Committee 1987–1993.

Mary A. Hermann, JD, PhD, is an assistant professor in the Department of Counselor Education at Mississippi State University, and is a member of the ACA Ethics Committee 2004–2006.

Michael M. Kocet, PhD, is an assistant professor of Counselor Education at Bridgewater State College and was cochair of the ACA Ethics Committee 2002–2004.

Courtland C. Lee, PhD, is a professor in the Counselor Education Program at the University of Maryland, and is past president of the American Counseling Association 1997–1998.

Mary E. Moline, PhD, is chair and professor in the Department of Counseling and Family Sciences at Loma Linda University.

Gerra Wellman Perkins, MEd, NCC, is a doctoral candidate in the Counselor Education Program at the University of New Orleans.

Mark Salo, MEd, NCC, is a counselor at Sacajewea Middle School in Bozeman, Montana, and was cochair of the ACA Ethics Committee 1994–1996.

Danielle Shareef, MEd, NCC, NCSC, is a doctoral candidate in the Counselor Education Program at the University of New Orleans.

Zarus E. Watson, PhD, is an associate professor in the Counselor Education Program at the University of New Orleans.

James L. Werth Jr., PhD, is an associate professor in the Department of Psychology at the University of Akron.

George T. Williams, EdD, is a professor in the Department of Counseling at The Citadel.

Robert E. Wubbolding, EdD, is professor emeritus of counseling at Xavier University, Cincinnati, Ohio, and director of the Center for Reality Therapy.

Mary Ellen Young, PhD, CRC, is in private practice as a research consultant for Tropical Research, and holds adjunct faculty appointments in rehabilitation counseling at the University of Florida, the University of North Florida, and Western Washington University.

Making the Best Use of the *Casebook*

We hope that both students and seasoned practitioners of counseling will find this casebook to be a valuable resource. We believe the casebook can be effectively utilized in an ethics course or in a practicum or internship experience to help future members of our profession learn about their ethical responsibilities and ways to address ethical dilemmas. The incidents that illustrate the standards help to clarify their intent and provide examples of appropriate practice.

The 10 chapters in this book examine an array of ethical issues: client rights and informed consent, ethical issues in multicultural counseling, confidentiality, competence, working with multiple clients, counseling minor clients, avoiding detrimental multiple relationships, working with clients who may harm themselves, counselor education and supervision, and the relationship between law and ethics.

Each of the 10 chapters is followed by two case studies that illustrate some of the issues examined in the chapter. Each case study presents an ethical dilemma and is followed by questions for thought and discussion, an analysis of the case, and additional questions for further reflection. Students have often told us that they had never thought about certain ethical questions until they were confronted with cases that raised difficult issues or posed dilemmas that could not be neatly resolved. This casebook gives students an opportunity to examine many ethical issues before they confront them in practice. As you read each of the case studies, put yourself in the role of a consultant to the professional described in the case. If this person were to consult you regarding the case, what would you want to say? You can also assume the role of the counselor, student, supervisor, or professor in the case and reflect on how you might deal with the situation.

For experienced counselors, we hope that the casebook serves as a vehicle for continuing education and that you use the material to further your aspirational ethics. As you read, reflect, and discuss the material with your colleagues, ask yourselves "How can I best monitor my own behavior?" "How can I apply relevant standards to situations I encounter?" "How can I develop increased ethical sensitivity?" "How can I ensure that I am thinking about what is best for my clients, my students, or my supervisees?"

We believe that ethics is best viewed from a developmental perspective. We may look at issues in one way as students; later, with time and experience, our views are likely to have evolved. Ethical reasoning takes on new meaning as we encounter a variety of ethical dilemmas. Professional maturity entails our willingness to question ourselves, to discuss our doubts with colleagues, and to engage in continual self-monitoring.

Part I

Introduction

Introduction

Evolution of the ACA Ethical Standards and the *Casebook*

Soon after the American Personnel and Guidance Association (APGA) was formed in 1952, it was recognized that a group of practitioners cannot actually be considered a profession without an established code of ethics (Allen, 1986). In 1953 Donald Super, then president of this new association, charged a committee to develop a code of ethics. Work was commenced, and 8 years later, in 1961, the first code of ethics for APGA was adopted. In 1963 the Ethics Committee began to solicit and compile incidents having ethical implications that could illustrate the standards. The first edition of the *Ethical Standards Casebook* was published in 1965, 4 years after the ethical standards were adopted.

About 1972 it was recognized that the ethical standards needed to be revised, and that the casebook would also require revision. Two committees were appointed to work simultaneously: one to revise the standards and the other to collect illustrative incidents for the casebook. The revised *APGA Ethical Standards* were adopted in 1974, and a single editor collated the collected incidents and prepared the second edition of the casebook, which was published in 1976.

The *APGA Ethical Standards* were again revised and a new code was adopted in 1981. The editor of the second edition of the casebook prepared the third edition with the assistance of two coeditors. This third edition was published in 1982. The association, then the American Association for Counseling and Development (AACD), adopted another revision of the code of ethics in 1988. Soon after the adoption of the revised code, the chair and a member of the Ethics Committee undertook the revision of the casebook. Input was solicited from a wide variety of sources to determine what changes were needed in the casebook to maximize its usefulness. The fourth edition was published in 1990.

An extensive revision of the ethical standards was embarked upon during the fall of 1991, with several goals in mind: (1) to develop a comprehensive set of ethical standards, (2) to produce a user-friendly document, and (3) to conduct an open revision process that would allow all ACA members opportunities to provide input. The need for a comprehensive set of standards grew out of a concern that there had been a proliferation of ethics documents for counselors. Historically the ACA ethical standards were generic and did not include the unique concerns of ACA divisions, and as a result, several divisions had published their own ethical guidelines. National voluntary certifying bodies that credential counselors as well as the counselor licensure boards in various states also had established their own codes of ethics. The existence of multiple codes of ethics created a situation that was confusing both for professional counselors and for consumers of our services (Herlihy & Remley, 1995). Therefore, the Ethics Committee carefully studied the ethics documents of ACA divisions and of other mental health professional associations, with the goal of incorporating standards applicable to all counselors into a single, comprehensive document. The 1995 *Code of Ethics and Standards of Practice* was the end result of this process.

A second need was to reorganize the ACA ethical standards into a more readable format. The result was a new organization that included sections on the counseling relationship; confidentiality; professional responsibility; relationships with other professionals; evaluation, assessment, and interpretation; teaching, training, and supervision; research and publication; and resolving ethical issues.

Finally, the Ethics Committee wanted to have an inclusive revision process, providing members, leaders, and relevant professional groups opportunity for input and suggestions. A first draft of the proposed revised ethical standards was presented to the membership in September 1993 and underwent a lengthy comment period. A second draft that reflected input and suggestions was presented a year later, in September and October 1994. A final version was adopted in April 1995 and went into effect on July 1, 1995.

At the beginning of the revision process, applications for the position of editor of the fifth edition of the casebook were solicited, the editors were selected by the ACA Media Committee, and work was begun on the casebook in conjunction with the standards revision process. The fifth edition of the casebook was published in 1996.

In 2002 David Kaplan, then president of ACA, appointed an ACA Ethics Code Revision Taskforce to once again revise and update the ethics code. In the following section Michael M. Kocet, Chair of that Taskforce, describes the process that was used to revise the *Code,* highlights major changes that were made, and offers a personal perspective on the revision process.

The 2005 *ACA Code of Ethics*

Michael M. Kocet

Selection of members of the ACA Ethics Code Revision Taskforce, appointed in 2002, was based on their professional areas of expertise, scholarly activities, and service to ACA. Several members were either current or past members of the ACA Ethics Committee. The taskforce members were: John Bloom, Tammy Bringaze, Rocco Cottone, Harriet Glosoff, Barbara Herlihy, Michael Kocet (Chair), Courtland Lee, Judy Miranti, Christine Moll, and Vilia Tarvydas. Two graduate students, Anna Harpster and Michael Hartley, served as note-takers throughout the process. The taskforce was given two main charges: (1) propose revisions to the 1995 *ACA Code of Ethics and*

Standards of Practice and (2) make recommendations for changes within the *Code of Ethics* with special (but not exclusive) focus on multiculturalism, diversity, and social justice.

The Revision Process

The taskforce initially met once a month by telephone conference calls and held a face-to-face meeting during the annual ACA convention. Taskforce members communicated regularly using e-mail, as well as a listserv created for the taskforce, which enabled members to continue their work between formal meetings. Smaller "working groups" were created, each of which was responsible for reviewing and creating recommendations for one of the eight main sections of the *Code*. The entire group then reviewed the recommendations of each working group and discussed new additions, changes, and deletions for each section. As work progressed, members of the taskforce met bi-weekly and sometimes on weekends to create a draft *Code of Ethics* that would be made available to the general ACA membership for review and feedback.

During the revision process, multiple formats enabled ACA members to provide feedback and commentary on the work of the taskforce and to give a "voice" to their concerns. A draft *Code of Ethics* was placed in *Counseling Today* as well as on the ACA Web site. An online feedback mechanism enabled members to provide their comments, concerns, and general suggestions in an electronic format. Feedback was also sought by leadership within ACA divisions, state leaders, national counseling leaders, and legal and outside experts to provide input on relevant sections of the draft. Counselor educators used the *Code* revision process as an educational opportunity, assigning graduate students in ethics courses to review the entire draft and write a detailed analysis including input as to its strengths or limitations. Engaging students directly in such an assignment was an excellent learning experience. It helped students become more knowledgeable about the *Code of Ethics* and gave them an opportunity to make a contribution to the profession by providing their own perspectives.

Two town hall meetings were held during the 2004 and 2005 ACA national conventions. Members of the association met with members of the taskforce and discussed highlights of the draft document. Members provided feedback that was instrumental in causing additional changes to be made to the initial draft. Throughout the process of creating the 2005 *ACA Code of Ethics*, input was sought on all levels and through a variety of venues.

It Takes a Village

Reflecting on the process of what it takes to create a code of ethics for the counseling profession reminds me of the African proverb, "It takes a village to raise a child." In this case, it might be more aptly phrased as "it takes a village to create a code of ethics." It took more than 2 years to write, review, revise, discuss, re-revise, and finally approve and implement the *Code*. It truly was a journey—shared by a host of professionals committed to ethical excellence and creating a higher standard of counseling practice that respects the important work that takes place in the counseling relationship. When issues were discussed that were extremely challenging or when divergent perspectives existed, members of the taskforce consulted with experts in the field outside the taskforce and even outside the association who specialized in those issues. Oftentimes, members provided specific recommended language to incorporate into the document. Although members of the Code Revision Taskforce were the primary authors of the 2005 *Code of Ethics,* many hands, minds, and hearts contributed to its creation.

Changes in the 2005 *Code of Ethics*

Although it would be nearly impossible to highlight every change made to the 2005 *ACA Code of Ethics,* a brief overview is provided to acclimate readers to some of the main differences in the new *Code.* The Standards of Practice found in the 1995 document were removed as a separate section and were integrated into the body of the main document. The original intent of the Standards of Practice was to provide members and nonmembers of ACA with a concise outline of the minimum expectations for ethical behavior. This purpose became unclear, however, when it came to actual implementation and use of the document in ethical case adjudications and for personal study and use. An updated Preamble and clearly stated Purposes section are new additions to the 2005 document.

The 1995 *Code of Ethics and Standards of Practice* contained eight main sections, and these have been retained in the 2005 *Code of Ethics,* with slight variations in the titles of the sections: A. The Counseling Relationship; B. Confidentiality, Privileged Communication, and Privacy; C. Professional Responsibility; D. Relationships With Other Professionals; E. Evaluation, Assessment, and Interpretation; F. Supervision, Training, and Teaching; G. Research and Publication; and H. Resolving Ethical Issues. Some key areas new to the 2005 edition are: Potentially Beneficial Interactions (A.5.d.), End-of-Life Care for Terminally Ill Clients (A.9.), Technology Applications (A.12.), Deceased Clients (B.3.f.), Counselor Incapacitation or Termination of Practice (C.2.h.), Historical and Social Prejudices in the Diagnosis of Pathology (E.5.c.), Innovative Theories and Techniques (F.6.f.), use of the term research "participants" rather than "subjects" (Section G), Plagiarism (G.5.b.), and Conflicts Between Ethics and Laws (H.1.b.). The 2005 *Code* also infuses multicultural and diversity issues throughout the document. Readers are encouraged to review the entire 2005 *ACA Code of Ethics* and compare it to the 1995 document to see all the changes that were made.

Prescriptive Versus Aspirational Ethics

An ongoing struggle among the members of the Code Revision Taskforce was how to balance two needs: (1) to create more prescriptive guidelines that clearly demarcate ethical responsibilities of counseling professionals that could be used by the ACA Ethics Committee in the adjudication of ethical violations, and (2) to create a document that helps professionals aspire to a higher level of ethical thought, reflection, and practice. It is impossible to create a code of ethics that addresses every potential ethical dilemma that a counselor might encounter. Therefore, a code of ethics must be, in a sense, a living document that can assist with individual ethical quandaries and be broad enough to encompass many divergent ethical situations. In a new aspirational component in the 2005 *Code,* an Introduction is found at the beginning of each major section. Each aspirational introduction helps to set a tone that encourages readers to reflect on not just the ethical mandates or prescriptiveness of a particular section but also to strive to make ethical decisions that take into account their personal and professional values, along with the cultural and contextual layers of ethical dilemmas.

A Personal Perspective

The opportunity to chair a taskforce responsible for creating the new *Code of Ethics* for the counseling profession has been one of the most rewarding professional experiences of my career. What made the process especially rewarding was being witness to the vast array of knowledge and expertise within the group. During our deliberations, there were many intense and fruitful discussions on a range of ethical issues facing the profession. For example, a paradigm shift is taking place within the profession from a traditional view of dual or multiple relationships as black/white, yes/no, right/wrong to a deeper reflection on the complexities involved in the professional relationships and connections that occur between counselors and clients, counselor educators and students, and supervisors and supervisees. Hence, the new *Code of Ethics* focuses on examining the potential benefits of interactions with clients, students, and supervisees within and outside the clinical setting.

The taskforce had meaningful discussions on end-of-life issues and the ethical conundrum of what role counselors should or should not have when clients present with these issues in the counseling relationship. Some other professional associations intentionally have not addressed end-of-life issues in their codes of ethics. By including end-of-life standards, we hope to foster an open dialogue on this difficult and sensitive issue. To hear ethical and multicultural scholars debate and discuss critical issues of the day was a humbling and rewarding opportunity. During our many telephone conference calls, face-to-face meetings, and e-mail and listserv discussions, consummate mutual respect and admiration were maintained. Even when different viewpoints existed, voices were not raised and strained pauses in conversations did not occur. No one left a meeting disgruntled or upset. This was a testament to the professionalism and dedication that all the members brought to this historic task. For me, our journey as a taskforce was just as meaningful as the document we produced.

In my experience serving on the ACA Ethics Committee and chairing the Ethics Code Revision Taskforce, I have learned that some counseling professionals tend to think about ethics only when they encounter a significant professional ethical dilemma. I have even heard some counselors say that the study of ethics is "boring" or tedious. I sometimes see the look on the faces of graduate students who feel overwhelmed after gaining an initial exposure to the myriad ethical issues facing counselors in all work settings. But, for me, the study and examination of ethics is exciting and rich with intricacies that require many layers of understanding and decision making. Studying ethics is rewarding for the very reason that there are no simple answers. Through consultation, supervision, discussion with colleagues and experts, and our own personal reflection process, we create our own path of truth and strive to create a moral and ethical compass that supports best practices and helps the profession sharpen its collective values and beliefs. Through this process I have learned that a group of counselors who come from a variety of cultural backgrounds and professional perspectives can work together, support one another, and maneuver through differences of opinion with admiration and respect for each other to create a document that will make an impact on the work done by counselors in a variety of settings. It can sometimes be overwhelming to realize that the document we helped create will touch the lives of thousands of counselors and even many more clients, students, research participants, consultees, and supervisees. As counselors, we sometimes question whether the work we do makes a difference. After helping create the *Code of Ethics,* I have learned that the work we all do as counselors does, in fact, make a significant difference, in many ways that we will never even imagine.

Foundations of Codes of Ethics

Ethics codes of organizations of mental health professionals serve a number of purposes. Perhaps their most basic function is to educate members about sound ethical conduct. As professional counselors, we rely on the ethical standards of the American Counseling Association (ACA) to guide us in our work. Reading and reflecting on the standards can help us to expand our awareness, clarify our values, and subsequently inform clients about our professional responsibilities. Applying the standards to our own practices can assist us to raise significant questions, most of which may not have simple or definitive answers. The application of ethical guidelines to particular situations demands a keen ethical sensitivity.

A second function of ethical standards is to provide a mechanism for professional accountability. The ultimate end of a code of ethics is to protect the public. The American Counseling Association, through enforcement of its *Code of Ethics,* holds its members accountable to the standards it has set forth. As professional counselors, we have an obligation not only to monitor our own behavior but also to encourage ethical conduct in our colleagues.

Codes of ethics also can serve as a catalyst for improving practice (Herlihy & Corey, 1994). No ethics code, no matter how lengthy or precisely worded, can address every situation counselors might encounter in their work. Therefore, it is crucial that we read the *Code* with an eye to both its letter and its spirit, and that we strive to understand the intentions that underlie each standard. This requires us to consider both mandatory and aspirational ethics. There is a very real difference between merely following the *Code of Ethics* and living out a commitment to practice with the highest ideals. ***Mandatory ethics*** describes a level of ethical functioning at which counselors merely act in compliance with minimal standards. By complying with these basic *musts* and *must nots,* counselors can meet the letter of the ethical standards of their profession. ***Aspirational ethics*** describes the highest standards of conduct to which professional counselors can aspire, and it requires that we do more. To practice according to aspirational ethics, counselors need to understand the spirit behind the *Code* and the principles on which it rests, and to have a process for reasoning through the ethical dilemmas they encounter.

Two very different but complementary ways of reasoning about ethics are principle ethics and virtue ethics. ***Principle ethics*** traditionally has been espoused in the fields of medicine and bioethics (Cottone & Tarvydas, 2003) as well as by the counseling profession. In this approach, certain moral principles—or generally accepted assumptions or values in society—are seen as fundamental to ethical reasoning. They are viewed as *prima facie* binding; that is, they must always be considered when counselors work to resolve an ethical dilemma. The following five moral principles generally are seen as being essential to counseling practice.

- ***Autonomy*** refers to independence and self-determination. Under this principle, counselors respect the freedom of clients to choose their own directions, make their own choices, and control their own lives. We have an ethical obligation to decrease client dependency and foster independent decision making. We refrain from imposing goals, avoid being judgmental, and are accepting of different values.
- ***Nonmaleficence*** means to do no harm. As counselors, we must take care that our actions do not risk hurting clients, even inadvertently. We have a responsibility to avoid engaging in practices that cause harm or have the potential to result in harm.
- ***Beneficence*** means to promote good, or mental health and wellness. This principle mandates that counselors actively promote the growth and welfare of those they serve.
- ***Justice*** is the foundation of our commitment to fairness in our professional relationships. Justice includes consideration of such factors as quality of services, allocation of time and resources, establishment of fees, and access to counseling services. This principle also refers to the fair treatment of an individual when his or her interests need to be considered in the context of the rights and interests of others.

- ***Fidelity*** means that counselors make honest promises and honor their commitments to clients, students, and supervisees. This principle involves creating a trusting and therapeutic climate in which people can search for their own solutions, and taking care not to deceive or exploit clients.

Principle ethics asks the question "What shall I do?" when faced with an ethical dilemma, whereas virtue ethics addresses the question "Who shall I be?" ***Virtue ethics*** focuses on the *actor* rather than the *action*. Virtue ethicists believe that professional ethics involves more than moral action; it also involves traits of character, or virtues, such as discernment or prudence, respectfulness, integrity, and self-awareness (Jordan & Meara, 1991; Meara, Schmidt, & Day, 1996). Additionally, virtuous counselors recognize the role of emotion in judging ethical conduct and the importance of connectedness to the community. Some writers (Cottone & Tarvydas, 2003; Herlihy & Watson, 2006; Meara et al., 1996) believe that incorporating virtue ethics can provide a more culturally sensitive approach to ethical decision making than can reliance on principle ethics alone.

- ***Discernment or prudence*** involves the exercise of caution and deliberate reflection before taking action, along with foresight regarding possible consequences of any action. Discernment includes a tolerance for ambiguity, which is an essential trait because most ethical dilemmas are fraught with ambiguities. Discernment also involves perspective-taking, which helps counselors to be aware that a client's view of a situation may not be the same as the counselor's view.
- ***Respectfulness*** is a broader term than autonomy, which is a highly individualistic concept (Meara et al., 1996). When working with clients whose cultures are collectivistic or group-oriented, this virtue requires counselors to respect clients on terms that the clients themselves define.
- ***Integrity*** means that counselors have stable, coherent moral values along with active fidelity to those values in judgment and practice (Beauchamp & Childress, 1994).
- ***Self-awareness*** means that counselors know their own assumptions and biases and how these may affect their relationships with clients. This awareness is a prerequisite for effective cross-cultural counseling (Meara et al., 1996).
- ***Acknowledgment of the role of emotion*** in ethical decision making is an important component of the feminist approach to ethics (Rave & Larsen, 1995). Virtue ethicists caution against assuming that emotion clouds reason. Instead, they contend that emotions (such as compassion) can inform reason.
- ***Connectedness with the community*** is rooted in the realization that counseling takes place within a cultural context. Therefore, it is vital that counselors are connected to and understand the norms and values of the communities in which they practice.

Both approaches, principle ethics and virtue ethics, have much to offer as we struggle with ethical issues. Who we are and what we do are equally important considerations in ethical decision making.

Enforcement of the *ACA Code of Ethics*

All ACA members are required to adhere to the *ACA Code of Ethics,* which serves as the basis for processing complaints of ethical violations against members. The ACA Ethics Committee is responsible for adjudicating complaints. Because this aspect of the committee's work is strictly confidential, many ACA members may not be aware of how the committee performs this function. The process of dealing with complaints of unethical behavior is briefly described here. The complete document, *ACA Policies and Procedures for Processing Complaints of Ethical Violations* (2003), is available on the ACA Web site (www.counseling.org).

Dealing With Complaints

The Ethics Committee will consider a complaint if the individual who is the subject of the complaint is a current member of ACA or was a member when the alleged violation(s) occurred. The committee has no jurisdiction over nonmembers; thus, those who file complaints against nonmembers are advised of alternative avenues for addressing their complaints. If any legal action is filed after a complaint has been accepted, all Ethics Committee actions are stayed until the legal action has been concluded.

The Ethics Committee does not act on anonymous complaints. Only written complaints, signed by complainants, are considered. Any individuals who have reason to believe that ACA members have violated the *Code* may initiate complaints.

If you believe that an ACA member has acted or is acting unethically, you have an ethical responsibility to take action (H.2.a.). Your first step should be to try "to resolve the issue informally with the other counselor if feasible, provided such action does not violate confidentiality rights that may be involved (H.2.b.). If informal resolution is not feasible or if it is attempted without success, you should write a letter to the Ethics Committee outlining the nature of the complaint, sign it, and send it in an envelope marked "confidential." You will receive a formal complaint form identifying the ACA ethical standards that may have been violated if the accusations are true. You are asked to sign the complaint (or suggest modifications if needed) and a release-of-information form. With your authorization, the accused member then receives copies of the formal complaint and any evidence or documents you have submitted in support of the complaint.

After the accused member has responded to the charges and all pertinent materials have been gathered, the Ethics Committee deliberates and decides on the complaint. Each complaint is given the most careful consideration. Most complaints are complex, alleging violations of multiple standards and often including a considerable amount of documentation, and discussions of each case are typically lengthy and involved. All perspectives are fully examined before a decision is reached. Decisions are rendered based on the evidence and documents provided by the complainant, accused member, and others. The Ethics Committee has the following options for disposition of a complaint: (1) dismiss the complaint or dismiss charges within the complaint, or (2) determine that ethical standards have been violated and impose sanctions.

Possible sanctions include remedial requirements, a reprimand, probation or suspension for a specified period of time subject to Ethics Committee review of compliance, permanent expulsion from ACA membership, or other corrective action such as successful completion of specific education or training, supervision, and evaluation or treatment. A decision to expel a member requires a unanimous vote. Members found to be in violation may appeal the decision, but only on specific grounds. An Appeals Panel reviews such cases. After the appeals process has been completed or the deadline for appeal has passed, the sanctions of suspension and expulsion are published to the membership.

What to Do If a Complaint Is Filed Against You

Few events can be more distressing for counselors than to learn that they have been formally charged with an ethics violation. Although most counselors spend their lifelong careers without having to deal with this situation, it is wise to be prepared for such an event and know how to respond.

First, *take the complaint seriously*. Although you may believe the charges are unwarranted, it is not in your best interest to ignore them or to respond in a casual manner. Occasionally we have heard counselors make these statements: "Why worry about an ethics complaint to the professional association? The worst that could happen is that I would lose my membership." It is true that the most severe sanction available to the ACA Ethics Committee is permanent expulsion from the association; however, when a sanction of suspension or expulsion is imposed, notifications are made to counselor licensure, certification, or registry boards, other mental health boards, the ACA Insurance Trust, and other entities. This could very well trigger an investigation by a state licensing board that could result in loss of license to practice.

Second, *respond fully to the charges*. You are required to cooperate with the Ethics Committee in its investigation (H.3.). Keep in mind that the Ethics Committee members who will be deciding the outcome of the complaint do not know you personally and can deliberate only on information they have before them. We suggest that you write your response as deliberately and dispassionately as possible. Although you may be tempted to write an emotional, impassioned defense, the committee must deal with the factual material provided. The Ethics Committee is charged to compile an objective, factual account of the dispute and make the best possible recommendation for its resolution.

Attend to the details of the complaint "with scrupulous attention" (Crawford, 1994, p. 92). Gear your response to the specific charges, addressing each section of the *ACA Code of Ethics* you have been accused of violating and submitting documentation. For instance, if you have utilized a powerful or relatively new technique with a client who has filed a complaint, it is useful to submit documentation that you are trained in the specific technique, are working under supervision, have consulted about the case with an expert in the technique, and/or have taken other precautions to prevent harm as specified in the *Code of Ethics.*

Third, even if you are surprised that a client or colleague has made an accusation against you, *do not attempt to contact the complainant* to discuss the situation. Despite your best intentions, doing so could be deemed as an attempt to coerce or unduly influence the client or colleague (Crawford, 1994). Instead, immediately notify your professional liability insurance carrier that a complaint has been made.

Fourth, it is prudent to *consult with an attorney* who can help you prepare your response and provide you with legal counsel. Although an ethics committee is not a court of law, an attorney who is familiar with due process and is skilled at formulating responses to charges of wrongdoing can be a helpful resource. Follow the attorney's advice once you receive it. Having the assistance of an attorney will be crucial if the allegations in the ethical complaint are later used as the basis of a lawsuit against you (Chauvin & Remley, 1996).

Finally, it is vital that you *take care of yourself emotionally* throughout the process. Your reactions to learning that you are the subject of an ethics complaint may include strong emotions such as shock and disbelief, indignation and anger, and fear. Your first impulse may be to unburden yourself to a family member, friend, or colleague for emotional support. If you do this, take care not to divulge the details of the complaint. Remember, you are bound by the same confidentiality requirement toward the accuser as is required with any other client (Chauvin & Remley, 1996). Processing your own emotional reactions with your supervisors or seeking personal counseling (without discussing the details of the complaint) can be important steps in helping you survive the ordeal with your self-confidence and emotional well-being intact.

Developing a Personal Ethical Stance

As we have noted, ethically conscientious counselors require more of themselves than simply following the letter of the ethical standards. Their decisions are not motivated by a desire to avoid charges of unethical or unprofessional conduct but rather by a desire to provide the best possible services to clients, students, or supervisees. Thus, although it is important for us to familiarize ourselves thoroughly with the *Code of Ethics,* it is also necessary for each of us to develop a personal ethical sense. We need to examine our own practices, looking for subtle ways that we might not be acting as ethically as we could. Gross unethical conduct can be detected, and enforcement is possible. Yet there are many less obvious situations in which counselors can fail to do what is appropriate. Here are a few examples of ways counselors might engage in ethically questionable behavior that would be difficult for others to detect and, thus, difficult to enforce:

- Prolonging the number of counseling sessions to satisfy the counselor's emotional needs or financial considerations
- Being unaware of countertransference reactions to a client, student, or supervisee, thus inadvertently increasing resistance and thwarting growth
- Imposing values, goals, or strategies on clients that are not congruent with their cultural background
- Using techniques or strategies that are comfortable for the counselor rather than those that are aimed at helping clients achieve their therapeutic goals
- Practicing with little enthusiasm or tolerating boredom and apathy

As Golden (1992) notes, the work of the counselor is fraught with ambiguities. When we find ourselves navigating in waters not clearly charted by our profession's *Code of Ethics,* we must be guided by an internal ethical compass.

We hope that you use the 2005 *ACA Code of Ethics,* and this casebook, as a means to further your own aspirational ethics. The *Code of Ethics* can help to guide us, but in the final analysis each of us is responsible for our own actions. We must be willing to grapple with the gray areas, raise questions, discuss our ethical concerns with colleagues, and monitor our own behavior.

The Ethical Decision-Making Process

Counselors are often faced with situations that require sound decision-making ability. Determining the appropriate course to take when faced with a difficult ethical dilemma can be a challenge. Because ethical dilemmas can be complex, it helps to have a model or a systematic process to guide one's reasoning. Several ethical decision-making models are available in the literature, including those offered by Corey, Corey, and Callanan (2007); Cottone (2001); Forester-Miller and Davis (1996); Rave and Larsen (1995); Remley and Herlihy (2005); Tarvydas (1998); and Welfel (2006). We urge you to examine them and then select a model or combination of models that works best for you. Although no two of these models are alike, many recommend the following steps in the ethical decision-making process:

1. *Identify the problem.* The first steps in resolving an ethical dilemma are to recognize that a problem exists and then to gather as much information as possible about the situation. Ask yourself whether this is an ethical, legal, professional, or clinical problem. If a legal question exists, it may be necessary to consult an attorney. Try to examine the

problem from several perspectives and avoid searching for simplistic solutions. It is good practice to begin a collaborative process with your client at this initial stage. This collaboration continues throughout the process of working toward an ethical decision, as does the process of documenting your decisions and actions.

2. *Examine the relevant codes of ethics and the professional literature.* Once you have clarified the problem, consult ethics codes to see if the issue is addressed there. If there is an applicable standard or several standards and they are specific and clear, following the course of action indicated may lead to a resolution of the problem. To be able to apply the ethical standards, it is essential that you have read them carefully and that you understand their implications. In addition, reading the recent literature on the particular ethical issue at hand will help ensure that you are using the most current professional knowledge and thinking as you work to resolve the dilemma.
3. *Consider the moral principles of autonomy, nonmaleficence, beneficence, justice, and fidelity.* Decide which principles apply to the situation, and keep in mind that the moral principles can compete with each other and thus suggest different courses of action. In theory, each principle is of equal value, which means that it is your challenge to determine which one takes priority for you in this case.
4. *Consult with colleagues, supervisors, or experts.* Colleagues can be extremely helpful in raising other issues relevant to the situation and in providing a perspective you may have overlooked. They may be able to identify aspects of the dilemma that you are not viewing objectively. Additionally, consultation serves as an important element of your defense in court if your decision is later challenged legally. Consultation is important in court cases because it illustrates an attempt to adhere to community standards by finding out what your colleagues in the community would do in the same situation. It is wise to document your consultations.
5. *Attend to your emotions.* Consider what emotions you are experiencing as you contemplate the situation. Check to see whether you are being influenced by feelings such as fear, self-doubt, frustration, disappointment, or an overwhelming sense of responsibility. Being aware of your emotions can help you assess whether you are seeing the situation accurately.
6. *Involve your client in the decision-making process.* This should occur throughout the process of resolving the dilemma, to the extent possible. Walden (1997, 2006) reminds us that the client is an integral part of the ethical community of the counseling relationship, and that counselors should avoid making decisions *for* the client rather than *with* the client. Clients are empowered when they are active partners in the decision-making process.
7. *Identify desired outcomes and generate potential courses of action.* Even after the most thoughtful consideration, a single desired outcome rarely

emerges in an ethical dilemma. You may find that you want to achieve a number of outcomes; some may be essential and others may be desirable but not necessary. Brainstorm as many possible courses of action as possible. If possible, enlist colleagues to help you generate possibilities that may not have occurred to you.

8. *Consider the potential consequences of all options and determine a course of action.* Consider the information you have gathered and the priorities you have set, evaluate each option, and assess the potential consequences for all parties involved. Ponder the implications of each course of action for the client, for others who will be affected, and for yourself as a counselor. Eliminate the options that clearly do not give the desired results or cause even more problematic consequences. Review the remaining options to determine which option or combination of options best fits the situation and addresses the priorities you and your client have identified.
9. *Evaluate the selected course of action.* Review the selected course of action to determine whether it presents any new ethical considerations. Stadler (1986) suggests applying three simple tests to ensure that the selected course of action is appropriate. In applying the test of justice, assess your own sense of fairness by determining whether you would treat others the same in this situation. For the test of publicity, ask yourself whether you would want your behavior reported in the press. The test of universality asks you to assess whether you could recommend the same course of action to another counselor in the same situation. If you can answer in the affirmative to each of these three tests and are satisfied that you have selected an appropriate course of action, you are ready to move on to implementation. If the course of action you have selected seems to present new ethical issues, you need to go back to the beginning and reevaluate each step of the process. Perhaps you have chosen the wrong option or identified the problem incorrectly.
10. *Implement the course of action.* Taking the appropriate action in an ethical dilemma is often difficult. The final step involves strengthening your ego to allow you to carry out your plan. After implementing your course of action, it is a good practice to follow up on the situation to assess whether your actions had the anticipated effect and consequences.

The procedural steps we have described should not be thought of as a simple linear way to reach a resolution on ethical matters. Ethical decision making is a process that involves a great deal of reflection, collaboration with the client, consultation with colleagues, and courage to make a decision based on this process. There is rarely one right answer to a complex ethical dilemma. However, if you follow a systematic model, you can be assured that you will be able to give a professional explanation for the course of action you chose.

An Inventory of Your Attitudes and Beliefs About Ethical Issues

As a way to encourage you to think critically about the *ACA Code of Ethics,* we have created a self-inventory to help you examine your reactions to many of the ethical issues that are addressed by the *Code.* This inventory is intended to promote critical thinking and to help you identify and assess your beliefs about ethical guidelines. There is no one correct answer to any of the items. For each item, identify the letter (or letters) of the response (or responses) that most accurately identifies your thinking about the issue. If none of the choices seems appropriate to you, write your own response on the blank line. If all of the choices seem appropriate, write "all of the above" on the blank line.

1. The counselor's primary obligation is to
   a. avoid a malpractice suit.
   b. enlist the family's involvement to help the client reach counseling goals.
   c. promote the values of society.
   d. respect the integrity and promote the welfare of the client.
   e. ______________________________.
2. Counselors who work with clients from cultural backgrounds different from their own
   a. are likely to find a referral necessary because of basic conflicts in values.
   b. respect these differences.
   c. do all that they can to gain knowledge about the client.
   d. attempt to influence the client to adjust to the values of society.
   e. ______________________________.
3. It is ethically imperative to secure the client's informed consent
   a. except for clients who are unable to give consent.
   b. except for minor clients.
   c. except for involuntary clients.
   d. for all clients.
   e. ______________________________.
4. Informed consent implies that clients have a right to
   a. expect absolute confidentiality.
   b. have information about counseling explained to them.
   c. refuse any recommended services.
   d. expect a guarantee that counseling will be effective.
   e. ______________________________.
5. Informed consent should be
   a. completed at the first session with a client.
   b. considered to be an ongoing process.
   c. gotten in writing from the client.

d. secured verbally from the client.
e. ________________________________.

6. With respect to the personal values of counselors, it is
   a. sometimes necessary for counselors to impose their values on clients.
   b. essential that counselors understand how their values influence the counseling process.
   c. a good policy for counselors to accept a client only if the client holds values similar to their own.
   d. important that counselors realize how their values and beliefs apply in a diverse society.
   e. ________________________________.
7. Having another relationship with a client (such as also being a friend, employer, or supervisor) is
   a. best avoided whenever possible.
   b. fraught with possibilities for exploitation and therefore is always unethical.
   c. generally unethical, illegal, and unprofessional.
   d. best decided in each situation, by balancing potential risks and benefits.
   e. ________________________________.
8. Sexual intimacies with current clients
   a. are unethical.
   b. are never justified.
   c. may be justified if the client initiates the relationship.
   d. represent a serious exploitation of the client's trust.
   e. ________________________________.
9. Counselors who offer group counseling have an ethical obligation to
   a. conduct a screening interview with potential group members.
   b. protect clients against physical and psychological trauma resulting from interactions within the group.
   c. provide follow-up assistance after termination, if needed.
   d. develop safety measures when using experimental methods.
   e. ________________________________.
10. In establishing fees for counseling services, counselors
    a. consider the financial status of clients in the local area.
    b. decide how much they want to charge and never lower their set fee.
    c. provide a referral for clients who cannot afford their fee.
    d. may engage in bartering with clients who cannot afford the fee.
    e. ________________________________.
11. If counselors determine that they are unable to be of professional assistance to a client,
    a. ethical practice dictates that they terminate the relationship.
    b. they should refer the client.

c. they should discuss the situation with the client.
d. they should continue seeing the client if the client declines a suggested referral.
e. ______________________________.

12. Ethical practice dictates that counselors terminate a counseling relationship when

a. it is reasonably clear that the client is no longer benefiting.
b. counseling services are no longer necessary.
c. counseling no longer serves the client's needs or interests.
d. clients do not pay the fees charged.
e. ______________________________.

13. Counselors demonstrate their respect for privacy of their clients by

a. avoiding unnecessary disclosures of confidential information.
b. recognizing that the right to privacy belongs to counselors and may be waived if it is in the best interests of the client.
c. consulting with another mental health professional when they are unsure about legal exceptions to confidentiality.
d. securing the client's written permission before making any disclosure of confidential information.
e. ______________________________.

14. With respect to records of counseling sessions, counselors

a. have no ethical obligation to maintain unnecessary records.
b. maintain records that are necessary to render quality service to clients.
c. must legally and ethically keep records for 10 years.
d. obtain the client's permission to disclose or transfer records to third parties.
e. ______________________________.

15. Counselors must practice within their boundaries of competence, which implies that they

a. should develop a clearly defined specialty area.
b. take steps to maintain competence in the skills they use.
c. consult with other professionals when they have concerns about ethical and professional practice.
d. practice strictly within the scope of their education and training.
e. ______________________________.

16. When the personal problems or conflicts of counselors are likely to lead to harm to a client, counselors

a. seek assistance for their own problems.
b. may limit, suspend, or terminate their relationship with a client.
c. are honest with the client about their difficulties and engage in detailed self-disclosure with the client.

d. make it a practice to consult with other professionals about the matter.
e. ______________________________.

17. In recruiting clients, counselors should realize
    a. it is acceptable to split fees with another professional who has referred a client to a private practitioner.
    b. they have an ethical right to expect to receive a fee for making a referral to another counselor.
    c. they do not accept fees for referring clients.
    d. they should expect to receive referrals in return when they make referrals to another professional.
    e. ______________________________.
18. It is not ethical for counselors to discriminate based on differences in
    a. age.
    b. sexual orientation.
    c. religion.
    d. culture.
    e. ______________________________.
19. In selecting assessment techniques, making evaluations, and interpreting the performance of special populations, ethical practice involves
    a. proceeding with caution.
    b. recognizing the effects of age, culture, disability, ethnicity, race, gender, religion, sexual orientation, and socioeconomic status on test administration and interpretation.
    c. treating all clients alike to ensure uniformity of practice.
    d. not allowing diversity issues to interfere with the quality of testing procedures.
    e. ______________________________.
20. With respect to nonprofessional interactions with their students, counselor educators
    a. serve as role models for professional behavior.
    b. are aware of the power differential and take steps to minimize any risks to students.
    c. explain to students the potential for such a relationship to become exploitive.
    d. always refrain from getting involved in any kind of dual relationship.
    e. ______________________________.
21. Counselor education programs should provide an orientation session prior to accepting students. The orientation should include information about
    a. the subject matter to be covered in the program.
    b. training components that encourage or require self-growth and self-disclosure as part of the training process.
    c. the history of the counseling profession.

d. up-to-date employment prospects for graduates.
e. ______________________________.

22. It is an ethical responsibility of counselor education programs to
    a. present varied theoretical positions.
    b. teach a single theoretical position to minimize confusion among students about how theory translates into practice.
    c. insist that students master a single theoretical orientation early in their program of study.
    d. provide information about the scientific bases of professional practice.
    e. ______________________________.
23. Regarding self-growth experiences as part of a training program, it is
    a. ethical to grade students on how self-disclosing and genuine they are in their interpersonal relationships in the classroom.
    b. important to develop safeguards so that risks to students are minimized.
    c. essential to have clear purposes in mind and maintain appropriate boundaries.
    d. unethical to use these techniques because students can easily be put into situations that are uncomfortable for them.
    e. ______________________________.
24. In conducting research involving use of human participants, ethical practice demands that counselors
    a. are sensitive to diversity issues with special populations.
    b. use deception only when good research design indicates its value.
    c. seek consultation and develop safeguards to protect the rights of research participants.
    d. obtain adequate informed consent of the research participants.
    e. ______________________________.
25. Involuntary participation in a research project is appropriate only when
    a. it can be demonstrated that participation will have no harmful effects on subjects.
    b. it is essential to the investigation.
    c. the participants are paid.
    d. the researcher is studying ways that involuntary participation might influence outcomes.
    e. ______________________________.
26. In reporting results of research, ethical practice involves
    a. presenting accurate results.
    b. reporting unfavorable results.
    c. disguising the identities of those who participated in the study.
    d. making available enough information so that other researchers could replicate the study.
    e. ______________________________.

27. When counselors have reason to believe that another counselor is violating an ethical standard, an appropriate first step is to
    a. seek informal resolution.
    b. ignore the situation.
    c. report the suspected violation to an ethics committee.
    d. seek out clients of this counselor to discover more details about the suspected behavior.
    e. ________________________________.
28. If a counselor confronts a colleague about a suspected ethical violation and this informal process does not resolve the situation, the appropriate course for the counselor to follow is to
    a. respect the differences of opinion with the colleague.
    b. report the colleague to an ethics committee.
    c. seek consultation from a supervisor.
    d. continue talking with the colleague in hopes of changing his or her behavior.
    e. ________________________________.
29. Counselors who refuse to offer pro bono services by giving some of their time and talent to endeavors for which there is little or no financial return
    a. should be considered unethical.
    b. should cancel their membership in ACA.
    c. are clearly motivated by self-interest and financial gain and should leave the counseling profession.
    d. can be considered ethical if they are financially stressed.
    e. ________________________________.
30. The practice of bartering may be acceptable when
    a. the relationship is not exploitive.
    b. the client requests it.
    c. the counselor feels comfortable with the practice.
    d. a clear contract is established.
    e. ________________________________.
31. My position on bartering with a client in exchange for counseling services is that
    a. it all depends on the circumstances of the individual case.
    b. I would consider this practice if the client had no way to pay for my continued services and was making progress in counseling.
    c. the practice is almost always unethical.
    d. I would seek consultation before agreeing to barter.
    e. ________________________________.
32. If a client were to offer me a gift, I would
    a. generally accept it, so that I would not offend the client by refusing it.

b. never accept it under any circumstances.
c. explore with the client the meaning of the gift.
d. accept the gift only if gift-giving is expected in the client's culture.
e. ______________________________.

33. Regarding the role of spiritual and religious values, as a counselor I would be inclined to
    a. ignore such values for fear that I would impose my own beliefs on my clients.
    b. consider a client's spirituality to be an important aspect of diversity.
    c. avoid bringing up the topic unless my client initiated such a discussion.
    d. conduct an assessment of my client's spiritual and religious beliefs during the intake session.
    e. ______________________________.

34. My position on end-of-life decisions is that I would
    a. always use the principle of a client's self-determination as the key in any decision about this issue.
    b. provide appropriate referral information to ensure that clients receive the necessary help.
    c. examine the options of breaking confidentiality to protect the client or not breaking confidentiality to respect the client's wishes.
    d. encourage my client to find meaning in life, regardless of his or her psychological or physical condition.
    e. ______________________________.

35. I would tend to refer a client to another professional
    a. if I had a major conflict in values with the client.
    b. if I did not have much experience working with the kind of problem the client is presenting.
    c. only as a last resort, after exploring all other options.
    d. if the client questioned whether I would be able to help her or him.
    e. ______________________________.

Part II

ACA Code of Ethics

ACA Code of Ethics

ACA Code of Ethics Preamble

The American Counseling Association is an educational, scientific, and professional organization whose members work in a variety of settings and serve in multiple capacities. ACA members are dedicated to the enhancement of human development throughout the life span. Association members recognize diversity and embrace a cross-cultural approach in support of the worth, dignity, potential, and uniqueness of people within their social and cultural contexts.

Professional values are an important way of living out an ethical commitment. Values inform principles. Inherently held values that guide our behaviors or exceed prescribed behaviors are deeply ingrained in the counselor and developed out of personal dedication, rather than the mandatory requirement of an external organization.

ACA Code of Ethics Purpose

The *ACA Code of Ethics* serves five main purposes:

1. The *Code* enables the association to clarify to current and future members, and to those served by members, the nature of the ethical responsibilities held in common by its members.
2. The *Code* helps support the mission of the association.
3. The *Code* establishes principles that define ethical behavior and best practices of association members.
4. The *Code* serves as an ethical guide designed to assist members in constructing a professional course of action that best serves those utilizing counseling services and best promotes the values of the counseling profession.
5. The *Code* serves as the basis for processing of ethical complaints and inquiries initiated against members of the association.

The *ACA Code of Ethics* contains eight main sections that address the following areas:

Section A: The Counseling Relationship
Section B: Confidentiality, Privileged Communication, and Privacy
Section C: Professional Responsibility
Section D: Relationships With Other Professionals
Section E: Evaluation, Assessment, and Interpretation
Section F: Supervision, Training, and Teaching
Section G: Research and Publication
Section H: Resolving Ethical Issues

Each section of the *ACA Code of Ethics* begins with an Introduction. The introductions to each section discuss what counselors should aspire to with regard to ethical behavior and responsibility. The Introduction helps set the tone for that particular section and provides a starting point that invites reflection on the ethical mandates contained in each part of the *ACA Code of Ethics.*

When counselors are faced with ethical dilemmas that are difficult to resolve, they are expected to engage in a carefully considered ethical decision-making process. Reasonable differences of opinion can and do exist among counselors with respect to the ways in which values, ethical principles, and ethical standards would be applied when they conflict. While there is no specific ethical decision-making model that is most effective, counselors are expected to be familiar with a credible model of decision making that can bear public scrutiny and its application.

Through a chosen ethical decision-making process and evaluation of the context of the situation, counselors are empowered to make decisions that help expand the capacity of people to grow and develop.

A brief glossary is given to provide readers with a concise description of some of the terms used in the *ACA Code of Ethics.*

Section A

The Counseling Relationship

Introduction

Counselors encourage client growth and development in ways that foster the interest and welfare of clients and promote formation of healthy relationships. Counselors actively attempt to understand the diverse cultural backgrounds of the clients they serve. Counselors also explore their own cultural identities and how these affect their values and beliefs about the counseling process.

Counselors are encouraged to contribute to society by devoting a portion of their professional activity to services for which there is little or no financial return (pro bono publico).

A.1. Welfare of Those Served by Counselors

A.1.a. Primary Responsibility

The primary responsibility of counselors is to respect the dignity and to promote the welfare of clients.

A.1.b. Records

Counselors maintain records necessary for rendering professional services to their clients and as required by laws, regulations, or agency or institution procedures. Counselors include sufficient and timely documentation in their client records to facilitate the delivery and continuity of needed services. Counselors take reasonable steps to ensure that documentation in records accurately reflects client progress and services provided. If errors are made in client records, counselors take steps to properly note the correction of such errors according to agency or institutional policies. *(See A.12.g.7., B.6., B.6.g., G.2.j.)*

A.1.c. Counseling Plans

Counselors and their clients work jointly in devising integrated counseling plans that offer reasonable promise of success and are consistent with abilities and circumstances of clients. Counselors and clients regularly review counseling plans to assess their continued viability and effectiveness, respecting the freedom of choice of clients. *(See A.2.a., A.2.d., A.12.g.)*

A.1.d. Support Network Involvement

Counselors recognize that support networks hold various meanings in the lives of clients and consider enlisting the support, understanding, and involvement of others (e.g., religious/spiritual/community leaders, family members, friends) as positive resources, when appropriate, with client consent.

A.1.e. Employment Needs

Counselors work with their clients considering employment in jobs that are consistent with the overall abilities, vocational limitations, physical restrictions, general temperament, interest and aptitude patterns, social skills, education, general qualifications, and other relevant characteristics and needs of clients. When appropriate, counselors appropriately trained in career development will assist in the placement of clients in positions that are consistent with the interest, culture, and the welfare of clients, employers, and/or the public.

A.2. Informed Consent in the Counseling Relationship

(See A.12.g., B.5., B.6.b., E.3., E.13.b., F.1.c., G.2.a.)

A.2.a. Informed Consent

Clients have the freedom to choose whether to enter into or remain in a counseling relationship and need adequate information about the counseling process and the counselor. Counselors have an obligation to review in writing and verbally with clients the rights and responsibilities of both the counselor and the client. Informed consent is an ongoing part of the counseling process, and counselors appropriately document discussions of informed consent throughout the counseling relationship.

A.2.b. Types of Information Needed

Counselors explicitly explain to clients the nature of all services provided. They inform clients about issues such as, but not limited to, the following: the purposes, goals, techniques, procedures, limitations, potential risks, and benefits of services; the counselor's qualifications, credentials, and relevant experience; continuation of services upon the incapacitation or death of a counselor; and other pertinent information. Counselors take steps to ensure that clients understand the implications of diagnosis, the intended use of tests and reports, fees, and billing arrangements. Clients have the right to confidentiality and to be provided with an explanation of its limitations (including how supervisors and/or treatment team professionals are involved); to obtain clear information about their records to participate in the ongoing counseling plans; and to refuse any services or modality change and to be advised of the consequences of such refusal.

A.2.c. Developmental and Cultural Sensitivity

Counselors communicate information in ways that are both developmentally and culturally appropriate. Counselors use clear and understandable language when discussing issues related to informed consent. When clients have difficulty understanding the language used by counselors, they provide necessary services (e.g., arranging for a qualified interpreter or translator) to ensure comprehension by clients. In collaboration with clients, counselors consider cultural implications of informed consent procedures and, where possible, counselors adjust their practices accordingly.

A.2.d. Inability to Give Consent

When counseling minors or persons unable to give voluntary consent, counselors seek the assent of clients to services, and include them in decision making as appropriate. Counselors recognize the need to balance the ethical rights of clients to make choices, their capacity to give consent or assent to receive services, and parental or familial legal rights and responsibilities to protect these clients and make decisions on their behalf.

A.3. Clients Served by Others

When counselors learn that their clients are in a professional relationship with another mental health professional, they request release from clients to inform the other professionals and strive to establish positive and collaborative professional relationships.

A.4. Avoiding Harm and Imposing Values

A.4.a. Avoiding Harm

Counselors act to avoid harming their clients, trainees, and research participants and to minimize or to remedy unavoidable or unanticipated harm.

A.4.b. Personal Values

Counselors are aware of their own values, attitudes, beliefs, and behaviors and avoid imposing values that are inconsistent with counseling goals. Counselors respect the diversity of clients, trainees, and research participants.

A.5. Roles and Relationships With Clients

(See F.3., F.10., G.3.)

A.5.a. Current Clients

Sexual or romantic counselor–client interactions or relationships with current clients, their romantic partners, or their family members are prohibited.

A.5.b. Former Clients

Sexual or romantic counselor–client interactions or relationships with former clients, their romantic partners, or their family members are prohibited for a period of 5 years following the last professional contact. Counselors, before engaging in sexual or romantic interactions or relationships with clients, their romantic partners, or client family members after 5 years following the last professional contact, demonstrate forethought and document (in written form) whether the interactions or relationship can be viewed as exploitive in some way and/or whether there is still potential to harm the former client; in cases of potential exploitation and/or harm, the counselor avoids entering such an interaction or relationship.

A.5.c. Nonprofessional Interactions or Relationships (Other Than Sexual or Romantic Interactions or Relationships)

Counselor–client nonprofessional relationships with clients, former clients, their romantic partners, or their family members should be avoided, except when the interaction is potentially beneficial to the client. *(See A.5.d.)*

A.5.d. Potentially Beneficial Interactions

When a counselor–client nonprofessional interaction with a client or former client may be potentially beneficial to the client or former client, the counselor must document in case records, prior to the interaction (when feasible), the rationale for such an interaction, the potential benefit, and anticipated consequences for the client or former client and other individuals significantly involved with the client or former client. Such interactions should be initiated with appropriate client consent. Where unintentional harm occurs to the client or former client, or to an individual significantly involved with the client or former client, due to the nonprofessional interaction, the counselor must show evidence of an attempt to remedy such harm. Examples of potentially beneficial interactions include, but are not limited to, attending a formal ceremony (e.g., a wedding/commitment ceremony or graduation); purchasing a service or product provided by a client or former client (excepting unrestricted bartering); hospital visits to an ill family member; mutual membership in a professional association, organization, or community. *(See A.5.c.)*

A.5.e. Role Changes in the Professional Relationship

When a counselor changes a role from the original or most recent contracted relationship, he or she obtains informed consent from the client and explains the right of the client to refuse services related to the change. Examples of role changes include

1. changing from individual to relationship or family counseling, or vice versa;
2. changing from a nonforensic evaluative role to a therapeutic role, or vice versa;
3. changing from a counselor to a researcher role (i.e., enlisting clients as research participants), or vice versa; and
4. changing from a counselor to a mediator role, or vice versa.

Clients must be fully informed of any anticipated consequences (e.g., financial, legal, personal, or therapeutic) of counselor role changes.

A.6. Roles and Relationships at Individual, Group, Institutional, and Societal Levels

A.6.a. Advocacy

When appropriate, counselors advocate at individual, group, institutional, and societal levels to examine potential barriers and obstacles that inhibit access and/or the growth and development of clients.

A.6.b. Confidentiality and Advocacy

Counselors obtain client consent prior to engaging in advocacy efforts on behalf of an identifiable client to improve the provision of services and to work toward removal of systemic barriers or obstacles that inhibit client access, growth, and development.

A.7. Multiple Clients

When a counselor agrees to provide counseling services to two or more persons who have a relationship, the counselor clarifies at the outset which person or persons are clients and the nature of the relationships the counselor will have with each involved person. If it becomes apparent that the counselor may be called upon to perform potentially conflicting roles, the counselor will clarify, adjust, or withdraw from roles appropriately. *(See A.8.a., B.4.)*

A.8. Group Work

(See B.4.a.)

A.8.a. Screening

Counselors screen prospective group counseling/therapy participants. To the extent possible, counselors select members whose needs and goals are compatible with goals of the group, who will not impede the group process, and whose well-being will not be jeopardized by the group experience.

A.8.b. Protecting Clients

In a group setting, counselors take reasonable precautions to protect clients from physical, emotional, or psychological trauma.

A.9. End-of-Life Care for Terminally Ill Clients

A.9.a. Quality of Care

Counselors strive to take measures that enable clients

1. to obtain high-quality end-of-life care for their physical, emotional, social, and spiritual needs;
2. to exercise the highest degree of self-determination possible;
3. to be given every opportunity possible to engage in informed decision making regarding their end-of-life care; and
4. to receive complete and adequate assessment regarding their ability to make competent, rational decisions on their own behalf from a mental health professional who is experienced in end-of-life care practice.

A.9.b. Counselor Competence, Choice, and Referral

Recognizing the personal, moral, and competence issues related to end-of-life decisions, counselors may choose to work or not work with terminally ill clients who wish to explore their end-of-life options. Counselors provide appropriate referral information to ensure that clients receive the necessary help.

A.9.c. Confidentiality

Counselors who provide services to terminally ill individuals who are considering hastening their own deaths have the option of breaking or not breaking confidentiality, depending on applicable laws and the specific circumstances of the situation and after seeking consultation or supervision from appropriate professional and legal parties. *(See B.5.c., B.7.c.)*

A.10. Fees and Bartering

A.10.a. Accepting Fees From Agency Clients

Counselors refuse a private fee or other remuneration for rendering services to persons who are entitled to such services through the counselor's employing agency or institution. The policies of a particular agency may make explicit provisions for agency clients to receive counseling services from members of its staff in private practice. In such instances, the clients must be informed of other options open to them should they seek private counseling services.

A.10.b. Establishing Fees

In establishing fees for professional counseling services, counselors consider the financial status of clients and locality. In the event that the established fee structure is inappropriate for a client, counselors assist clients in attempting to find comparable services of acceptable cost.

A.10.c. Nonpayment of Fees

If counselors intend to use collection agencies or take legal measures to collect fees from clients who do not pay for services as agreed upon, they first inform clients of intended actions and offer clients the opportunity to make payment.

A.10.d. Bartering

Counselors may barter only if the relationship is not exploitive or harmful and does not place the counselor in an unfair advantage, if the client requests it, and if such arrangements are an accepted practice among professionals in the community. Counselors consider the cultural implications of bartering and discuss relevant concerns with clients and document such agreements in a clear written contract.

A.10.e. Receiving Gifts

Counselors understand the challenges of accepting gifts from clients and recognize that in some cultures, small gifts are a token of respect and showing gratitude. When determining whether or not to accept a gift from clients, counselors take into account the therapeutic relationship, the monetary value of the gift, a client's motivation for giving the gift, and the counselor's motivation for wanting or declining the gift.

A.11. Termination and Referral

A.11.a. Abandonment Prohibited

Counselors do not abandon or neglect clients in counseling. Counselors assist in making appropriate arrangements for the continuation of treatment, when necessary, during interruptions such as vacations, illness, and following termination.

A.11.b. Inability to Assist Clients

If counselors determine an inability to be of professional assistance to clients, they avoid entering or continuing counseling relationships. Counselors are knowledgeable about culturally and clinically appropriate referral resources and suggest these alternatives. If clients decline the suggested referrals, counselors should discontinue the relationship.

A.11.c. Appropriate Termination

Counselors terminate a counseling relationship when it becomes reasonably apparent that the client no longer needs assistance, is not likely to benefit, or is being harmed by continued counseling. Counselors may terminate counseling when in jeopardy of harm by the client, or another person with whom the client has a relationship, or when clients do not pay fees as agreed upon. Counselors provide pretermination counseling and recommend other service providers when necessary.

A.11.d. Appropriate Transfer of Services

When counselors transfer or refer clients to other practitioners, they ensure that appropriate clinical and administrative processes are completed and open communication is maintained with both clients and practitioners.

A.12. Technology Applications

A.12.a. Benefits and Limitations

Counselors inform clients of the benefits and limitations of using information technology applications in the counseling process and in business/billing procedures. Such technologies include but are not limited to computer hardware and software, telephones, the World Wide Web, the Internet, online assessment instruments, and other communication devices.

A.12.b. Technology-Assisted Services

When providing technology-assisted distance counseling services, counselors determine that clients are intellectually, emotionally, and physically capable of using the application and that the application is appropriate for the needs of clients.

A.12.c. Inappropriate Services

When technology-assisted distance counseling services are deemed inappropriate by the counselor or client, counselors consider delivering services face to face.

A.12.d. Access

Counselors provide reasonable access to computer applications when providing technology-assisted distance counseling services.

A.12.e. Laws and Statutes

Counselors ensure that the use of technology does not violate the laws of any local, state, national, or international entity and observe all relevant statutes.

A.12.f. Assistance

Counselors seek business, legal, and technical assistance when using technology applications, particularly when the use of such applications crosses state or national boundaries.

A.12.g. Technology and Informed Consent

As part of the process of establishing informed consent, counselors do the following:

1. Address issues related to the difficulty of maintaining the confidentiality of electronically transmitted communications.
2. Inform clients of all colleagues, supervisors, and employees, such as Informational Technology (IT) administrators, who might have authorized or unauthorized access to electronic transmissions.
3. Urge clients to be aware of all authorized or unauthorized users including family members and fellow employees who have access to any technology clients may use in the counseling process.
4. Inform clients of pertinent legal rights and limitations governing the practice of a profession over state lines or international boundaries.
5. Use encrypted Web sites and e-mail communications to help ensure confidentiality when possible.
6. When the use of encryption is not possible, counselors notify clients of this fact and limit electronic transmissions to general communications that are not client specific.
7. Inform clients if and for how long archival storage of transaction records are maintained.
8. Discuss the possibility of technology failure and alternate methods of service delivery.
9. Inform clients of emergency procedures, such as calling 911 or a local crisis hotline, when the counselor is not available.
10. Discuss time zone differences, local customs, and cultural or language differences that might impact service delivery.
11. Inform clients when technology-assisted distance counseling services are not covered by insurance. *(See A.2.)*

A.12.h. Sites on the World Wide Web
Counselors maintaining sites on the World Wide Web (the Internet) do the following:

1. Regularly check that electronic links are working and professionally appropriate.
2. Establish ways clients can contact the counselor in case of technology failure.
3. Provide electronic links to relevant state licensure and professional certification boards to protect consumer rights and facilitate addressing ethical concerns.
4. Establish a method for verifying client identity.
5. Obtain the written consent of the legal guardian or other authorized legal representative prior to rendering services in the event the client is a minor child, an adult who is legally incompetent, or an adult incapable of giving informed consent.
6. Strive to provide a site that is accessible to persons with disabilities.
7. Strive to provide translation capabilities for clients who have a different primary language while also addressing the imperfect nature of such translations.
8. Assist clients in determining the validity and reliability of information found on the World Wide Web and other technology applications.

Section B

Confidentiality, Privileged Communication, and Privacy

Introduction

Counselors recognize that trust is a cornerstone of the counseling relationship. Counselors aspire to earn the trust of clients by creating an ongoing partnership, establishing and upholding appropriate boundaries, and maintaining confidentiality. Counselors communicate the parameters of confidentiality in a culturally competent manner.

B.1. Respecting Client Rights

B.1.a. Multicultural/Diversity Considerations
Counselors maintain awareness and sensitivity regarding cultural meanings of confidentiality and privacy. Counselors respect

differing views toward disclosure of information. Counselors hold ongoing discussions with clients as to how, when, and with whom information is to be shared.

B.1.b. Respect for Privacy
Counselors respect client rights to privacy. Counselors solicit private information from clients only when it is beneficial to the counseling process.

B.1.c. Respect for Confidentiality
Counselors do not share confidential information without client consent or without sound legal or ethical justification.

B.1.d. Explanation of Limitations
At initiation and throughout the counseling process, counselors inform clients of the limitations of confidentiality and seek to identify foreseeable situations in which confidentiality must be breached. *(See A.2.b.)*

B.2. Exceptions

B.2.a. Danger and Legal Requirements
The general requirement that counselors keep information confidential does not apply when disclosure is required to protect clients or identified others from serious and foreseeable harm or when legal requirements demand that confidential information must be revealed. Counselors consult with other professionals when in doubt as to the validity of an exception. Additional considerations apply when addressing end-of-life issues. *(See A.9.c.)*

B.2.b. Contagious, Life-Threatening Diseases
When clients disclose that they have a disease commonly known to be both communicable and life threatening, counselors may be justified in disclosing information to identifiable third parties, if they are known to be at demonstrable and high risk of contracting the disease. Prior to making a disclosure, counselors confirm that there is such a diagnosis and assess the intent of clients to inform the third parties about their disease or to engage in any behaviors that may be harmful to an identifiable third party.

B.2.c. Court-Ordered Disclosure
When subpoenaed to release confidential or privileged information without a client's permission, counselors obtain written, informed consent from the client or take steps to prohibit the disclosure or have it limited as narrowly as possible due to potential harm to the client or counseling relationship.

B.2.d. Minimal Disclosure
To the extent possible, clients are informed before confidential information is disclosed and are involved in the disclosure decision-making process. When circumstances require the disclosure of confidential information, only essential information is revealed.

B.3. Information Shared With Others

B.3.a. Subordinates
Counselors make every effort to ensure that privacy and confidentiality of clients are maintained by subordinates, including employees, supervisees, students, clerical assistants, and volunteers. *(See F.1.c.)*

B.3.b. Treatment Teams
When client treatment involves a continued review or participation by a treatment team, the client will be informed of the team's existence and composition, information being shared, and the purposes of sharing such information.

B.3.c. Confidential Settings
Counselors discuss confidential information only in settings in which they can reasonably ensure client privacy.

B.3.d. Third-Party Payers
Counselors disclose information to third-party payers only when clients have authorized such disclosure.

B.3.e. Transmitting Confidential Information
Counselors take precautions to ensure the confidentiality of information transmitted through the use of computers, electronic mail, facsimile machines, telephones, voicemail, answering machines, and other electronic or computer technology. *(See A.12.g.)*

B.3.f. Deceased Clients
Counselors protect the confidentiality of deceased clients, consistent with legal requirements and agency or setting policies.

B.4. Groups and Families

B.4.a. Group Work
In group work, counselors clearly explain the importance and parameters of

confidentiality for the specific group being entered.

B.4.b. Couples and Family Counseling

In couples and family counseling, counselors clearly define who is considered "the client" and discuss expectations and limitations of confidentiality. Counselors seek agreement and document in writing such agreement among all involved parties having capacity to give consent concerning each individual's right to confidentiality and any obligation to preserve the confidentiality of information known.

B.5. Clients Lacking Capacity to Give Informed Consent

B.5.a. Responsibility to Clients

When counseling minor clients or adult clients who lack the capacity to give voluntary, informed consent, counselors protect the confidentiality of information received in the counseling relationship as specified by federal and state laws, written policies, and applicable ethical standards.

B.5.b. Responsibility to Parents and Legal Guardians

Counselors inform parents and legal guardians about the role of counselors and the confidential nature of the counseling relationship. Counselors are sensitive to the cultural diversity of families and respect the inherent rights and responsibilities of parents/guardians over the welfare of their children/charges according to law. Counselors work to establish, as appropriate, collaborative relationships with parents/guardians to best serve clients.

B.5.c. Release of Confidential Information

When counseling minor clients or adult clients who lack the capacity to give voluntary consent to release confidential information, counselors seek permission from an appropriate third party to disclose information. In such instances, counselors inform clients consistent with their level of understanding and take culturally appropriate measures to safeguard client confidentiality.

B.6. Records

B.6.a. Confidentiality of Records

Counselors ensure that records are kept in a secure location and that only authorized persons have access to records.

B.6.b. Permission to Record

Counselors obtain permission from clients prior to recording sessions through electronic or other means.

B.6.c. Permission to Observe

Counselors obtain permission from clients prior to observing counseling sessions, reviewing session transcripts, or viewing recordings of sessions with supervisors, faculty, peers, or others within the training environment.

B.6.d. Client Access

Counselors provide reasonable access to records and copies of records when requested by competent clients. Counselors limit the access of clients to their records, or portions of their records, only when there is compelling evidence that such access would cause harm to the client. Counselors document the request of clients and the rationale for withholding some or all of the record in the files of clients. In situations involving multiple clients, counselors provide individual clients with only those parts of records that related directly to them and do not include confidential information related to any other client.

B.6.e. Assistance With Records

When clients request access to their records, counselors provide assistance and consultation in interpreting counseling records.

B.6.f. Disclosure or Transfer

Unless exceptions to confidentiality exist, counselors obtain written permission from clients to disclose or transfer records to legitimate third parties. Steps are taken to ensure that receivers of counseling records are sensitive to their confidential nature. *(See A.3., E.4.)*

B.6.g. Storage and Disposal After Termination

Counselors store records following termination of services to ensure reasonable future access, maintain records in accordance with state and federal statutes governing records, and dispose of client records and other sensitive materials in a manner that protects client confidentiality. When records are of an artistic nature, counselors obtain client (or guardian) consent with regard to handling of such records or documents. *(See A.1.b.)*

B.6.h. Reasonable Precautions

Counselors take reasonable precautions to protect client confidentiality in the event of the counselor's termination of practice, incapacity, or death. *(See C.2.h.)*

B.7. Research and Training

B.7.a. Institutional Approval

When institutional approval is required, counselors provide accurate information about their research proposals and obtain approval prior to conducting their research. They conduct research in accordance with the approved research protocol.

B.7.b. Adherence to Guidelines

Counselors are responsible for understanding and adhering to state, federal, agency, or institutional policies or applicable guidelines regarding confidentiality in their research practices.

B.7.c. Confidentiality of Information Obtained in Research

Violations of participant privacy and confidentiality are risks of participation in research involving human participants. Investigators maintain all research records in a secure manner. They explain to participants the risks of violations of privacy and confidentiality and disclose to participants any limits of confidentiality that reasonably can be expected. Regardless of the degree to which confidentiality will be maintained, investigators must disclose to participants any limits of confidentiality that reasonably can be expected. *(See G.2.e.)*

B.7.d. Disclosure of Research Information

Counselors do not disclose confidential information that reasonably could lead to the identification of a research participant unless they have obtained the prior consent of the person. Use of data derived from counseling relationships for purposes of training, research, or publication is confined to content that is disguised to ensure the anonymity of the individuals involved. *(See G.2.a., G.2.d.)*

B.7.e. Agreement for Identification

Identification of clients, students, or supervisees in a presentation or publication is permissible only when they have reviewed the material and agreed to its presentation or publication. *(See G.4.d.)*

B.8. Consultation

B.8.a. Agreements

When acting as consultants, counselors seek agreements among all parties involved concerning each individual's rights to confidentiality, the obligation of each individual to preserve confidential information, and the limits of confidentiality of information shared by others.

B.8.b. Respect for Privacy

Information obtained in a consulting relationship is discussed for professional purposes only with persons directly involved with the case. Written and oral reports present only data germane to the purposes of the consultation, and every effort is made to protect client identity and to avoid undue invasion of privacy.

B.8.c. Disclosure of Confidential Information

When consulting with colleagues, counselors do not disclose confidential information that reasonably could lead to the identification of a client or other person or organization with whom they have a confidential relationship unless they have obtained the prior consent of the person or organization or the disclosure cannot be avoided. They disclose information only to the extent necessary to achieve the purposes of the consultation. *(See D.2.d.)*

Section C

Professional Responsibility

Introduction

Counselors aspire to open, honest, and accurate communication in dealing with the public and other professionals. They practice in a non-discriminatory manner within the boundaries of professional and personal competence and have a responsibility to abide by the *ACA Code of Ethics.* Counselors actively participate in local, state, and national associations that foster the development and improvement of counseling. Counselors advocate to promote change at the individual, group, institutional, and societal levels that improves the quality of life for individuals and groups and removes potential barriers to the provision or access of appropriate services being offered. Counselors have a responsibility to the public to engage in counseling practices that are based on rigorous research methodologies. In addition, counselors engage in self-care activities to maintain and promote their emotional, physical, mental, and spiritual well-being to best meet their professional responsibilities.

C.1. Knowledge of Standards

Counselors have a responsibility to read, understand, and follow the *ACA Code of Ethics* and adhere to applicable laws and regulations.

C.2. Professional Competence

C.2.a. Boundaries of Competence

Counselors practice only within the boundaries of their competence, based on their education, training, supervised experience, state and national professional credentials, and appropriate professional experience. Counselors gain knowledge, personal awareness, sensitivity, and skills pertinent to working with a diverse client population. *(See A.9.b., C.4.e., E.2., F.2., F.11.b.)*

C.2.b. New Specialty Areas of Practice

Counselors practice in specialty areas new to them only after appropriate education, training, and supervised experience. While developing skills in new specialty areas, counselors take steps to ensure the competence of their work and to protect others from possible harm. *(See F.6.f.)*

C.2.c. Qualified for Employment

Counselors accept employment only for positions for which they are qualified by education, training, supervised experience, state and national professional credentials, and appropriate professional experience. Counselors hire for professional counseling positions only individuals who are qualified and competent for those positions.

C.2.d. Monitor Effectiveness

Counselors continually monitor their effectiveness as professionals and take steps to improve when necessary. Counselors in private practice take reasonable steps to seek peer supervision as needed to evaluate their efficacy as counselors.

C.2.e. Consultation on Ethical Obligations

Counselors take reasonable steps to consult with other counselors or related professionals when they have questions regarding their ethical obligations or professional practice.

C.2.f. Continuing Education

Counselors recognize the need for continuing education to acquire and maintain a reasonable level of awareness of current scientific and professional information in their fields of activity. They take steps to maintain competence in the skills they use, are open to new procedures, and keep current with the diverse populations and specific populations with whom they work.

C.2.g. Impairment

Counselors are alert to the signs of impairment from their own physical, mental, or emotional problems and refrain from offering or providing professional services when such impairment is likely to harm a client or others. They seek assistance for problems that reach the level of professional impairment, and, if necessary, they limit, suspend, or terminate their professional responsibilities until such time it is determined that they may safely resume their work. Counselors assist colleagues or supervisors in recognizing their own professional impairment and provide consultation and assistance when warranted with colleagues or supervisors showing signs of impairment and intervene as appropriate to prevent imminent harm to clients. *(See A.11.b., F.8.b.)*

C.2.h. Counselor Incapacitation or Termination of Practice

When counselors leave a practice, they follow a prepared plan for transfer of clients and files. Counselors prepare and disseminate to an identified colleague or "records custodian" a plan for the transfer of clients and files in the case of their incapacitation, death, or termination of practice.

C.3. Advertising and Soliciting Clients

C.3.a. Accurate Advertising

When advertising or otherwise representing their services to the public, counselors identify their credentials in an accurate manner that is not false, misleading, deceptive, or fraudulent.

C.3.b. Testimonials

Counselors who use testimonials do not solicit them from current clients nor former clients nor any other persons who may be vulnerable to undue influence.

C.3.c. Statements by Others

Counselors make reasonable efforts to ensure that statements made by others about them or the profession of counseling are accurate.

C.3.d. Recruiting Through Employment

Counselors do not use their places of employment or institutional affiliation to recruit or gain clients, supervisees, or consultees for their private practices.

C.3.e. Products and Training Advertisements

Counselors who develop products related to their profession or conduct workshops or training events ensure that the advertisements concerning these products or events are accurate and disclose adequate information for consumers to make informed choices. *(See C.6.d.)*

C.3.f. Promoting to Those Served

Counselors do not use counseling, teaching, training, or supervisory relationships to promote their products or training events in a manner that is deceptive or would exert undue influence on individuals who may be vulnerable. However, counselor educators may adopt textbooks they have authored for instructional purposes.

C.4. Professional Qualifications

C.4.a. Accurate Representation

Counselors claim or imply only professional qualifications actually completed and correct any known misrepresentations of their qualifications by others. Counselors truthfully represent the qualifications of their professional colleagues. Counselors clearly distinguish between paid and volunteer work experience and accurately describe their continuing education and specialized training. *(See C.2.a.)*

C.4.b. Credentials

Counselors claim only licenses or certifications that are current and in good standing.

C.4.c. Educational Degrees

Counselors clearly differentiate between earned and honorary degrees.

C.4.d. Implying Doctoral-Level Competence

Counselors clearly state their highest earned degree in counseling or closely related field. Counselors do not imply doctoral-level competence when only possessing a master's degree in counseling or a related field by referring to themselves as "Dr." in a counseling context when their doctorate is not in counseling or a related field.

C.4.e. Program Accreditation Status

Counselors clearly state the accreditation status of their degree programs at the time the degree was earned.

C.4.f. Professional Membership

Counselors clearly differentiate between current, active memberships and former memberships in associations. Members of the American Counseling Association must clearly differentiate between professional membership, which implies the possession of at least a master's degree in counseling, and regular membership, which is open to individuals whose interests and activities are consistent with those of ACA but are not qualified for professional membership.

C.5. Nondiscrimination

Counselors do not condone or engage in discrimination based on age, culture, disability, ethnicity, race, religion/spirituality, gender, gender identity, sexual orientation, marital status/partnership, language preference, socioeconomic status, or any basis proscribed by law. Counselors do not discriminate against clients, students, employees, supervisees, or research participants in a manner that has a negative impact on these persons.

C.6.Public Responsibility

C.6.a. Sexual Harassment
Counselors do not engage in or condone sexual harassment. Sexual harassment is defined as sexual solicitation, physical advances, or verbal or nonverbal conduct that is sexual in nature, that occurs in connection with professional activities or roles, and that either

1. is unwelcome, is offensive, or creates a hostile workplace or learning environment, and counselors know or are told this; or
2. is sufficiently severe or intense to be perceived as harassment to a reasonable person in the context in which the behavior occurred.

Sexual harassment can consist of a single intense or severe act or multiple persistent or pervasive acts.

C.6.b. Reports to Third Parties
Counselors are accurate, honest, and objective in reporting their professional activities and judgments to appropriate third parties, including courts, health insurance companies, those who are the recipients of evaluation reports, and others. *(See B.3., E.4.)*

C.6.c. Media Presentations
When counselors provide advice or comment by means of public lectures, demonstrations, radio or television programs, prerecorded tapes, technology-based applications, printed articles, mailed material, or other media, they take reasonable precautions to ensure that

1. the statements are based on appropriate professional counseling literature and practice,
2. the statements are otherwise consistent with the *ACA Code of Ethics*, and
3. the recipients of the information are not encouraged to infer that a professional counseling relationship has been established.

C.6.d. Exploitation of Others
Counselors do not exploit others in their professional relationships. *(See C.3.e.)*

C.6.e. Scientific Bases for Treatment Modalities
Counselors use techniques/ procedures/modalities that are grounded in theory and/or have an empirical or scientific foundation. Counselors who do not must define the techniques/procedures as "unproven" or "developing" and explain the potential risks and ethical considerations of using such techniques/procedures and take steps to protect clients from possible harm. *(See A.4.a., E.5.c., E.5.d.)*

C.7. Responsibility to Other Professionals

C.7.a. Personal Public Statements
When making personal statements in a public context, counselors clarify that they are speaking from their personal perspectives and that they are not speaking on behalf of all counselors or the profession.

Section D

Relationships With Other Professionals

Introduction

Professional counselors recognize that the quality of their interactions with colleagues can influence the quality of services provided to clients. They work to become knowledgeable about colleagues within and outside the field of counseling. Counselors develop positive working relationships and systems of communication with colleagues to enhance services to clients.

D.1. Relationships With Colleagues, Employers, and Employees

D.1.a. Different Approaches

Counselors are respectful of approaches to counseling services that differ from their own. Counselors are respectful of traditions and practices of other professional groups with which they work.

D.1.b. Forming Relationships

Counselors work to develop and strengthen interdisciplinary relations with colleagues from other disciplines to best serve clients.

D.1.c. Interdisciplinary Teamwork

Counselors who are members of interdisciplinary teams delivering multifaceted services to clients keep the focus on how to best serve the clients. They participate in and contribute to decisions that affect the well-being of clients by drawing on the perspectives, values, and experiences of the counseling profession and those of colleagues from other disciplines. *(See A.1.a.)*

D.1.d. Confidentiality

When counselors are required by law, institutional policy, or extraordinary circumstances to serve in more than one role in judicial or administrative proceedings, they clarify role expectations and the parameters of confidentiality with their colleagues. *(See B.1.c., B.1.d., B.2.c., B.2.d., B.3.b.)*

D.1.e. Establishing Professional and Ethical Obligations

Counselors who are members of interdisciplinary teams clarify professional and ethical obligations of the team as a whole and of its individual members. When a team decision raises ethical concerns, counselors first attempt to resolve the concern within the team. If they cannot reach resolution among team members, counselors pursue other avenues to address their concerns consistent with client well-being.

D.1.f. Personnel Selection and Assignment

Counselors select competent staff and assign responsibilities compatible with their skills and experiences.

D.1.g. Employer Policies

The acceptance of employment in an agency or institution implies that counselors are in agreement with its general policies and principles. Counselors strive to reach agreement with employers as to acceptable standards of conduct that allow for changes in institutional policy conducive to the growth and development of clients.

D.1.h. Negative Conditions

Counselors alert their employers of inappropriate policies and practices. They attempt to effect changes in such policies or procedures through constructive action within the organization. When such policies are potentially disruptive or damaging to clients or may limit the effectiveness of services provided and change cannot be effected, counselors take appropriate further action. Such action may include referral to appropriate certification, accreditation, or state licensure organizations, or voluntary termination of employment.

D.1.i. Protection From Punitive Action

Counselors take care not to harass or dismiss an employee who has acted in a responsible and ethical manner to expose inappropriate employer policies or practices.

D.2. Consultation

D.2.a. Consultant Competency

Counselors take reasonable steps to ensure that they have the appropriate resources and competencies when providing consultation services. Counselors provide appropriate referral resources when requested or needed. *(See C.2.a.)*

D.2.b. Understanding Consultees

When providing consultation, counselors attempt to develop with their consultees a clear understanding of problem definition, goals for change, and predicted consequences of interventions selected.

D.2.c. Consultant Goals

The consulting relationship is one in which consultee adaptability and growth toward self-direction are consistently encouraged and cultivated.

D.2.d. Informed Consent in Consultation

When providing consultation, counselors have an obligation to review, in writing and verbally, the rights and responsibilities of both counselors and consultees. Counselors use clear and understandable language to inform all parties involved about the purpose of the services to be provided, relevant costs, potential risks and benefits, and the limits of confidentiality. Working in conjunction with the consultee, counselors attempt to develop a clear definition of the problem, goals for change, and predicted consequences of interventions that are culturally responsive and appropriate to the needs of consultees. *(See A.2.a., A.2.b.)*

Section E

Evaluation, Assessment, and Interpretation

Introduction

Counselors use assessment instruments as one component of the counseling process, taking into account the client personal and cultural context. Counselors promote the well-being of individual clients or groups of clients by developing and using appropriate educational, psychological, and career assessment instruments.

E.1. General

E.1.a. Assessment

The primary purpose of educational, psychological, and career assessment is to provide measurements that are valid and reliable in either comparative or absolute terms. These include, but are not limited to, measurements of ability, personality, interest, intelligence, achievement, and performance. Counselors recognize the need to interpret the statements in this section as applying to both quantitative and qualitative assessments.

E.1.b. Client Welfare

Counselors do not misuse assessment results and interpretations, and they take reasonable steps to prevent others from misusing the information these techniques provide. They respect the client's right to know the results, the interpretations made, and the bases for counselors' conclusions and recommendations.

E.2. Competence to Use and Interpret Assessment Instruments

E.2.a. Limits of Competence

Counselors utilize only those testing and assessment services for which they have been trained and are competent. Counselors using technology-assisted test interpretations are trained in the construct being measured and the specific instrument being used prior to using its technology-based application. Counselors take reasonable measures to ensure the proper use of psychological and career assessment techniques by persons under their supervision. *(See A.12.)*

E.2.b. Appropriate Use

Counselors are responsible for the appropriate application, scoring, interpretation, and use of assessment instruments relevant to the needs of the client, whether they score and interpret such assessments themselves or use technology or other services.

E.2.c. Decisions Based on Results

Counselors responsible for decisions involving individuals or policies that are based on assessment results have a thorough understanding of educational, psychological, and career measurement, including validation criteria, assessment research, and guidelines for assessment development and use.

E.3. Informed Consent in Assessment

E.3.a. Explanation to Clients

Prior to assessment, counselors explain the nature and purposes of assessment and the specific use of results by potential recipients. The explanation will be given in the language of the client (or other legally authorized person on behalf of the client), unless an explicit exception has been agreed upon in advance. Counselors consider the client's personal or cultural context, the level of the client's understanding of the results, and the impact of the results on the client. *(See A.2., A.12.g., F.1.c.)*

E.3.b. Recipients of Results

Counselors consider the examinee's welfare, explicit understandings, and prior agreements in determining who receives the assessment results. Counselors include accurate and appropriate interpretations with any release of individual or group assessment results. *(See B.2.c., B.5.)*

E.4. Release of Data to Qualified Professionals

Counselors release assessment data in which the client is identified only with the consent of the client or the client's legal representative. Such data are released only to persons recognized by counselors as qualified to interpret the data. *(See B.1., B.3., B.6.b.)*

E.5. Diagnosis of Mental Disorders

E.5.a. Proper Diagnosis

Counselors take special care to provide proper diagnosis of mental disorders. Assessment techniques (including personal interview) used to determine client care (e.g., locus of treatment, type of treatment, or recommended follow-up) are carefully selected and appropriately used.

E.5.b. Cultural Sensitivity

Counselors recognize that culture affects the manner in which clients' problems are defined. Clients' socioeconomic and cultural experiences are considered when diagnosing mental disorders. *(See A.2.c.)*

E.5.c. Historical and Social Prejudices in the Diagnosis of Pathology

Counselors recognize historical and social prejudices in the misdiagnosis and pathologizing of certain individuals and groups and the role of mental health professionals in perpetuating these prejudices through diagnosis and treatment.

E.5.d. Refraining From Diagnosis

Counselors may refrain from making and/or reporting a diagnosis if they believe it would cause harm to the client or others.

E.6. Instrument Selection

E.6.a. Appropriateness of Instruments

Counselors carefully consider the validity, reliability, psychometric limitations, and appropriateness of instruments when selecting assessments.

E.6.b. Referral Information

If a client is referred to a third party for assessment, the counselor provides specific referral questions and sufficient objective data about the client to ensure that appropriate assessment instruments are utilized. *(See A.9.b., B.3.)*

E.6.c. Culturally Diverse Populations

Counselors are cautious when selecting assessments for culturally diverse populations to avoid the use of instruments that lack appropriate psychometric properties for the client population. *(See A.2.c., E.5.b.)*

E.7. Conditions of Assessment Administration

(See A.12.b, A.12.d.)

E.7.a. Administration Conditions

Counselors administer assessments under the same conditions that were established in their standardization. When assessments are not administered under standard conditions, as may be necessary to accommodate clients with disabilities, or when unusual behavior or irregularities occur during the administration, those conditions are noted in interpretation, and the results may be designated as invalid or of questionable validity.

E.7.b. Technological Administration

Counselors ensure that administration programs function properly and provide clients with accurate results when technological or other electronic methods are used for assessment administration.

E.7.c. Unsupervised Assessments

Unless the assessment instrument is designed, intended, and validated for self-administration and/or scoring, counselors do not permit inadequately supervised use.

E.7.d. Disclosure of Favorable Conditions

Prior to administration of assessments, conditions that produce most favorable assessment results are made known to the examinee.

E.8. Multicultural Issues/ Diversity in Assessment

Counselors use with caution assessment techniques that were normed on populations other than that of the client. Counselors recognize the effects of age, color, culture, disability, ethnic group, gender, race, language preference, religion, spirituality, sexual orientation, and socioeconomic status on test administration and interpretation, and place test results in proper perspective with other relevant factors. *(See A.2.c., E.5.b.)*

E.9. Scoring and Interpretation of Assessments

E.9.a. Reporting

In reporting assessment results, counselors indicate reservations that exist regarding validity or reliability due to circumstances of the assessment or the inappropriateness of the norms for the person tested.

E.9.b. Research Instruments

Counselors exercise caution when interpreting the results of research instruments not having sufficient technical data to support respondent results. The specific purposes for the use of such instruments are stated explicitly to the examinee.

E.9.c. Assessment Services

Counselors who provide assessment scoring and interpretation services to support the assessment process confirm the validity of such interpretations. They accurately describe the purpose, norms, validity, reliability, and applications of the procedures and any special qualifications applicable to their use. The public offering of an automated test interpretations service is considered a professional-to-professional consultation. The formal responsibility of the consultant is to the consultee, but the ultimate and overriding responsibility is to the client. *(See D.2.)*

E.10. Assessment Security

Counselors maintain the integrity and security of tests and other assessment techniques consistent with legal and contractual obligations. Counselors do not appropriate, reproduce, or modify published assessments or parts thereof without acknowledgment and permission from the publisher.

E.11. Obsolete Assessments and Outdated Results

Counselors do not use data or results from assessments that are obsolete or outdated for the current purpose. Counselors make every effort to prevent the misuse of obsolete measures and assessment data by others.

E.12. Assessment Construction

Counselors use established scientific procedures, relevant standards, and current professional knowledge for assessment design in the development, publication, and utilization of educational and psychological assessment techniques.

E.13. Forensic Evaluation: Evaluation for Legal Proceedings

E.13.a. Primary Obligations

When providing forensic evaluations, the primary obligation of counselors is to produce objective findings that can be substantiated based on information and techniques appropriate to the evaluation, which may include examination of the individual and/or review of records. Counselors are entitled to form professional opinions based on their professional knowledge and expertise that can be supported by the data gathered in evaluations. Counselors will define the limits of their reports or testimony, especially when an examination of the individual has not been conducted.

E.13.b. Consent for Evaluation

Individuals being evaluated are informed in writing that the relationship is for the purposes of an evaluation and is not counseling in nature, and entities or individuals who will receive the evaluation report are identified. Written consent to be evaluated is obtained from those being evaluated unless a court orders evaluations to be conducted without the written consent of individuals being evaluated. When children or vulnerable adults are being evaluated, informed written consent is obtained from a parent or guardian.

E.13.c. Client Evaluation Prohibited

Counselors do not evaluate individuals for forensic purposes they currently counsel or individuals they have counseled in the past. Counselors do not accept as counseling clients individuals they are evaluating or individuals they have evaluated in the past for forensic purposes.

E.13.d. Avoid Potentially Harmful Relationships

Counselors who provide forensic evaluations avoid potentially harmful professional or personal relationships with family members, romantic partners, and close friends of individuals they are evaluating or have evaluated in the past.

Section F

Supervision, Training, and Teaching

Introduction

Counselors aspire to foster meaningful and respectful professional relationships and to maintain appropriate boundaries with supervisees and students. Counselors have theoretical and pedagogical foundations for their work and aim to be fair, accurate, and honest in their assessments of counselors-in-training.

F.1. Counselor Supervision and Client Welfare

F.1.a. Client Welfare

A primary obligation of counseling supervisors is to monitor the services provided by other counselors or counselors-in-training. Counseling supervisors monitor client welfare and supervisee clinical performance and professional development. To fulfill these obligations, supervisors meet regularly with supervisees to review case notes, samples of clinical work, or live observations. Supervisees have a responsibility to understand and follow the *ACA Code of Ethics*.

F.1.b. Counselor Credentials

Counseling supervisors work to ensure that clients are aware of the qualifications of the supervisees who render services to the clients. *(See A.2.b.)*

F.1.c. Informed Consent and Client Rights

Supervisors make supervisees aware of client rights including the protection of client privacy and confidentiality in the counseling relationship. Supervisees provide clients with professional disclosure information and inform them of how the supervision process influences the limits of confidentiality. Supervisees make clients aware of who will have access to records of the counseling relationship and how these records will be used. *(See A.2.b., B.1.d.)*

F.2. Counselor Supervision Competence

F.2.a. Supervisor Preparation

Prior to offering clinical supervision services, counselors are trained in supervision methods and techniques. Counselors who offer clinical supervision services regularly pursue continuing education activities including both counseling and supervision topics and skills. *(See C.2.a., C.2.f.)*

F.2.b. Multicultural Issues/ Diversity in Supervision

Counseling supervisors are aware of and address the role of multiculturalism/ diversity in the supervisory relationship.

F.3. Supervisory Relationships

F.3.a. Relationship Boundaries With Supervisees

Counseling supervisors clearly define and maintain ethical professional, personal, and social relationships with their supervisees. Counseling supervisors avoid nonprofessional relationships with current supervisees. If supervisors must assume other professional roles (e.g., clinical and administrative supervisor, instructor) with supervisees, they work to minimize potential conflicts and explain to supervisees the expectations and responsibilities associated with each role. They do not engage in any form of nonprofessional interaction that may compromise the supervisory relationship.

F.3.b. Sexual Relationships

Sexual or romantic interactions or relationships with current supervisees are prohibited.

F.3.c. Sexual Harassment

Counseling supervisors do not condone or subject supervisees to sexual harassment. *(See C.6.a.)*

F.3.d. Close Relatives and Friends

Counseling supervisors avoid accepting close relatives, romantic partners, or friends as supervisees.

F.3.e. Potentially Beneficial Relationships

Counseling supervisors are aware of the power differential in their relationships with supervisees. If they believe nonprofessional relationships with a supervisee may be potentially beneficial to the supervisee, they take precautions similar to those taken by counselors when working with clients. Examples of potentially beneficial interactions or relationships include attending a formal ceremony; hospital visits; providing support during a stressful event; or mutual membership in a professional association, organization, or community. Counseling supervisors engage in open discussions with supervisees when they consider entering into relationships with them outside of their roles as clinical and/or administrative supervisors. Before engaging in nonprofessional relationships, supervisors discuss with supervisees and document the rationale for such interactions, potential benefits or drawbacks, and anticipated consequences for the supervisee. Supervisors clarify the specific nature and limitations of the additional role(s) they will have with the supervisee.

F.4. Supervisor Responsibilities

F.4.a. Informed Consent for Supervision

Supervisors are responsible for incorporating into their supervision the principles of informed consent and participation. Supervisors inform supervisees of the policies and procedures to which they are to adhere and the mechanisms for due process appeal of individual supervisory actions.

F.4.b. Emergencies and Absences

Supervisors establish and communicate to supervisees procedures for contacting them or, in their absence, alternative on-call supervisors to assist in handling crises.

F.4.c. Standards for Supervisees

Supervisors make their supervisees aware of professional and ethical standards and legal responsibilities. Supervisors of postdegree counselors encourage these counselors to adhere to professional standards of practice. *(See C.1.)*

F.4.d. Termination of the Supervisory Relationship

Supervisors or supervisees have the right to terminate the supervisory relationship with adequate notice. Reasons for withdrawal are provided to the other party. When cultural, clinical, or professional issues are crucial to the viability of the supervisory relationship, both parties make efforts to resolve differences. When termination is warranted, supervisors make appropriate referrals to possible alternative supervisors.

F.5. Counseling Supervision Evaluation, Remediation, and Endorsement

F.5.a. Evaluation

Supervisors document and provide supervisees with ongoing performance appraisal and evaluation feedback and schedule periodic formal evaluative sessions throughout the supervisory relationship.

F.5.b. Limitations

Through ongoing evaluation and appraisal, supervisors are aware of the limitations of supervisees that might impede performance. Supervisors assist supervisees in securing remedial assistance when needed. They recommend dismissal from training programs, applied counseling settings, or state or voluntary professional credentialing processes when those supervisees are unable to provide competent professional services. Supervisors seek consultation and document their decisions to dismiss or refer supervisees for assistance. They ensure that supervisees are aware of options available to them to address such decisions. *(See C.2.g.)*

F.5.c. Counseling for Supervisees

If supervisees request counseling, supervisors provide them with acceptable referrals. Counselors do not provide counseling services to supervisees. Supervisors address interpersonal competencies in terms of the impact of these issues on clients, the supervisory relationship, and professional functioning. *(See F.3.a.)*

F.5.d. Endorsement

Supervisors endorse supervisees for certification, licensure, employment, or completion of an academic or training program only when they believe supervisees are qualified for the endorsement. Regardless of qualifications, supervisors do not endorse supervisees whom they believe to be impaired in any way that would interfere with the performance of the duties associated with the endorsement.

F.6. Responsibilities of Counselor Educators

F.6.a. Counselor Educators

Counselor educators who are responsible for developing, implementing, and supervising educational programs are skilled as teachers and practitioners. They are knowledgeable regarding the ethical, legal, and regulatory aspects of the profession, are skilled in applying that knowledge, and make students and supervisees aware of their responsibilities. Counselor educators conduct counselor education and training programs in an ethical manner and serve as role models for professional behavior. *(See C.1., C.2.a., C.2.c.)*

F.6.b. Infusing Multicultural Issues/Diversity

Counselor educators infuse material related to multiculturalism/diversity into all courses and workshops for the development of professional counselors.

F.6.c. Integration of Study and Practice

Counselor educators establish education and training programs that integrate academic study and supervised practice.

F.6.d. Teaching Ethics

Counselor educators make students and supervisees aware of the ethical responsibilities and standards of the profession and the ethical responsibilities of students to the profession. Counselor educators infuse ethical considerations throughout the curriculum. *(See C.1.)*

F.6.e. Peer Relationships

Counselor educators make every effort to ensure that the rights of peers are not compromised when students or supervisees lead counseling groups or provide clinical supervision. Counselor educators take steps to ensure that students and supervisees understand they have the same ethical obligations as counselor educators, trainers, and supervisors.

F.6.f. Innovative Theories and Techniques

When counselor educators teach counseling techniques/procedures that are innovative, without an empirical foundation, or without a well-grounded theoretical foundation, they define the counseling techniques/procedures as "unproven" or "developing" and explain to students the potential risks and ethical considerations of using such techniques/procedures.

F.6.g. Field Placements

Counselor educators develop clear policies within their training programs regarding field placement and other clinical experiences. Counselor educators provide clearly stated roles and responsibilities for the student or supervisee, the site supervisor, and the program supervisor. They confirm that site supervisors are qualified to provide supervision and inform site supervisors of their professional and ethical responsibilities in this role.

F.6.h. Professional Disclosure

Before initiating counseling services, counselors-in-training disclose their status as students and explain how this status affects the limits of confidentiality.

Counselor educators ensure that the clients at field placements are aware of the services rendered and the qualifications of the students and supervisees rendering those services. Students and supervisees obtain client permission before they use any information concerning the counseling relationship in the training process. *(See A.2.b.)*

F.7. Student Welfare

F.7.a. Orientation

Counselor educators recognize that orientation is a developmental process that continues throughout the educational and clinical training of students. Counseling faculty provide prospective students with information about the counselor education program's expectations:

1. The type and level of skill and knowledge acquisition required for successful completion of the training
2. Program training goals, objectives, and mission, and subject matter to be covered
3. Bases for evaluation
4. Training components that encourage self-growth or self-disclosure as part of the training process
5. The type of supervision settings and requirements of the sites for required clinical field experiences
6. Student and supervisee evaluation and dismissal policies and procedures
7. Up-to-date employment prospects for graduates

F.7.b. Self-Growth Experiences

Counselor education programs delineate requirements for self-disclosure or self-growth experiences in their admission and program materials. Counselor educators use professional judgment when designing training experiences they conduct that require student and supervisee self-growth or self-disclosure. Students and supervisees are made aware of the ramifications their self-disclosure may have when counselors whose primary role as teacher, trainer, or supervisor requires acting on ethical obligations to the profession. Evaluative components of experiential training experiences explicitly delineate predetermined academic standards that are separate and do not depend on the student's level of self-disclosure. Counselor educators may require trainees to seek professional help to address any personal concerns that may be affecting their competency.

F.8. Student Responsibilities

F.8.a. Standards for Students

Counselors-in-training have a responsibility to understand and follow the *ACA Code of Ethics* and adhere to applicable laws, regulatory policies, and rules and policies governing professional staff behavior at the agency or placement setting. Students have the same obligation to clients as those required of professional counselors. *(See C.1., H.1.)*

F.8.b. Impairment

Counselors-in-training refrain from offering or providing counseling services when their physical, mental, or emotional problems are likely to harm a client or others. They are alert to the signs of impairment, seek assistance for problems, and notify their program supervisors when they are aware that they are unable to effectively provide services. In addition, they seek appropriate professional services for themselves to remediate the problems that are interfering with their ability to provide services to others. *(See A.1., C.2.d., C.2.g.)*

F.9. Evaluation and Remediation of Students

F.9.a. Evaluation

Counselors clearly state to students, prior to and throughout the training program, the levels of competency expected, appraisal methods, and timing of evaluations for both didactic and clinical competencies. Counselor educators provide students with ongoing performance appraisal and evaluation feedback throughout the training program.

F.9.b. Limitations

Counselor educators, throughout ongoing evaluation and appraisal, are aware of and address the inability of some students to achieve counseling competencies that might impede performance. Counselor educators

1. assist students in securing remedial assistance when needed,
2. seek professional consultation and document their decision to dismiss or refer students for assistance, and
3. ensure that students have recourse in a timely manner to address decisions to require them to seek assistance or to dismiss them and provide students with due process according to institutional policies and procedures. *(See C.2.g.)*

F.9.c. Counseling for Students
If students request counseling or if counseling services are required as part of a remediation process, counselor educators provide acceptable referrals.

F. 10. Roles and Relationships Between Counselor Educators and Students

F.10.a. Sexual or Romantic Relationships
Sexual or romantic interactions or relationships with current students are prohibited.

F.10.b. Sexual Harassment
Counselor educators do not condone or subject students to sexual harassment. *(See C.6.a.)*

F.10.c. Relationships With Former Students
Counselor educators are aware of the power differential in the relationship between faculty and students. Faculty members foster open discussions with former students when considering engaging in a social, sexual, or other intimate relationship. Faculty members discuss with the former student how their former relationship may affect the change in relationship.

F.10.d. Nonprofessional Relationships
Counselor educators avoid nonprofessional or ongoing professional relationships with students in which there is a risk of potential harm to the student or that may compromise the training experience or grades assigned. In addition, counselor educators do not accept any form of professional services, fees, commissions, reimbursement, or remuneration from a site for student or supervisee placement.

F.10.e. Counseling Services
Counselor educators do not serve as counselors to current students unless this is a brief role associated with a training experience.

F.10.f. Potentially Beneficial Relationships
Counselor educators are aware of the power differential in the relationship between faculty and students. If they believe a nonprofessional relationship with a student may be potentially beneficial to the student, they take precautions similar to those taken by counselors when working with clients. Examples of potentially beneficial interactions or relationships include, but are not limited to, attending a formal ceremony; hospital visits; providing support during a stressful event; or mutual membership in a professional association, organization, or community. Counselor educators engage in open discussions with students when they consider entering into relationships with students outside of their roles as teachers and supervisors. They discuss with students the rationale for such interactions, the potential benefits and drawbacks, and the anticipated consequences for the student. Educators clarify the specific nature and limitations of the additional role(s) they will have with the student prior to engaging in a nonprofessional relationship. Nonprofessional relationships with students should be time-limited and initiated with student consent.

F.11. Multicultural/Diversity Competence in Counselor Education and Training Programs

F.11.a. Faculty Diversity
Counselor educators are committed to recruiting and retaining a diverse faculty.

F.11.b. Student Diversity
Counselor educators actively attempt to recruit and retain a diverse student body. Counselor educators demonstrate commitment to multicultural/diversity competence by recognizing and valuing diverse cultures and types of abilities students bring to the training experience. Counselor educators provide appropriate accommodations that enhance and support diverse student well-being and academic performance.

F.11.c. Multicultural/Diversity Competence
Counselor educators actively infuse multicultural/diversity competency in their training and supervision practices. They actively train students to gain awareness, knowledge, and skills in the competencies of multicultural practice. Counselor educators include case examples, role-plays, discussion questions, and other classroom activities that promote and represent various cultural perspectives.

Section G

Research and Publication

Introduction

Counselors who conduct research are encouraged to contribute to the knowledge base of the profession and promote a clearer understanding of the conditions that lead to a healthy and more just society. Counselors support efforts of researchers by participating fully and willingly whenever possible. Counselors minimize bias and respect diversity in designing and implementing research programs.

G.1. Research Responsibilities

G.1.a. Use of Human Research Participants
Counselors plan, design, conduct, and report research in a manner that is consistent with pertinent ethical principles, federal and state laws, host institutional regulations, and scientific standards governing research with human research participants.

G.1.b. Deviation From Standard Practice
Counselors seek consultation and observe stringent safeguards to protect the rights of research participants when a research problem suggests a deviation from standard or acceptable practices.

G.1.c. Independent Researchers
When independent researchers do not have access to an Institutional Review Board (IRB), they should consult with researchers who are familiar with IRB procedures to provide appropriate safeguards.

G.1.d. Precautions to Avoid Injury
Counselors who conduct research with human participants are responsible for the welfare of participants throughout the research process and should take reasonable precautions to avoid causing injurious psychological, emotional, physical, or social effects to participants.

G.1.e. Principal Researcher Responsibility
The ultimate responsibility for ethical research practice lies with the principal researcher. All others involved in the research activities share ethical obligations and responsibility for their own actions.

G.1.f. Minimal Interference
Counselors take reasonable precautions to avoid causing disruptions in the lives of research participants that could be caused by their involvement in research.

G.1.g. Multicultural/Diversity Considerations in Research
When appropriate to research goals, counselors are sensitive to incorporating research procedures that take into account cultural considerations. They seek consultation when appropriate.

G.2. Rights of Research Participants

(See A.2., A.7.)

G.2.a. Informed Consent in Research
Individuals have the right to consent to become research participants. In seeking consent, counselors use language that

1. accurately explains the purpose and procedures to be followed,

2. identifies any procedures that are experimental or relatively untried,
3. describes any attendant discomforts and risks,
4. describes any benefits or changes in individuals or organizations that might be reasonably expected,
5. discloses appropriate alternative procedures that would be advantageous for participants,
6. offers to answer any inquiries concerning the procedures,
7. describes any limitations on confidentiality,
8. describes the format and potential target audiences for the dissemination of research findings, and
9. instructs participants that they are free to withdraw their consent and to discontinue participation in the project at any time without penalty.

G.2.b. Deception

Counselors do not conduct research involving deception unless alternative procedures are not feasible and the prospective value of the research justifies the deception. If such deception has the potential to cause physical or emotional harm to research participants, the research is not conducted, regardless of prospective value. When the methodological requirements of a study necessitate concealment or deception, the investigator explains the reasons for this action as soon as possible during the debriefing.

G.2.c. Student/Supervisee Participation

Researchers who involve students or supervisees in research make clear to them that the decision regarding whether or not to participate in research activities does not affect one's academic standing or supervisory relationship. Students or supervisees who choose not to participate in educational research are provided with an appropriate alternative to fulfill their academic or clinical requirements.

G.2.d. Client Participation

Counselors conducting research involving clients make clear in the informed consent process that clients are free to choose whether or not to participate in research activities. Counselors take necessary precautions to protect clients from adverse consequences of declining or withdrawing from participation.

G.2.e. Confidentiality of Information

Information obtained about research participants during the course of an investigation is confidential. When the possibility exists that others may obtain access to such information, ethical research practice requires that the possibility, together with the plans for protecting confidentiality, be explained to participants as a part of the procedure for obtaining informed consent.

G.2.f. Persons Not Capable of Giving Informed Consent

When a person is not capable of giving informed consent, counselors provide an appropriate explanation to, obtain agreement for participation from, and obtain the appropriate consent of a legally authorized person.

G.2.g. Commitments to Participants

Counselors take reasonable measures to honor all commitments to research participants. *(See A.2.c.)*

G.2.h. Explanations After Data Collection

After data are collected, counselors provide participants with full clarification of the nature of the study to remove any misconceptions participants might have regarding the research. Where scientific or human values justify delaying or withholding information, counselors take reasonable measures to avoid causing harm.

G.2.i. Informing Sponsors

Counselors inform sponsors, institutions, and publication channels regarding research procedures and outcomes. Counselors ensure that appropriate bodies and authorities are given pertinent information and acknowledgment.

G.2.j. Disposal of Research Documents and Records

Within a reasonable period of time following the completion of a research project or study, counselors take steps to destroy records or documents (audio, video, digital, and written) containing confidential data or information that identifies research participants. When records are of an artistic nature, researchers obtain participant consent with regard to handling of such records or documents. *(See B.4.a., B.4.g.)*

G.3. Relationships With Research Participants (When Research Involves Intensive or Extended Interactions)

G.3.a. Nonprofessional Relationships

Nonprofessional relationships with research participants should be avoided.

G.3.b. Relationships With Research Participants

Sexual or romantic counselor–research participant interactions or relationships with current research participants are prohibited.

G.3.c. Sexual Harassment and Research Participants

Researchers do not condone or subject research participants to sexual harassment.

G.3.d. Potentially Beneficial Interactions

When a nonprofessional interaction between the researcher and the research participant may be potentially beneficial, the researcher must document, prior to the interaction (when feasible), the rationale for such an interaction, the potential benefit, and anticipated consequences for the research participant. Such interactions should be initiated with appropriate consent of the research participant. Where unintentional harm occurs to the research participant due to the nonprofessional interaction, the researcher must show evidence of an attempt to remedy such harm.

G.4. Reporting Results

G.4.a. Accurate Results

Counselors plan, conduct, and report research accurately. They provide thorough discussions of the limitations of their data and alternative hypotheses. Counselors do not engage in misleading or fraudulent research, distort data, misrepresent data, or deliberately bias their results. They explicitly mention all variables and conditions known to the investigator that may have affected the outcome of a study or the interpretation of data. They describe the extent to which results are applicable for diverse populations.

G.4.b. Obligation to Report Unfavorable Results

Counselors report the results of any research of professional value. Results that reflect unfavorably on institutions, programs, services, prevailing opinions, or vested interests are not withheld.

G.4.c. Reporting Errors

If counselors discover significant errors in their published research, they take reasonable steps to correct such errors in a correction erratum, or through other appropriate publication means.

G.4.d. Identity of Participants

Counselors who supply data, aid in the research of another person, report research results, or make original data available take due care to disguise the identity of respective participants in the absence of specific authorization from the participants to do otherwise. In situations where participants self-identify their involvement in research studies, researchers take active steps to ensure that data are adapted/changed to protect the identity and welfare of all parties and that discussion of results does not cause harm to participants.

G.4.e. Replication Studies

Counselors are obligated to make available sufficient original research data to qualified professionals who may wish to replicate the study.

G.5. Publication

G.5.a. Recognizing Contributions

When conducting and reporting research, counselors are familiar with and give recognition to previous work on the topic, observe copyright laws, and give full credit to those to whom credit is due.

G.5.b. Plagiarism

Counselors do not plagiarize; that is, they do not present another person's work as their own work.

G.5.c. Review/Republication of Data or Ideas
Counselors fully acknowledge and make editorial reviewers aware of prior publication of ideas or data where such ideas or data are submitted for review or publication.

G.5.d. Contributors
Counselors give credit through joint authorship, acknowledgment, footnote statements, or other appropriate means to those who have contributed significantly to research or concept development in accordance with such contributions. The principal contributor is listed first, and minor technical or professional contributions are acknowledged in notes or introductory statements.

G.5.e. Agreement of Contributors
Counselors who conduct joint research with colleagues or students/supervisees establish agreements in advance regarding allocation of tasks, publication credit, and types of acknowledgment that will be received.

G.5.f. Student Research
For articles that are substantially based on students' course papers, projects, dissertations or theses, and on which students have been the primary contributors, they are listed as principal authors.

G.5.g. Duplicate Submission
Counselors submit manuscripts for consideration to only one journal at a time. Manuscripts that are published in whole or in substantial part in another journal or published work are not submitted for publication without acknowledgment and permission from the previous publication.

G.5.h. Professional Review
Counselors who review material submitted for publication, research, or other scholarly purposes respect the confidentiality and proprietary rights of those who submitted it. Counselors use care to make publication decisions based on valid and defensible standards. Counselors review article submissions in a timely manner and based on their scope and competency in research methodologies. Counselors who serve as reviewers at the request of editors or publishers make every effort to only review materials that are within their scope of competency and use care to avoid personal biases.

Section H
Resolving Ethical Issues

Introduction
Counselors behave in a legal, ethical, and moral manner in the conduct of their professional work. They are aware that client protection and trust in the profession depend on a high level of professional conduct. They hold other counselors to the same standards and are willing to take appropriate action to ensure that these standards are upheld.

Counselors strive to resolve ethical dilemmas with direct and open communication among all parties involved and seek consultation with colleagues and supervisors when necessary. Counselors incorporate ethical practice into their daily professional work. They engage in ongoing professional development regarding current topics in ethical and legal issues in counseling.

H.1. Standards and the Law
(See F.9.a.)

H.1.a. Knowledge
Counselors understand the *ACA Code of Ethics* and other applicable ethics codes from other professional organizations or from certification and licensure bodies of which they are members. Lack of knowledge or misunderstanding of an ethical responsibility is not a defense against a charge of unethical conduct.

H.1.b. Conflicts Between Ethics and Laws
If ethical responsibilities conflict with law, regulations, or other governing legal authority, counselors make known their commitment to the *ACA Code of Ethics* and take steps to resolve the conflict. If the conflict cannot be resolved by such means, counselors may adhere to the requirements of law, regulations, or other governing legal authority.

H.2. Suspected Violations

H.2.a. Ethical Behavior Expected
Counselors expect colleagues to adhere

to the *ACA Code of Ethics.* When counselors possess knowledge that raises doubts as to whether another counselor is acting in an ethical manner, they take appropriate action. *(See H.2.b., H.2.c.)*

H.2.b. Informal Resolution

When counselors have reason to believe that another counselor is violating or has violated an ethical standard, they attempt first to resolve the issue informally with the other counselor if feasible, provided such action does not violate confidentiality rights that may be involved.

H.2.c. Reporting Ethical Violations

If an apparent violation has substantially harmed, or is likely to substantially harm, a person or organization and is not appropriate for informal resolution or is not resolved properly, counselors take further action appropriate to the situation. Such action might include referral to state or national committees on professional ethics, voluntary national certification bodies, state licensing boards, or to the appropriate institutional authorities. This standard does not apply when an intervention would violate confidentiality rights or when counselors have been retained to review the work of another counselor whose professional conduct is in question.

H.2.d. Consultation

When uncertain as to whether a particular situation or course of action may be in violation of the *ACA Code of Ethics,* counselors consult with other counselors who are knowledgeable about ethics and the *ACA Code of Ethics,* with colleagues, or with appropriate authorities

H.2.e. Organizational Conflicts

If the demands of an organization with which counselors are affiliated pose a conflict with the *ACA Code of Ethics,* counselors specify the nature of such conflicts and express to their supervisors or other responsible officials their commitment to the *ACA Code of Ethics.* When possible, counselors work toward change within the organization to allow full adherence to the *ACA Code of Ethics.* In doing so, they address any confidentiality issues.

H.2.f. Unwarranted Complaints

Counselors do not initiate, participate in, or encourage the filing of ethics complaints that are made with reckless disregard or willful ignorance of facts that would disprove the allegation.

H.2.g. Unfair Discrimination Against Complainants and Respondents

Counselors do not deny persons employment, advancement, admission to academic or other programs, tenure, or promotion based solely upon their having made or their being the subject of an ethics complaint. This does not preclude taking action based upon the outcome of such proceedings or considering other appropriate information.

H.3. Cooperation With Ethics Committees

Counselors assist in the process of enforcing the *ACA Code of Ethics.* Counselors cooperate with investigations, proceedings, and requirements of the ACA Ethics Committee or ethics committees of other duly constituted associations or boards having jurisdiction over those charged with a violation. Counselors are familiar with the *ACA Policies and Procedures for Processing Complaints of Ethical Violations* and use it as a reference for assisting in the enforcement of the *ACA Code of Ethics.*

Glossary of Terms

Advocacy – promotion of the well-being of individuals and groups, and the counseling profession within systems and organizations. Advocacy seeks to remove barriers and obstacles that inhibit access, growth, and development.

Assent – to demonstrate agreement, when a person is otherwise not capable or competent to give formal consent (e.g., informed consent) to a counseling service or plan.

Client – an individual seeking or referred to the professional services of a counselor for help with problem resolution or decision making.

Counselor – a professional (or a student who is a counselor-in-training) engaged in a counseling practice or other counseling-related services. Counselors fulfill many roles and responsibilities such as counselor educators, researchers, supervisors, practitioners, and consultants.

Counselor Educator – a professional counselor engaged primarily in developing, implementing, and supervising the educational preparation of counselors-in-training.

Counselor Supervisor – a professional counselor who engages in a formal relationship with a practicing counselor or counselor-in-training for the purpose of overseeing that individual's counseling work or clinical skill development.

Culture – membership in a socially constructed way of living, which incorporates collective values, beliefs, norms, boundaries, and lifestyles that are cocreated with others who share similar worldviews comprising biological, psychosocial, historical, psychological, and other factors.

Diversity – the similarities and differences that occur within and across cultures, and the intersection of cultural and social identities.

Documents – any written, digital, audio, visual, or artistic recording of the work within the counseling relationship between counselor and client.

Examinee – a recipient of any professional counseling service that includes educational, psychological, and career appraisal utilizing qualitative or quantitative techniques.

Forensic Evaluation – any formal assessment conducted for court or other legal proceedings.

Multicultural/Diversity Competence – a capacity whereby counselors possess cultural and diversity awareness and knowledge about self and others, and how this awareness and knowledge is applied effectively in practice with clients and client groups.

Multicultural/Diversity Counseling – counseling that recognizes diversity and embraces approaches that support the worth, dignity, potential, and uniqueness of individuals within their historical, cultural, economic, political, and psychosocial contexts.

Student – an individual engaged in formal educational preparation as a counselor-in-training.

Supervisee – a professional counselor or counselor-in-training whose counseling work or clinical skill development is being overseen in a formal supervisory relationship by a qualified trained professional.

Supervisor – counselors who are trained to oversee the professional clinical work of counselors and counselors-in-training.

Teaching – all activities engaged in as part of a formal educational program designed to lead to a graduate degree in counseling.

Training – the instruction and practice of skills related to the counseling profession. Training contributes to the ongoing proficiency of students and professional counselors.

Part III

ACA Code of Ethics With Illustrative Vignettes

This section of the casebook presents the revised *ACA Code of Ethics,* adopted by the association in July 2005, together with illustrative vignettes. Each of the individual ethical standards that comprise the code is followed by a vignette, which clarifies the meaning of the standard. The vignettes are not intended to be comprehensive examples and do not address every aspect of each standard.

After many standards, a note in parentheses directs you to another standard or standards. In reviewing the vignettes, it is important to keep in mind that the individual standards are very much interrelated.

A series of questions (Study and Discussion Guide) is presented at the beginning of each major section of the *Code of Ethics.* We hope these questions will stimulate thought and discussion with fellow students or colleagues. They are designed to guide you in thinking through the application of the standards to your own practice.

Section A

The Counseling Relationship

Study and Discussion Guide

- **Client Welfare:** What steps can you take to ensure that the welfare of your client is the guiding principle for your practice?
- **Respecting Diversity:** How can you ensure that you are aware of any subtle biases you may have that could affect your work with diverse client populations? How can you guard against racial and sexual stereotyping in your counseling relationships with clients?
- **Informed Consent:** What procedures do you use to inform prospective clients about the nature of counseling? What types of information do prospective clients need to receive to make an informed decision to enter a counseling relationship?
- **Counselor's Personal Values:** What are some of your strongly held values, beliefs, and attitudes? How will you avoid imposing these values on your clients, even inadvertently?
- **Relationship Boundaries:** Why do you think counselors generally should avoid having another, nonprofessional relationship with a client?
- **Sexual Intimacies With Current and Former Clients:** What might you say to a client who told you that she and her previous counselor had been involved in a sexual relationship for several months before she terminated the professional relationship? What would you do? What are your thoughts on the matter of sexual intimacies with former clients?
- **Advocacy:** As a counselor, what are some ways that you can serve as an advocate for your clients?
- **Group Work:** What do you consider to be the main ethical issues in working with groups?
- **End-of-Life Care:** Would you be able to provide effective, unbiased counseling services to clients who are terminally ill and want to choose the time and manner of ending their lives?
- **Establishing Fees:** How might you determine an appropriate fee structure for your counseling practice? In what ways might you meet your ethical obligation to provide some pro bono service?
- **Bartering:** What are your thoughts about the advantages and disadvantages of bartering with clients? Can you think of any circumstances under which you would agree to barter with a client?
- **Termination and Referral:** What might you do if you thought you could not help a client, yet the client wanted to continue seeing you?

What action might you take if this client refused to accept a referral? What ethical issues are involved in termination with clients?

- **Technologies:** What ethical issues need to be considered when using technologies such as facsimile machines or the Internet, or when providing distance counseling services?

Section A

The Counseling Relationship

Introduction

Counselors encourage client growth and development in ways that foster the interest and welfare of clients and promote formation of healthy relationships. Counselors actively attempt to understand the diverse cultural backgrounds of the clients they serve. Counselors also explore their own cultural identities and how these affect their values and beliefs about the counseling process.

Counselors are encouraged to contribute to society by devoting a portion of their professional activity to services for which there is little or no financial return (pro bono publico).

A.1. Welfare of Those Served By Counselors

A.1.a. Primary Responsibility

The primary responsibility of counselors is to respect the dignity and to promote the welfare of clients.

Mary, age 78, has suffered a stroke that has left her with halting speech that can be difficult to understand. Although she moves slowly, she has regained much of her mobility. She seeks counseling at a community agency for help in deciding whether to sell her home and move into an assisted-living facility. Alex, the counselor, listens patiently and checks to ensure that he understands Mary accurately. He learns that Mary prizes her independence, which she has gained over 20 years as a widow, takes great joy in her flower garden, and looks forward to having her neighbors stop by to visit. Alex helps Mary clarify that she wants to remain in her home. Together they explore options that would further this goal, such as having a hot meal delivered daily by a local organization, hiring a gardener to help her, and arranging for a speech therapist to make home visits.

A.1.b. Records

Counselors maintain records necessary for rendering professional services to their clients and as required by laws, regulations, or agency or institution procedures. Counselors include sufficient and timely documentation in their client records to facilitate the delivery and continuity of needed services. Counselors take reasonable steps to ensure that documentation in records accurately reflects client progress and services provided. If errors are made in client records, counselors take steps to properly note the correction of such errors according to agency or institutional policies. *(See A.12.g.7., B.6., B.6.g., G.2.j.)*

Yolanda, a licensed professional counselor in private practice, keeps careful records pertaining to each of her clients, including dates and length of sessions, types of services provided, progress notes, diagnoses rendered, and billing and payment information. She routinely leaves time between client sessions to maintain her records so that she can write them while her memory is fresh. She keeps the complete records of adult clients for 7 years as required by her state's licensure law.

A.1.c. Counseling Plans

Counselors and their clients work jointly in devising integrated counseling plans that offer reasonable promise of success and are consistent with abilities and circumstances of clients. Counselors and clients regularly review counseling plans to assess their continued viability and effectiveness, respecting the freedom of choice of clients. *(See A.2.a., A.2.d., A.12.g.)*

Sarah, a high school counselor, works with students who have been referred to her because of disruptive classroom behavior. She works with her clients to determine their goals and which aspects of their behavior they are willing to change. Once they identify specific thoughts and actions, she works collaboratively with them in designing individualized action plans. She helps them develop plans that are clear, attainable, and realistic, and works to ensure that these plans are *their* plans. Sarah teaches her clients how to monitor their plans and modify them as needed. With clients' permission, she enlists the cooperation of teachers and parents to help clients succeed in meeting their goals.

A.1.d. Support Network Involvement

Counselors recognize that support networks hold various meanings in the lives of clients and consider enlisting the support, understanding, and involvement of others (e.g., religious/spiritual/community leaders, family members, friends) as positive resources, when appropriate, with client consent.

Marlene has been seeing Bill, an LPC, to deal with her depression. Through the counseling process, she has become aware that she has been so involved in meeting the needs of her husband and children that she has lost touch with her own needs. With Bill's assistance, she realizes that she wants to develop some aspects of her life that are separate from her family. Marlene and the counselor decide together to invite her husband and children to a family session in which Marlene can feel supported as she expresses her feelings and wishes. They also discuss the importance to Marlene of her church community, and they decide to enlist the support of her pastor in involving her in church activities.

A.1.e. Employment Needs

Counselors work with their clients considering employment in jobs that are consistent with the overall abilities, vocational limitations, physical restrictions, general temperament, interest and aptitude patterns, social skills, education, general qualifications, and other relevant characteristics and needs of clients. When appropriate, counselors appropriately trained in career development will assist in the placement of clients in positions that are consistent with the interest, culture, and the welfare of clients, employers, and/or the public.

Bart, a 55-year-old geologist, has accepted an offer of early retirement from the company where he had worked for 25 years. He seeks the assistance of a career counselor when he realizes he was not really ready to retire. During the initial session, he states that he wants a change from geology and wants an interesting job, and that salary is not an issue because he is financially secure. The counselor gathers pertinent information and administers a battery of career assessment measures. Their third session focuses on examining the results of the inventories, which indicate a possible interest in retail work, specifically in sporting goods. Because Bart is an athletic person who has spent much leisure time hunting and fishing, this idea appeals to him. In looking at the results of the inventories, he and the counselor also note that Bart's mathematical and organizational skills might qualify him for managerial duties. Bart leaves the session with plans to put together a résumé and begin to look for a job in sporting goods management.

A.2. Informed Consent in the Counseling Relationship

(See A.12.g., B.5., B.6.b., E.3., E.13.b., F.1.c., G.2.a.)

A.2.a. Informed Consent

Clients have the freedom to choose whether to enter into or remain in a counseling relationship and need adequate information about the counseling process and the counselor. Counselors have an obligation to review in writing and verbally with clients the rights and responsibilities of both the counselor and the client. Informed consent is an ongoing part of the counseling process, and counselors appropriately document discussions of informed consent throughout the counseling relationship.

Iman, who has never sought counseling before, comes to an initial session with Carla, a counselor in private practice. Iman describes her reservations about coming to see a counselor who does not share her Middle Eastern heritage and her fears that Carla may harbor some of the prejudices that Iman encounters in her daily life. She adds that she came anyway, though, because a friend who is a former client of Carla's had highly recommended Carla. Carla explores these concerns with Iman and provides her with information about herself and how she generally conducts the counseling process. Together they review Carla's professional disclosure statement and a document provided by the National Board for Certified Counselors (NBCC) that describes client rights and responsibilities. Carla gives Iman copies of both documents to take home. At the end of the session, Iman, with some hesitation, tells Carla that she believes she can be comfortable in this counseling relationship. Hearing her hesitation, Carla schedules a second appointment and also suggests that Iman think over her decision for a few days and call her. She adds that if, at that time, Iman has decided to look for a different counselor, Carla will assist her in finding a counselor who either is of Middle Eastern origin or who has considerable experience in working with clients with this cultural heritage.

A.2.b. Types of Information Needed

Counselors explicitly explain to clients the nature of all services provided. They inform clients about issues such as, but not limited to, the following:

the purposes, goals, techniques, procedures, limitations, potential risks, and benefits of services; the counselor's qualifications, credentials, and relevant experience; continuation of services upon the incapacitation or death of a counselor; and other pertinent information. Counselors take steps to ensure that clients understand the implications of diagnosis, the intended use of tests and reports, fees, and billing arrangements. Clients have the right to confidentiality and to be provided with an explanation of its limitations (including how supervisors and/or treatment team professionals are involved); to obtain clear information about their records; to participate in the ongoing counseling plans; and to refuse any services or modality change and to be advised of the consequences of such refusal.

Arnold seeks counseling at a community counseling and training center where services are provided by licensed professional counselors and by counselor interns from a local counselor education program. Arnold's intake session is with Donna, a counselor intern. During the session, Donna provides Arnold with information about the counseling services provided at the center and explains that even if she completes her internship before Arnold is ready to terminate counseling, center policy is that he will continue to receive counseling from one of the counselors on staff. Together, they review Donna's professional disclosure statement, which describes Donna's qualifications and, in general terms, the goals of counseling, techniques, and risks and benefits. Donna reviews confidentiality and the limitations that are created by her status as an intern. They discuss possible diagnoses and use of any tests or reports that might be a part of the counseling process, and how the center's sliding fee scale will be applied for Arnold. Donna explains to Arnold that he will be an active partner in establishing the counseling goals and plans.

A.2.c. Developmental and Cultural Sensitivity

Counselors communicate information in ways that are both developmentally and culturally appropriate. Counselors use clear and understandable language when discussing issues related to informed consent. When clients have difficulty understanding the language used by counselors, they provide necessary services (e.g., arranging for a qualified interpreter or translator) to ensure comprehension by clients. In collaboration with clients, counselors consider cultural implications of informed consent procedures and, where possible, counselors adjust their practices accordingly.

Danielle, a counselor in a community college counseling center, meets for the first time with Guillermo, an 18-year-old freshman. Guillermo is from Guatemala; he came to the United States with his family 8 months ago. He speaks English haltingly and struggles to find words to express himself. Danielle speaks no Spanish and is uncertain whether Guillermo fully comprehends her explanations of the counseling process. With Guillermo's permission, she enlists Jesus, another counselor at the center who is fluent in Spanish, to sit in on their session. At the end of the session, Jesus explains to Danielle that Guillermo's English comprehension skills are excellent although his expressive skills are developing more slowly. Guillermo states that he wants to continue in counseling with Danielle, but that he wants his family to know about and approve of his decision. They arrange for Jesus to translate

Danielle's disclosure statement into Spanish for Guillermo to take home and share with his family. Danielle and Jesus also tell Guillermo that they are willing to arrange to have a counseling session that includes his family, if Guillermo wishes.

A.2.d. Inability to Give Consent

When counseling minors or persons unable to give voluntary consent, counselors seek the assent of clients to services, and include them in decision making as appropriate. Counselors recognize the need to balance the ethical rights of clients to make choices, their capacity to give consent or assent to receive services, and parental or familial legal rights and responsibilities to protect these clients and make decisions on their behalf.

Danny is an 11-year-old prospective client who is brought by his mother to Adriane's office for counseling. Even though Danny is too young to give legally valid informed consent, Adriane includes Danny along with his mother in a verbal explanation of all information contained in her disclosure statement, using language that Danny can understand. Adriane is careful to check to ensure that Danny comprehends the information and to ascertain his willingness to participate in counseling. At the end of the session, Adriane asks both Danny and his mother to sign the written disclosure statement.

A.3. Clients Served by Others

When counselors learn that their clients are in a professional relationship with another mental health professional, they request release from clients to inform the other professionals and strive to establish positive and collaborative professional relationships.

Jorge offers a group counseling experience through a community mental health agency. Elizabeth requests to join the group and reveals during her screening interview that she is currently seeing a counselor at another agency for individual counseling. Jorge requests permission to contact the other counselor, and Elizabeth agrees. Jorge and the individual counselor agree that concurrent group and individual counseling would be advisable for Elizabeth. They also agree that, with Elizabeth's permission, they will communicate with each other as needed to help ensure that the best possible services are provided.

A.4. Avoiding Harm and Imposing Values

A.4.a. Avoiding Harm

Counselors act to avoid harming their clients, trainees, and research participants and to minimize or to remedy unavoidable or unanticipated harm.

Tim, a counselor in private practice, has been seeing Ellen for several months related to issues surrounding her divorce. Ellen has reported recently that she doesn't have much of an appetite any more and is having trouble sleeping at night. Ellen now discloses that she believes that her divorce was a result of her husband's dissatisfaction with her weight, and therefore she feels that she must lose weight rapidly to look better and begin dating again. Ellen also discloses that on several occasions she has eaten much more than she should have and purged immediately to rid herself of the calories. Tim realizes that Ellen is exhibiting behaviors related to an eating disorder. Tim has no training in working with eating disorders, and he informs Ellen that he will have to refer her to someone specializing in eating disorders. Ellen says that she already trusts Tim and would prefer to keep working with him. Tim explains the reasons for the referral and helps her to make an appointment with another counselor who has training and experience in working with eating disorders.

A.4.b. Personal Values

Counselors are aware of their own values, attitudes, beliefs, and behaviors and avoid imposing values that are inconsistent with counseling goals. Counselors respect the diversity of clients, trainees, and research participants.

Katy, a school counselor, has strong personal beliefs against abortion. Mandy, a 15-year-old girl, comes to see the counselor because she is pregnant and wants information about the physical and emotional effects of an abortion. Katy responds with factual information about the emotional effects and suggests that Mandy talk with the school nurse about physical effects. Katy asks Mandy whether she has discussed this decision with her parents. Mandy asks if she can bring her parents in to talk about the situation in the counselor's presence. Katy agrees to the request. Throughout the family session, Katy remains objective and does not try to promote her antiabortion beliefs.

A.5. Roles and Relationships With Clients

(See F.3., F.10., G.3.)

A.5.a. Current Clients

Sexual or romantic counselor–client interactions or relationships with current clients, their romantic partners, or their family members are prohibited.

Davita, a client, suggests to Steve, her counselor, that they see each other socially, on a dating basis, because they have such a close relationship. Davita also indicates that she finds Steve sexually attractive. Steve is careful to be sensitive to her reactions as he lets her know that this will not be possible, nor would it be ethically appropriate. He carefully explains the potential for exploitation involved.

A.5.b. Former Clients

Sexual or romantic counselor–client interactions or relationships with former clients, their romantic partners, or their family members are prohibited for a period of 5 years following the last professional contact. Counselors, before engaging in sexual or romantic interactions or relationships with clients, their romantic partners, or client family members after 5 years following the last professional contact, demonstrate forethought and document (in written form) whether the interactions or relationship can be viewed as exploitive in some way and/or whether there is still potential to harm the former client; in cases of potential exploitation and/or harm, the counselor avoids entering such an interaction or relationship.

Susan served as Frank's counselor for 6 months. While in counseling, Frank worked on his fears of intimacy and learned assertiveness skills in asking for what he wanted. Nearly 3 years after counseling ended, Susan and Frank meet at a social function. Frank tells Susan that he wants to strike up a personal relationship. He feels that enough time has passed since their professional relationship ended and states that he is sexually attracted to her. Susan responds that, although she finds Frank to be a most interesting person, she feels uncomfortable in pursuing a personal relationship at any time because of the nature of their former relationship. She explains the ethics of her profession and her personal beliefs about keeping her personal and professional lives separate. She lets Frank know that a personal relationship between them will not be possible.

A.5.c. Nonprofessional Interactions or Relationships (Other Than Sexual or Romantic Interactions or Relationships)

Counselor–client nonprofessional relationships with clients, former clients, their romantic partners, or their family members should be avoided, except when the interaction is potentially beneficial to the client. *(See A.5.d.)*

Lakiesha, a school counselor, worked with Tyrone, a fourth grader, in individual counseling for several weeks after Tyrone was referred by his teacher because his academic performance had deteriorated suddenly. Through the counseling process, Lakiesha learns that Tyrone's parents are divorced and that his father, with whom he lives, has recently remarried. One evening, at a political function, Lakiesha is approached by a woman who introduces herself as Tyrone's stepmother. The woman thanks Lakiesha for being so helpful to Tyrone and then suggests that the two of them go out for a drink after the function ends and talk about ways they could work together to further the political causes in which they are both interested. Lakiesha thanks the woman for the invitation but, thinking ahead to the potential complexities involved, she declines.

A.5.d. Potentially Beneficial Interactions

When a counselor–client nonprofessional interaction with a client or former client may be potentially beneficial to the client or former client, the counselor must document in case records, prior to the interaction (when feasible), the rationale for such an interaction, the potential benefit, and anticipated consequences for the client or former client and other individuals significantly involved with the client or former client. Such interactions should be initiated with appropriate client consent. Where unintentional harm occurs to the client or former client, or to an individual significantly involved with the client or former client, due to the nonprofessional interaction, the counselor must show evidence of an attempt to remedy such harm. Examples of potentially beneficial interactions include, but are not limited to, attending a formal ceremony (e.g., a wedding/commitment ceremony or graduation); purchasing a service or product provided by a client or former client (excepting unrestricted bartering); hospital visits to an ill family member; mutual membership in a professional association, organization, or community. *(See A.5.c.)*

Sandra and Roger, who have been married for 24 years, seek marriage counseling from Jake, stating that their relationship has become "hollow" now that the children are grown and have left home. They tell Jake that they both believe in the sanctity of marriage but cannot seem to connect with each other in a meaningful way. Over the course of several months in counseling, Sandra and Roger learn new communication skills, find some shared interests, and clarify their feelings toward each other. They come to a session with the news that counseling has helped them tremendously to strengthen their relationship and that they are planning a renewal-of-vows ceremony. They ask Jake to come to the ceremony, adding that it would mean a lot to them if he would attend. After reviewing with them the possible risks, Jake agrees to attend the ceremony.

A.5.e. Role Changes in the Professional Relationship

When a counselor changes a role from the original or most recent contracted relationship, he or she obtains informed consent from the client and explains the right of the client to refuse services related to the change. Examples of role changes include

1. changing from individual to relationship or family counseling or vice versa;
2. changing from a nonforensic evaluative role to a therapeutic role, or vice versa;
3. changing from a counselor to a researcher role (i.e., enlisting clients as research participants), or vice versa; and
4. changing from a counselor to a mediator role, or vice versa.

Clients must be fully informed of any anticipated consequences (e.g., financial, legal, personal, or therapeutic) of counselor role changes.

Mai-Jing, an LPC in private practice, works part-time under contract with the Juvenile Probation and Parole Department to provide counseling services to court-referred youth. In this role, she is asked to counsel Kendra, a 15-year-old girl who has received deferred adjudication after being apprehended for shoplifting. When Mai-Jing meets with Kendra for the first time, she is careful to explain that she is required to make a report to the court regarding Kendra's progress in counseling. Kendra agrees to this condition, and they meet for the court-mandated eight sessions. During the final session, Kendra asks if she can continue to see Mai-Jing in Mai-Jing's private practice. Mai-Jing explains to Kendra the changes in the counseling relationship this would entail, including differences in confidentiality, reporting, and payment arrangements. Kendra agrees to allow Mai-Jing to contact her legal guardian to arrange for Kendra to become a client in her private practice.

A.6. Roles and Relationships at Individual, Group, Institutional, and Societal Levels

A.6.a. Advocacy

When appropriate, counselors advocate at individual, group, institutional, and societal levels to examine potential barriers and obstacles that inhibit access and/or the growth and development of clients.

Paul is a college counselor who specializes in career counseling. Jose came to the counseling center to discuss career options with Paul. Jose reports that he has always dreamed of getting a degree in computer science but doesn't believe that this is an option for him. Jose is legally blind, and in the first session he explains how this disability affects all areas of his life, including his ability to make career choices. Jose states that his adviser in the computer science department has encouraged him to change majors to something that doesn't require many visual tasks. Jose explained to the adviser that accommodative equipment is available that would enable him to see the computer screen, and that if the department would provide this, he would be able to complete the course work easily. (Jose's adviser dismissed the idea, saying that there was no money in the department for such things.) Paul assists Jose in contacting Student Disability Services on campus, and together they find that this equipment can be provided. Paul arranges a meeting with several faculty members and begins a task force that will examine how the needs of students with disabilities are being met on campus. Paul also collaborates with other counselors in the center to begin offering diversity training to professors at the university.

A.6.b. Confidentiality and Advocacy

Counselors obtain client consent prior to engaging in advocacy efforts on behalf of an identifiable client to improve the provision of services and to work toward removal of systemic barriers or obstacles that inhibit client access, growth, and development.

Claudia is a rehabilitation counselor working in a Veteran's hospital. She notices that one of her clients, John, is not receiving proper medical care. John complains that he is constantly in pain; he reports that he usually receives his medicine late and sometimes does not receive it at all. Claudia discusses the matter with John, focusing on his rights as a patient in this facility. John states that he needs help, but he does not have any family members who can speak to the hospital administration about the quality of his care. Claudia agrees to be an advocate for John, with his consent. Claudia explains to John exactly with whom she will be speaking and what information will be disclosed. They discuss possible outcomes of these actions and how John might be affected. John agrees that this is the best course of action and signs a waiver of confidentiality so that Claudia can begin taking steps to see that he receives proper care.

A.7. Multiple Clients

When a counselor agrees to provide counseling services to two or more persons who have a relationship, the counselor clarifies at the outset which person or persons are clients and the nature of the relationship the counselor will have with each involved person. If it becomes apparent that the counselor may be called upon to perform potentially conflicting roles, the counselor will clarify, adjust, or withdraw from roles appropriately. *(See A.8.a., B.4.)*

A marriage and family counselor agrees to see Linda and Tom for marriage counseling. The counselor explains at the outset that she will begin working with them conjointly but may wish at times to see each of them individually. She secures their understanding and agreement that she will not divulge to either of them what the other has said in individual sessions. Several weeks into the counseling process, during an individual session, Linda voices her suspicion that Tom is having an affair. Linda asks the counselor to tell her whether Tom has said anything in his sessions that might confirm this. The counselor reiterates her policy regarding confidentiality of individual sessions and explores with Linda the possibility of expressing her concern directly to Tom.

A.8. Group Work

(See B.4.a.)

A.8.a. Screening

Counselors screen prospective group counseling/therapy participants. To the extent possible, counselors select members whose needs and goals are compatible with goals of the group, who will not impede the group process, and whose well-being will not be jeopardized by the group experience.

Several women apply to join a group being formed at a counseling center for women over 30 who are searching for educational, occupational, or personal alternatives to their present situation. Danica, the counselor who will facilitate the group, interviews and gives a personality inventory to each applicant. The inventory suggests the presence of a severe personality disorder in the case of one woman who applied. Danica meets with her and suggests that her needs might be better filled by other services that are offered at the counseling center. Arrangements are made for a referral.

A.8.b. Protecting Clients

In a group setting, counselors take reasonable precautions to protect clients from physical, emotional, or psychological trauma.

Martin, an LPC, is facilitating the first session of a growth group. This first session is a "trial" session that individuals may attend to help them decide whether they want to make a commitment to the group. At one point, a member expresses some personal concerns that indicate he may have serious emotional problems. Martin guides the group focus away from that member. After the group session, Martin meets privately with the member and refers him for individual counseling.

A.9. End-of-Life Care for Terminally Ill Clients

A.9.a. Quality of Care

Counselors take measures that enable clients

1. to obtain high-quality end-of-life care for their physical, emotional, social, and spiritual needs;
2. to exercise the highest degree of self-determination possible;
3. to be given every opportunity possible to engage in informed decision making regarding their end-of-life care; and
4. to receive complete and adequate assessment regarding their ability to make competent, rational decisions on their own behalf from a mental health professional who is experienced in end-of-life care practice.

Anna, a counselor who works on the oncology ward of a hospital, has been counseling Dana, who has been diagnosed as terminally ill. Dana has been evaluated by a psychiatrist on staff who is experienced in working with terminally ill clients. The psychiatrist concluded that Dana is mentally capable of making decisions regarding her end-of-life care. Anna explores with Dana a range of physical, emotional, social, and spiritual issues that are important to Dana. This exploration helps Dana determine what end-of-life services she does and does not desire to receive.

A.9.b. Counselor Competence, Choice, and Referral

Recognizing the personal, moral, and competence issues related to end-of-life decisions, counselors may choose to work or not work with terminally ill clients who wish to explore their end-of-life options. Counselors provide appropriate referral information to ensure that clients receive the necessary help.

John, a counselor, had been seeing Robert for 2 months when Robert was diagnosed as terminally ill with cancer. They have several sessions that focus on helping Robert come to terms with his illness, and Robert then tells John that he wants to explore his end-of-life options, including assisted suicide. John's personal and moral stance is that no individual should consider making such a decision. After consulting with his supervisor, John explains his beliefs to Robert and provides him with a referral list of counselors who work regularly with terminally ill clients.

A.9.c. Confidentiality

Counselors who provide services to terminally ill individuals who are considering hastening their own deaths have the option of breaking or not breaking confidentiality, depending on applicable laws and the specific circumstances of the situation and after seeking consultation or supervision from appropriate professional and legal parties. *(See B.5.c., B.7.c.)*

Mary is a counselor who is working with Daniel, age 22, who has been diagnosed with a terminal illness. During a session, Daniel informs Mary that he is considering taking his own life so as not to be a burden to his family. After consulting with her supervisor and with an attorney who represents terminally ill clients, Mary has a conversation with Daniel in which she expresses her concern for his welfare and explains to him that she would like him to talk to his family about this matter. She offers to be a part of the family discussion to help Daniel and his family members express their feelings and find a resolution.

A.10. Fees and Bartering

A.10.a. Accepting Fees From Agency Clients

Counselors refuse a private fee or other remuneration for rendering services to persons who are entitled to such services through the counselor's employing agency or institution. The policies of a particular agency may make explicit provisions for agency clients to receive counseling services from members of its staff in private practice. In such instances, the clients must be informed of other options open to them should they seek private counseling services.

Beverly is an LPC who works half time as a counselor in a university counseling center and half time in independent private practice. The university counseling center's policy is that students are allowed six visits for personal counseling at no charge. If further counseling is needed, they are referred to practitioners in the community. Beverly's contract with the university as a part-time employee allows her to include herself as a private practitioner on a referral list that is given to students who request additional services. When Beverly provides the referral list to her student clients, she carefully explains the benefits and services provided by other providers and does not attempt in any way to persuade them to select her name from the list.

A.10.b. Establishing Fees

In establishing fees for professional counseling services, counselors consider the financial status of clients and locality. In the event that the established fee structure is inappropriate for a client, counselors assist clients in attempting to find comparable services of acceptable cost.

Gregory, a counselor who has been in private practice in Los Angeles, moves to a small midwestern town. He goes to the department chair of the counselor education program at the local university, introduces himself, and indicates he is interested in opening his own practice. He asks the department chair to recommend four professionals who are established in private practice in the town. After speaking with these four people, he decides to establish a fee that is in keeping with local practice and is considerably lower than what he had been charging in Los Angeles.

A.10.c. Nonpayment of Fees

If counselors intend to use collection agencies or take legal measures to collect fees from clients who do not pay for services as agreed upon, they first inform clients of intended actions and offer clients the opportunity to make payment.

Jennifer is an LPC in private practice. Debbie and Malcolm came to see Jennifer for couples counseling for nine sessions. Jennifer allowed the couple to postpone paying for the last three sessions due to some financial difficulties they were having. Debbie and Malcolm did not return to counseling after the ninth session and left an outstanding balance. Jennifer attempted to contact the couple by telephone, but they did not return her calls. She sent a letter informing them that they had 30 days to remit payment before the debt would be transferred to a collection agency.

A.10.d. Bartering

Counselors may barter only if the relationship is not exploitive or harmful and does not place the counselor in an unfair advantage, if the client requests it, and if such arrangements are an accepted practice among professionals in the community. Counselors consider the cultural implications of bartering and discuss relevant concerns with clients and document such agreements in a clear written contract.

A client is undergoing an expensive divorce and tells Sandra, his counselor, that he will have to terminate his weekly counseling sessions unless they can make other financial arrangements. The client has noticed that Sandra's office is furnished with period furniture and some inexpensive antiques. Because he owns an antiques and collectibles shop, he asks if she might be willing to exchange counseling services for some furniture she could select at the shop. Bartering is not customary among professionals in the area where

Sandra practices. Sandra explains to the client the potential problems she sees with his proposal. Although she declines the offer to barter, she does agree to reduce her fee and suggests that he come for counseling every other week for the time being.

A.10.e. Receiving Gifts

Counselors understand the challenges of accepting gifts from clients and recognize that in some cultures, small gifts are a token of respect and showing gratitude. When determining whether or not to accept a gift from clients, counselors take into account the therapeutic relationship, the monetary value of the gift, a client's motivation for giving the gift, and the counselor's motivation for wanting or declining the gift.

Bonita has been counseling David on a weekly basis for 3 months. The counseling process has been successful in helping David achieve the goals he had set for himself. During their session last week, Bonita and David had agreed that today's session would be their termination session. David arrives at today's session carrying a potted plant, which he offers to Bonita as a gift for her office and as a way of thanking her for her assistance. Bonita considers David's motivation for offering this gift, the fact that David can easily afford to give it, and the fact that this is their final session together. She decides to accept the gift.

A.11. Termination and Referral

A.11.a. Abandonment Prohibited

Counselors do not abandon or neglect clients in counseling. Counselors assist in making appropriate arrangements for the continuation of treatment, when necessary, during interruptions such as vacations, illness, and following termination.

Mary Lou knows that she is going to spend 4 weeks in Europe during the summer. She informs her clients in February and lets them know that it is possible for them to see one of her colleagues during her absence. Early in the spring, she informs prospective clients who call her that she will not be accepting any new clients until she returns from her trip, and she gives them the names and telephone numbers of several well-qualified counselors.

A.11.b. Inability to Assist Clients

If counselors determine an inability to be of professional assistance to clients, they avoid entering or continuing counseling relationships. Counselors are knowledgeable about culturally and clinically appropriate referral resources and suggest these alternatives. If clients decline the suggested referrals, counselors should discontinue the relationship.

Rafael, a counselor for the juvenile court system, is assigned to work with a young man who has serious problems relating to authority figures. This client constantly ridicules and insults police, administrators, and other authority figures with whom he interacts. After making several unsuccessful attempts to develop rapport with the client and after consulting with his clinical supervisor, Rafael determines that he is not able to establish a therapeutic relationship with this young man. With the client's permission, he refers the client to another counselor who has a record of success in working with rebellious young people.

A.11.c. Appropriate Termination

Counselors terminate a counseling relationship when it becomes reasonably apparent that the client no longer needs assistance, is not likely to benefit, or is being harmed by continued counseling. Counselors may terminate counseling when in jeopardy of harm by the client, or another person with whom the client has a relationship, or when clients do not pay fees as agreed upon. Counselors provide pretermination counseling and recommend other service providers when necessary.

> Gary has been in individual counseling with Loretta for almost 7 months. For the first few months, he was making steady gains toward meeting his goals. However, for the past month, Loretta has felt that Gary has been doing very little, either in the sessions or outside them. Loretta has shared her reactions with Gary, but he has been reluctant to consider terminating the counseling relationship. Finally, Gary acknowledges that he is not really interested in making more changes and that he has been avoiding the uncomfortable feelings that he knows will come with termination. After further discussion, they agree to have two more sessions devoted to preparing for termination.

A.11.d. Appropriate Transfer of Services

When counselors transfer or refer clients to other practitioners, they ensure that appropriate clinical and administrative processes are completed and open communication is maintained with both clients and practitioners.

> Lauren is a counselor who has been working with a client, Alex. When Alex tells her that he is moving to another city, they make a termination plan that includes Lauren helping Alex locate a qualified counselor in his new city. Lauren obtains the proper releases from Alex so that she can share information with his new counselor.

A.12. Technology Applications

A.12.a. Benefits and Limitations

Counselors inform clients of the benefits and limitations of using information technology applications in the counseling process and in business/billing procedures. Such technologies include but are not limited to computer hardware and software, telephones, the World Wide Web, the Internet, online assessment instruments, and other communication devices.

> Naomi, a career counselor, begins to interpret a career interest inventory to a client. When the client sees the computer-generated scores and narrative report, he remarks, "This is really impressive! Now I can find out what career I should choose." Naomi carefully explains that the inventory cannot tell the client what he should do and that the results are only one tool for helping him to make his own decision.

A.12.b. Technology-Assisted Services

When providing technology-assisted distance counseling services, counselors determine that clients are intellectually, emotionally, and physically capable of using the application and that the application is appropriate for the needs of clients.

> Rebecca contacts Patti, a counselor in private practice, to arrange for counseling for her 13-year-old daughter. Rebecca would like her daughter to receive services via e-mail, which is convenient for the family's busy schedule. Rebecca thinks her daughter's extensive experience with chat rooms on the Internet makes Web counseling appropriate for her. Patti explains that this type of counseling is not appropriate for therapeutic communication with a 13-year-old. Patti further explains that, although the child is technologically competent, e-mail would not be an adequate substitute for a face-to-face counseling relationship. Patti arranges face-to-face appointments that fit into the family's schedule.

A.12.c. Inappropriate Services
When technology-assisted distance counseling services are deemed inappropriate by the counselor or client, counselors consider delivering services face to face.

> Paulo, a counselor, is contacted by Rachel through his counseling services' Web site. Paulo determines that Rachel is using a computer at the public library. He recommends face-to-face counseling because the library's computer is not conducive to the privacy and confidentiality necessary to create a therapeutic environment.

A.12.d. Access
Counselors provide reasonable access to computer applications when providing technology-assisted distance counseling services.

> Sam is a counselor in a university career counseling center who routinely asks student clients to complete computerized career interest inventories between their face-to-face sessions. First, he ascertains that the students are competent in using the technology and understand how to complete the particular inventories on the computer. When students do not have home computers, he arranges for them to access the computers in the counseling center's computer laboratory.

A.12.e. Laws and Statutes
Counselors ensure that the use of technology does not violate the laws of any local, state, national, or international entity and observe all relevant statutes.

> Malik, an entering college freshman, has been quadriplegic since a diving accident left him paralyzed. He wants to major in business administration and meets with an adviser in the department. The adviser realizes that the department does not have some of the equipment necessary to accommodate Malik. The adviser immediately calls the student disability services offices on campus to arrange for Malik to have the necessary accommodations.

A.12.f. Assistance
Counselors seek business, legal, and technical assistance when using technology applications, particularly when the use of such applications crosses state or national boundaries.

Elijah, owner of a mental health rehabilitation agency, is responsible for his company's transition to new billing and records maintenance software, which was ordered by the previous owner. The new software will streamline operations and makes use of the Internet. Because this software has been on the market for less than a year, Elijah is concerned about confidential information getting lost if all the glitches aren't worked out. He contacts a computer consultant to determine whether his concerns are justified. He contacts his lawyer and his accountant to find out his rights if he cancels his contract for the software and to determine whether the company can afford the risk.

A.12.g. Technology and Informed Consent

As part of the process of establishing informed consent, counselors do the following:

1. Address issues related to the difficulty of maintaining the confidentiality of electronically transmitted communications.
2. Inform clients of all colleagues, supervisors, and employees, such as Informational Technology (IT) administrators, who might have authorized or unauthorized access to electronic transmissions.
3. Urge clients to be aware of all authorized or unauthorized users including family members and fellow employees who have access to any technology clients may use in the counseling process.
4. Inform clients of pertinent legal rights and limitations governing the practice of a profession over state lines or international boundaries.
5. Use encrypted Web sites and e-mail communications to help ensure confidentiality when possible.
6. When the use of encryption is not possible, counselors notify clients of this fact and limit electronic transmissions to general communications that are not client specific.
7. Inform clients if and for how long archival storage of transaction records are maintained.
8. Discuss the possibility of technology failure and alternate methods of service delivery.
9. Inform clients of emergency procedures, such as calling 911 or a local crisis hotline, when the counselor is not available.
10. Discuss time zone differences, local customs, and cultural or language differences that might impact service delivery.
11. Inform clients when technology-assisted distance counseling services are not covered by insurance. *(See A.2.)*

Audrey, a private practitioner, has developed a Web-based counseling center. She has prepared a declaration of practices and procedures specific to the use of this modality. She has established a procedure by which clients can receive services or referrals through an 800 number in cases of emergency or technology failure.

A.12.h. Sites on the World Wide Web

Counselors maintaining sites on the World Wide Web (the Internet) do the following:

1. Regularly check that electronic links are working and professionally appropriate.
2. Establish ways clients can contact the counselor in case of technology failure.
3. Provide electronic links to relevant state licensure and professional certification boards to protect consumer rights and facilitate addressing ethical concerns.
4. Establish a method for verifying client identity.
5. Obtain the written consent of the legal guardian or other authorized legal representative prior to rendering services in the event the client is a minor child, an adult who is legally incompetent, or an adult incapable of giving informed consent.
6. Strive to provide a site that is accessible to persons with disabilities.
7. Strive to provide translation capabilities for clients who have a different primary language while also addressing the imperfect nature of such translations.
8. Assist clients in determining the validity and reliability of information found on the World Wide Web and other technology applications.

Chuyonne, a licensed professional counselor, has established an Internet counseling service. Her Web site provides electronic links to her state counselor licensure board's Web site and to the American Counseling Association's Web site. Once she establishes counseling relationships with her clients, she ensures that they have the toll-free telephone number of her answering service, which has been instructed to call her on her pager if clients are unable to contact her through the usual technological means.

Section B

Confidentiality, Privileged Communication, and Privacy

Study and Discussion Guide

- **Explaining Confidentiality:** What information should you give clients about the nature and purpose of confidentiality, and how should you present it?
- **Exceptions to Confidentiality:** What might you want to tell clients about the exceptions to confidentiality? Do you think informing clients about the limits to confidentiality increases or decreases trust? What are your thoughts about confidentiality as it pertains to clients with contagious, life-threatening diseases? to minor clients?
- **Confidentiality With Groups and Families:** Do confidentiality requirements need to be tailored to individual, group, and family counseling? What are the limitations to confidentiality in groups? in working with families?
- **Cultural Considerations:** How might a client's culture affect his or her views about and expectations of confidentiality in counseling?
- **Sharing Confidential Information:** Under what circumstances would it be ethically acceptable to share confidential information about a client with a third party?
- **Records:** What guidelines should you have for maintaining adequate records on your clients? How would you respond if a client asked to see your records of your counseling sessions with him or her?

Section B

Confidentiality, Privileged Communication, and Privacy

Introduction

Counselors recognize that trust is a cornerstone of the counseling relationship. Counselors aspire to earn the trust of clients by creating an ongoing partnership, establishing and upholding appropriate boundaries, and maintaining confidentiality. Counselors communicate the parameters of confidentiality in a culturally competent manner.

B.1. Respecting Client Rights

B.1.a. Multicultural/Diversity Considerations

Counselors maintain awareness and sensitivity regarding cultural meanings of confidentiality and privacy. Counselors respect differing views toward disclosure of information. Counselors hold ongoing discussions with clients as to how, when, and with whom information is to be shared.

Patrice works as a counselor in a community agency. She goes to the reception area to greet her new client, Fatima, who is waiting with her husband. Fatima introduces Patrice to her husband and asks the counselor to allow her husband to sit with her through the intake session. When Patrice inquires as to the reason for this request, Fatima explains that in her native culture it is unacceptable for a wife to have secrets from her husband, and that she would not be comfortable in the session without him there. The intake session is held with the couple. Patrice clarifies that future sessions will be conducted with Fatima alone so that the counseling process can be focused on the concerns that prompted Fatima to call for an appointment. Patrice explains that the confidentiality of information shared during sessions belongs to Fatima, and that she may share information with her husband if she wishes. She checks to ensure that Fatima understands this plan and agrees to it.

B.1.b. Respect for Privacy

Counselors respect client rights to privacy. Counselors solicit private information from clients only when it is beneficial to the counseling process.

Ron, a counselor in an elementary school, has been asked to see Tawana, a second grader the referring teacher describes as being withdrawn and inattentive lately. Tawana's father is a well-known professional athlete whose name has been in the news recently due to a sex scandal allegedly involving several members of the sports team. Although Ron is curious about what may be happening with Tawana's father, he begins his counseling session with her by focusing on the reason for the referral. His intention is to discuss family problems with Tawana only if *she* introduces the subject.

B.1.c. Respect for Confidentiality

Counselors do not share confidential information without client consent, or without sound legal or ethical justification.

Arnetta, an elementary school counselor, conducts several short-term groups with children. The principal calls Arnetta in for a conference and says that due to a district push for accountability, he needs to know what progress each child in each of her groups is making. Arnetta explains to the principal that she believes it would be unprofessional and unethical to comply with this request. However, she is willing to summarize some key themes and general concerns of children in the groups and to give this information to the principal. In doing so, Arnetta takes care to ensure that no individual child can be identified based on this information.

B.1.d. Explanation of Limitations

At initiation and throughout the counseling process, counselors inform clients of the limitations of confidentiality and seek to identify foreseeable situations in which confidentiality must be breached. *(See A.2.b.)*

Joe, an 18-year-old high school senior, was arrested for possession of a controlled substance, was given deferred adjudication, and is now on probation. One condition of his deferred adjudication is a requirement that he participate in counseling with a substance abuse counselor. When Joe meets with Thalia, the counselor, she explains confidentiality and its limitations. She emphasizes that she will be required to make a report to the court when they complete their sessions, and she outlines the types of information her report must include.

B.2. Exceptions

B.2.a. Danger and Legal Requirements

The general requirement that counselors keep information confidential does not apply when disclosure is required to protect clients or identified others from serious and foreseeable harm or when legal requirements demand that confidential information must be revealed. Counselors consult with other professionals when in doubt as to the validity of an exception. Additional considerations apply when addressing end-of-life issues. *(See A.9.c.)*

Mark, a college freshman, comes to the university counseling center. In his first session with Renee, the counselor, he discloses that he is feeling despondent over breaking up with his girlfriend. He reveals that the previous evening he attempted to slash his wrists but stopped when he began to draw blood. After exploring his current emotional state, Renee suggests that he consider admission to the student health service. Mark refuses, although he admits that he cannot be sure that he will not attempt self-destructive behavior again. Renee assesses Mark as being at continuing high risk to himself, and she contacts the psychiatrist at the student health center after informing Mark of her intent to do so.

B.2.b. Contagious, Life-Threatening Diseases

When clients disclose that they have a disease commonly known to be both communicable and life threatening, counselors may be justified in disclosing information to identifiable third parties, if they are known to be at demonstrable and high risk of contracting the disease. Prior to making a disclosure, counselors confirm that there is such a diagnosis and assess the intent of clients to inform the third parties about their disease or to engage in any behaviors that may be harmful to an identifiable third party.

Darla has been counseling Walt for 3 weeks. Walt brings to his fourth session the results of an HIV test he took, which confirms that he is HIV positive. He is agitated, angry, and wanting revenge. From his perspective, he is a victim and doesn't see why he should be concerned about anybody but himself. Knowing that Walt has a new romantic partner, Darla asks him about his intentions to inform his partner of his HIV status. Walt adamantly states that he has no intention, now or in the future, of telling him or even of adopting safe sex practices. The counselor informs him that if he steadfastly holds to this decision, she will feel ethically compelled to inform his partner. (The state in which the counselor practices has a partner notification statute that would permit this.) During the remainder of the session, Darla continues to explore with Walt the ramifications of his decision to keep his HIV status from his partner.

B.2.c. Court-Ordered Disclosure

When subpoenaed to release confidential or privileged information without a client's permission, counselors obtain written, informed consent from the client or take steps to prohibit the disclosure or have it limited as narrowly as possible due to potential harm to the client or counseling relationship.

The court orders Johann, an LPC, to release the records of a minor client who is the subject of a custody suit. Because the child is highly anxious about being placed in the middle of his parents' conflict in court, Johann believes that it will not be in the child's best interest to disclose the specific content of the counseling sessions. Johann requests to the court that the child's records not be released and explains the importance of preserving the child's confidentiality and the counseling relationship.

B.2.d. Minimal Disclosure

To the extent possible, clients are informed before confidential information is disclosed and are involved in the disclosure decision-making process. When circumstances require the disclosure of confidential information, only essential information is revealed.

Francesca, who has a history of violent behavior when intoxicated, begins seeing a counselor at a mental health center soon after she completes an inpatient treatment program for addiction to alcohol. She maintains her sobriety for several months. Then one evening, obviously intoxicated, she calls the counselor. She threatens to kill her mother. Although the client is incoherent, the counselor discerns that she has a gun. The counselor attempts to explain his obligation to breach confidentiality in order to warn and protect someone in danger, but the client is not receptive. The counselor calls the mother but is unable to reach her. He then calls the police, telling them only the specific nature of the threat and the names and addresses of the client and her mother.

B.3. Information Shared With Others

B.3.a. Subordinates

Counselors make every effort to ensure that privacy and confidentiality of clients are maintained by subordinates, including employees, supervisees, students, clerical assistants, and volunteers. *(See F.1.c.)*

New clerical staff members are hired to work in a counseling agency. The agency director presents a training program for them that includes a discussion of the importance of confidentiality in counseling. Appropriate management of case files to protect client confidentiality is emphasized. The staff members are instructed not to reveal information about clients in response to inquiries made by phone, letter, or in person but to channel such inquiries to the director of the agency.

B.3.b. Treatment Teams

When client treatment involves a continued review or participation by a treatment team, the client will be informed of the team's existence and composition, information being shared, and the purposes of sharing such information.

Mahmoud, who works in an inpatient facility, informs his clients that certain members of the treatment staff will have access to his records. He also tells them that case conferences take place on a regular basis and assures them that the team approach is designed to include a variety of perspectives in providing services to clients. He encourages them to ask questions throughout their stay at the facility.

B.3.c. Confidential Settings

Counselors discuss confidential information only in settings in which they can reasonably ensure client privacy.

Roberto works as a counselor in the oncology unit of a hospital. He has spent much of his morning playing "telephone tag" with the unit's social worker, in an attempt to coordinate services for one of the patients with whom they both are working. As he is leaving the unit for lunch, Roberto steps into a crowded elevator and runs into the social worker. They both say simultaneously, "I've been trying to reach you!" They step out of the elevator, go into Roberto's office, and close the door behind them to confer.

B.3.d. Third-Party Payers

Counselors disclose information to third-party payers only when clients have authorized such disclosure.

Norman, a counselor in private practice, has entered into a contractual agreement with a managed care company. During his initial sessions with new clients who have been referred by the company, he devotes considerable time to discussing the specific limits that are placed on confidentiality by company policies and procedures. He tells them that he will release information to the managed care company only after clients have given him written authorization to do so. He further explains that their refusal to provide requested information could cause the company to deny claims for reimbursement.

B.3.e. Transmitting Confidential Information

Counselors take precautions to ensure the confidentiality of information transmitted through the use of computers, electronic mail, facsimile machines, telephones, voicemail, answering machines, and other electronic or computer technology. *(See A.12.g.)*

Dave, an LPC, receives a telephone call from a former client. The client tells Dave that he has moved to another state and asks that his records be sent to the clinic where he plans to resume his counseling. Dave explains that his policy is to secure written permission before releasing records, and he offers to send the client a written form that would grant authorization to have his records transferred. The client agrees to this procedure and returns the form with his signature. Dave includes with the records a cover letter that explains their confidential nature.

B.3.f. Deceased Clients

Counselors protect the confidentiality of deceased clients, consistent with legal requirements and agency or setting policies.

The agency in which Ophelia works has a policy that the counseling records of deceased clients may be released only if the person making the request produces a court order for the records. A year ago, Ophelia had worked with a woman client whom Ophelia had assessed to be at risk for suicide. Ophelia had referred the client to the agency's psychiatrist for further evaluation and possible antidepressant medication. Now, Ophelia receives a telephone call from the woman's husband, informing her that his wife committed suicide 3 weeks ago and demanding that she release his wife's counseling records to him. Ophelia explains that it is contrary to agency policy for her to release the records until he can provide her with a court order.

B.4. Groups and Families

B.4.a. Group Work

In group work, counselors clearly explain the importance and parameters of confidentiality for the specific group being entered.

Quentin, a high school counselor, regularly conducts groups. He informs students from the outset that confidentiality cannot be guaranteed and discusses the exceptions to confidentiality. He emphasizes the importance of respecting one another's confidences and explains that trust will not develop in the group unless confidentiality is maintained. From time to time, he reminds the members of how easy it would be to breach confidentiality unintentionally, and he clarifies this point using examples that are realistic for the students.

B.4.b. Couples and Family Counseling

In couples and family counseling, counselors clearly define who is considered "the client" and discuss expectations and limitations of confidentiality. Counselors seek agreement and document in writing such agreement among all involved parties having capacity to give consent concerning each individual's right to confidentiality and any obligation to preserve the confidentiality of information known.

Candace, a marriage and family counselor, tells all couples at the outset of the counseling relationship that she will usually work with them as a couple in conjoint sessions, but occasionally she will wish to see each of them individually. She explains that she will not disclose information that either of them may share during an individual session, but that it is important that they do not keep secrets from one another. She explains that such triangles work against the purposes of relationship counseling.

B.5. Clients Lacking Capacity to Give Informed Consent

B.5.a. Responsibility to Clients

When counseling minor clients or adult clients who lack the capacity to give voluntary, informed consent, counselors protect the confidentiality of information received in the counseling relationship as specified by federal and state laws, written policies, and applicable ethical standards.

Carol, a private practitioner, is counseling a child named Jonathan. When Jonathan's father comes to pick him up after a session, the father wants to know how his son is progressing. Carol reminds the father of their discussion held during the intake session, when she explained the importance of confidentiality as well as its limitations when working with minors. In Jonathan's presence and with Jonathan's permission, she gives the father a general idea about Jonathan's progress. The father demands more specific examples, and Carol invites him to participate in the second half of Jonathan's next session. Carol realizes that the father may have a legal right to the information he has requested, but she hopes she will be able to first talk with Jonathan about what he is willing to share with his father and to persuade the father to accept the information Jonathan is willing to disclose.

B.5.b. Responsibility to Parents and Legal Guardians

Counselors inform parents and legal guardians about the role of counselors and the confidential nature of the counseling relationship. Counselors are sensitive to the cultural diversity of families and respect the inherent rights and responsibilities of parents/guardians over the welfare of their children/charges according to law. Counselors work to establish, as appropriate, collaborative relationships with parents/guardians to best serve clients.

Jose is an elementary school counselor whose school district is experiencing an increase in enrollment of children whose parents have recently migrated from one South American country. Part of his job is to provide individual counseling to first and second graders who have been identified by their teachers as having adjustment problems. Typically, after Jose meets with a child and gains the child's consent, he invites the parents to a conference to talk about the best ways to proceed with the child. He realizes that his work with young children will be enhanced if the parents provide informed consent and are cooperative. Jose explains to the parents the importance of confidentiality as the foundation for trust in the counseling relationship.

B.5.c. Release of Confidential Information

When counseling minor clients or adult clients who lack the capacity to give voluntary consent to release confidential information, counselors seek permission from an appropriate third party to disclose information. In such instances, counselors inform clients consistent with their level of understanding and take culturally appropriate measures to safeguard client confidentiality.

Rowena is a counselor in a United Way funded agency that provides services to clients with chronic mental illnesses. About once every 3 or 4 months over the past 3 years she has seen Samantha, who suffers from schizophrenia and has been living with her adult son. The primary focus of their counseling sessions has been to ensure that Samantha continues to take her antipsychotic medications and to monitor the progression of her illness. Today, Rowena receives a telephone call from Samantha's son who requests Samantha's counseling records. The son explains that Samantha's condition has deteriorated to the point where he can no longer care for her in his home and that he plans to place her in a residential psychiatric facility. Rowena tells the son that she will need a signed release of confidential information form. If Samantha cannot sign it, his signed release must be accompanied by documentation that he has legal authority to make decisions on Samantha's behalf.

B.6. Records

B.6.a. Confidentiality of Records

Counselors ensure that records are kept in a secure location and that only authorized persons have access to records.

Kenneth, a school counselor, has stressed to his principal the importance of his maintaining control over his counseling session notes. The principal has provided a separate locking file for Kenneth's office. This permits the counseling notes to be kept confidential and separate from students' educational records that are accessible to others under provisions of the Family Educational Rights to Privacy Act (FERPA).

B.6.b. Permission to Record

Counselors obtain permission from clients prior to recording sessions through electronic or other means.

Qi-Ling is a master's degree student completing her internship in a counseling agency. She explains to each of her clients at the first session that she is a trainee and is working under supervision. She asks for permission to audiotape the sessions, explaining that she will be reviewing the tapes to assess her work and that her supervisor will also listen to portions of the tapes and provide her with feedback.

B.6.c. Permission to Observe

Counselors obtain permission from clients prior to observing counseling sessions, reviewing session transcripts, or viewing recordings of sessions with supervisors, faculty, peers, or others within the training environment.

Ellen has earned her master's degree and is working toward her licensure as a professional counselor. She works in an agency that has an observation facility, and her supervisor periodically observes from behind the one-way mirror. Ellen informs clients that she is working toward her license and that she is being supervised. She explains to clients about the one-way mirror and obtains their permission before proceeding to counsel them.

B.6.d. Client Access

Counselors provide reasonable access to records and copies of records when requested by competent clients. Counselors limit the access of clients to their records, or portions of their records, only when there is compelling evidence that such access would cause harm to the client. Counselors document the request of clients and the rationale for withholding some or all of the record in the files of clients. In situations involving multiple clients, counselors provide individual clients with only those parts of records that related directly to them and do not include confidential information related to any other client.

Fred receives a call from Marcia, a former client whom he saw individually for 3 months. Marcia's husband also attended several conjoint counseling sessions and came to see Fred twice for individual sessions. Marcia now tells Fred that she and her husband are divorced, she is moving to another state, and she wants a copy of her records. Fred agrees to send her a copy of the records of her individual sessions and explains that he cannot release those portions of the records that include confidential information about her former husband without the ex-husband's consent.

B.6.e. Assistance With Records

When clients request access to their records, counselors provide assistance and consultation in interpreting counseling records.

Margaret is a 40-year-old client who has been seeing a counselor in private practice. Margaret asks to look at the records the counselor is keeping of their sessions. When the counselor asks why she wants to examine the records, Margaret explains that she had a bad experience with a former boss who wrote negative comments about her and placed them in her file. Since that incident, she tends not to be very trusting about what is recorded about her. The counselor makes a copy of the records for Margaret and reviews their contents with her. The counselor checks to ensure that Margaret understands the content and meaning of the records.

B.6.f. Disclosure or Transfer

Unless exceptions to confidentiality exist, counselors obtain written permission from clients to disclose or transfer records to legitimate third parties. Steps are taken to ensure that receivers of counseling records are sensitive to their confidential nature. *(See A.3., E.4.)*

Wayne, an LPC, receives a request from a psychiatrist requesting the records of a former client. The psychiatrist's written request includes a written authorization from the client. Wayne sends the records with a cover letter stating that the records are confidential.

B.6.g. Storage and Disposal After Termination

Counselors store records following termination of services to ensure reasonable future access, maintain records in accordance with state and federal statutes governing records, and dispose of client records and other sensitive materials in a manner that protects client confidentiality. When records are of an artistic nature, counselors obtain client (or guardian) consent with regard to handling of such records or documents. *(See A.1.b.)*

Naomi routinely keeps her entire counseling records for 5 years following termination of services. After 5 years have passed, she shreds the records, keeping on a diskette only basic information such as client name and contact information, dates seen and services rendered, diagnoses, and a summary of the counseling process. She takes care, however, not to destroy any client files for which litigation might be anticipated.

B.6.h. Reasonable Precautions

Counselors take reasonable precautions to protect client confidentiality in the event of the counselor's termination of practice, incapacity, or death. *(See C.2.h.)*

Oliver is in a group private practice with three other LPCs. He has made a contractual arrangement with one of his partners that the partner will assume his client load and provide continuing counseling services if Oliver should die, become incapacitated, or terminate his practice. The partner has agreed to assume responsibility for maintaining clients' confidentiality.

B.7. Research and Training

B.7.a. Institutional Approval

When institutional approval is required, counselors provide accurate information about their research proposals and obtain approval prior to conducting their research. They conduct research in accordance with the approved research protocol.

Paula is a professor in a counselor education program. She is planning to conduct a research study using human participants. She prepares and submits to her university's Institutional Review Board (IRB) a formal request for permission to conduct the study. She undertakes her research project only after receiving written approval from the IRB.

B.7.b. Adherence to Guidelines

Counselors are responsible for understanding and adhering to state, federal, agency, or institutional policies or applicable guidelines regarding confidentiality in their research practices.

Janet is a new assistant professor in a counselor education program. Because this is her first faculty position, she attends an orientation session conducted by the university's Office of Sponsored Research. During the orientation, she learns about state, federal, and university policies and procedures for conducting research, including requirements for maintaining confidentiality in conducting research with human participants.

B.7.c. Confidentiality of Information Obtained in Research

Violations of participant privacy and confidentiality are risks of participation in research involving human participants. Investigators maintain all research records in a secure manner. They explain to participants the risks of violations of privacy and confidentiality and disclose to participants any limits of confidentiality that reasonably can be expected. Regardless of the degree to which confidentiality will be maintained, investigators must disclose to participants any limits of confidentiality that reasonably can be expected. *(See G.2.e.)*

Karl is a doctoral student in a counselor education program. He is about to begin his dissertation research. He plans to conduct survey research by electronic mail to investigate the level of multicultural awareness of master's-level counseling interns. Although he intends to use a software program that protects the anonymity of the respondents to the survey, his participant consent form explains that e-mail is not always 100% secure. Before beginning his study, he receives approval from his dissertation committee and the university Institutional Review Board (IRB). Both bodies verify that Karl has adequately explained the risks of violations of privacy.

B.7.d. Disclosure of Research Information

Counselors do not disclose confidential information that reasonably could lead to the identification of a research participant unless they have obtained the prior consent of the person. Use of data derived from counseling relationships for purposes of training, research, or publication is confined to content that is disguised to ensure the anonymity of the individuals involved. *(See G.2.a., G.2.d.)*

Laurie is a doctoral student who is conducting a qualitative dissertation study. To ensure participant anonymity, she assigns a pseudonym to each of her participants. In reporting her findings, she carefully constructs her participant profiles to avoid including any information that could potentially identify any participant to the readers.

B.7.e. Agreement for Identification

Identification of clients, students, or supervisees in a presentation or publication is permissible only when they have reviewed the material and agreed to its presentation or publication. *(See G.4.d.)*

Ernest is a counselor educator who is planning to give a presentation at a professional conference. The topic of his presentation is "critical incidents in counselor supervision." The presentation will include showing a videotape of three supervision sessions that Ernest conducted with his students. Ernest reviews each videotape with the student depicted and secures the student's permission to use the videotape in his presentation.

B.8. Consultation

B.8.a. Agreements

When acting as consultants, counselors seek agreements among all parties involved concerning each individual's rights to confidentiality, the obligation of each individual to preserve confidential information, and the limits of confidentiality of information shared by others.

Ibrahim is offered an opportunity to serve as a consultant at a psychiatric hospital. The director of the hospital asks him to conduct a training workshop for the staff in managing job-related stress. Before accepting the opportunity, Ibrahim clarifies that his report to the director will provide general information on the effectiveness of the workshop but will contain no information that could identify any particular staff member who participates. He obtains the director's pledge to respect the confidentiality of the report, and discusses the director's intended use of the report to ensure that there will be no negative repercussions for participating staff members.

B.8.b. Respect for Privacy

Information obtained in a consulting relationship is discussed for professional purposes only with persons directly involved with the case. Written and oral reports present only data germane to the purposes of the consultation, and every effort is made to protect client identity and to avoid undue invasion of privacy.

Germaine, an LPC in private practice, conducts a diversity sensitivity workshop for all the teachers in a particular elementary school. When she meets with the principal and is asked for information that might help him increase his teachers' ability to relate to students who are culturally different from themselves, she provides only general information about strategies to increase multicultural competence among educators. She takes care to avoid identifying any particular teacher who participated in the workshop.

B.8.c. Disclosure of Confidential Information

When consulting with colleagues, counselors do not disclose confidential information that reasonably could lead to the identification of a client or other person or organization with whom they have a confidential relationship unless they have obtained the prior consent of the person or organization or the disclosure cannot be avoided. They disclose information only to the extent necessary to achieve the purposes of the consultation. *(See D.2.d.)*

Jacqueline, an adjunct faculty member, is providing clinical supervision to Jerome, a counselor intern in the master's program. She becomes increasingly aware that Jerome is uncomfortable discussing personalization issues with her during their supervision sessions. She attempts to discuss this with Jerome, but he insists that there is no problem. Jacqueline wonders whether the difficulty lies in Jerome's resistance to supervision or in her inability to establish a trusting supervisory relationship with him. She seeks consultation from another faculty member, describing the issues as she perceives them but taking care not to provide information that would enable the consulting faculty member to identify Jerome.

Section C

Professional Responsibility

Study and Discussion Guide

- **Boundaries of Competence:** Assume that your employer asks you to perform services for which you do not have the needed training or experience. What might you say to your employer? If you wanted to develop and practice in a new area of specialty, how would you go about obtaining the appropriate education, training, and supervised experience?
- **Maintaining Expertise:** What steps do you need to take to maintain competence in the skills you use and to keep current with new developments? To what extent do you need to participate in continuing education activities to ensure that you are being ethical?
- **Seeking Consultation:** Under what circumstances might you consult with another professional regarding your ethical obligations to a client? How can you determine when a client's condition represents a clear and imminent danger to the client or others? How can you assess the degree of danger?
- **Impairment:** What are your opinions about impaired counselors who continue to practice? How do you recognize early signs of burnout or impairment in yourself? What would you do if you became aware that a condition was beginning to negatively impact your work?
- **Sexual Harassment:** Can you think of ways to prevent sexual harassment from occurring in your workplace?
- **Clients Served by Others:** If you discovered that one of your clients was also seeing another mental health professional, and the client did not want you to contact the other professional to coordinate services, what would you do?

Section C

Professional Responsibility

Introduction

Counselors aspire to open, honest, and accurate communication in dealing with the public and other professionals. They practice in a nondiscriminatory manner within the boundaries of professional and personal competence and have a responsibility to abide by the *ACA Code of Ethics.*

Counselors actively participate in local, state, and national associations that foster the development and improvement of counseling. Counselors advocate to promote change at the individual, group, institutional, and societal levels that improves the quality of life for individuals and groups and removes potential barriers to the provision or access of appropriate services being offered. Counselors have a responsibility to the public to engage in counseling practices that are based on rigorous research methodologies. In addition, counselors engage in self-care activities to maintain and promote their emotional, physical, mental, and spiritual well-being to best meet their professional responsibilities.

C.1. Knowledge of Standards

Counselors have a responsibility to read, understand, and follow the *ACA Code of Ethics* and adhere to applicable laws and regulations.

> Connie is a counselor who works in a group private practice with four other counselors. When the 2005 *ACA Code of Ethics* is published, she reads it carefully. She asks her partners in the practice to also read the document and requests that the five of them meet to discuss their understanding of the standards and how they apply to their practice.

C.2. Professional Competence

C.2.a. Boundaries of Competence

Counselors practice only within the boundaries of their competence, based on their education, training, supervised experience, state and national professional credentials, and appropriate professional experience. Counselors gain knowledge, personal awareness, sensitivity, and skills pertinent to working with a diverse client population. *(See A.9.b., C.4.e., E.2., F.2., F.11.b.)*

> Daniel is working in a community agency that serves a culturally diverse client population. Realizing that he has limited knowledge of some of the cultural groups with whom he works, he attends several workshops dealing with specific needs of these client groups. Daniel is aware that his graduate training did not equip him to effectively meet all the challenges that he is now facing, and he is committed to continuing his education as a means to fill this gap.

C.2.b. New Specialty Areas of Practice

Counselors practice in specialty areas new to them only after appropriate education, training, and supervised experience. While developing skills in new specialty areas, counselors take steps to ensure the competence of their work and to protect others from possible harm. *(See F.6.f.)*

> Will is asked to facilitate a support group for AIDS patients. Although he has attended several workshops on AIDS-related issues and counseling and has done extensive reading in journals and books on the subject, he has limited experience in working directly with persons with AIDS. He arranges to cofacilitate the group for the first 3 months with a colleague who is experienced in counseling people with AIDS. He also seeks ongoing supervision of his work.

C.2.c. Qualified for Employment
Counselors accept employment only for positions for which they are qualified by education, training, supervised experience, state and national professional credentials, and appropriate professional experience. Counselors hire for professional counseling positions only individuals who are qualified and competent for those positions.

Yin-Li, the director of a community counseling agency, has placed an advertisement seeking a counselor to staff its satellite center in a small community about 2 hours' drive from the main office where Yin-Li works. The person hired to staff the satellite center will need to work independently, with only minimal supervision from the director. Yin-Li interviews a man who recently completed his master's degree. Although she is favorably impressed with the applicant, she does not hire him because she realizes that this recent graduate lacks sufficient experience to work without closer supervision.

C.2.d. Monitor Effectiveness
Counselors continually monitor their effectiveness as professionals and take steps to improve when necessary. Counselors in private practice take reasonable steps to seek peer supervision as needed to evaluate their efficacy as counselors.

A counselor practices in a city whose population has expanded dramatically due to an influx of immigrants from Central American countries. The counselor's parents immigrated from Mexico, and he is fluent in Spanish, but he grew up in the United States and has little knowledge of Central American cultures. As he begins to see more clients who are recent immigrants, he seeks peer supervision regarding his work with these clients.

C.2.e. Consultation on Ethical Obligations
Counselors take reasonable steps to consult with other counselors or related professionals when they have questions regarding their ethical obligations or professional practice.

Mustafa, a counselor who works on an army base, encounters an ethical dilemma in working with a servicewoman and her family. He consults with two different professionals who have expertise in family counseling to explore his options for dealing with the dilemma. Both consultants offer similar suggestions, and he follows their advice. He documents the consultations in his case notes.

C.2.f. Continuing Education
Counselors recognize the need for continuing education to acquire and maintain a reasonable level of awareness of current scientific and professional information in their fields of activity. They take steps to maintain competence in the skills they use, are open to new procedures, and keep current with the diverse populations and specific populations with whom they work.

Peter is a counselor who has had no specialized training or course work in counseling gay and lesbian clients. He does not want to deny counseling services to this population, but he is concerned that some of his attitudes and his limited knowledge will hamper his effectiveness. Peter reads journal articles on counseling gay, lesbian, bisexual, and transgender (GLBT) people, and he purchases a book dealing with this client population. He then attends a professional development institute on counseling gay and lesbian clients and participates in several meetings of a local organization of gay and lesbian mental health professionals. Peter realizes that he needs to be open to learning and that he will have to challenge some of his assumptions.

C.2.g. Impairment

Counselors are alert to the signs of impairment from their own physical, mental, or emotional problems and refrain from offering or providing professional services when such impairment is likely to harm a client or others. They seek assistance for problems that reach the level of professional impairment, and, if necessary, they limit, suspend, or terminate their professional responsibilities until such time it is determined that they may safely resume their work. Counselors assist colleagues or supervisors in recognizing their own professional impairment and provide consultation and assistance when warranted with colleagues or supervisors showing signs of impairment and intervene as appropriate to prevent imminent harm to clients. *(See A.11.b., F.8.b.)*

Rhonda is a counselor in private practice who facilitates grief groups two evenings a week. She suffers the unexpected loss of both of her parents in an auto accident. As a result, she does not feel that she can provide competent counseling services for the group members. She informs them of the situation and, with their approval, makes arrangements for another qualified professional to conduct the sessions.

C.2.h. Counselor Incapacitation or Termination of Practice

When counselors leave a practice, they follow a prepared plan for transfer of clients and files. Counselors prepare and disseminate to an identified colleague or "records custodian" a plan for the transfer of clients and files in the case of their incapacitation, death, or termination of practice.

Katherine is planning to retire from her private practice in counseling. Long before her retirement, she began refusing new clients because she is concerned about not abandoning any of her current clients. Katherine has the best interests of her clients as a central concern, and she began planning over a year in advance of her intended retirement date. Her advance planning included the maintenance, custody, security, and transfer of her clients' records. She prepared a letter that she sent to all of her current and former clients announcing her eventual retirement, and she discussed with all of her current clients how her retirement plans might affect their present and future counseling relationship.

C.3. Advertising and Soliciting Clients

C.3.a. Accurate Advertising

When advertising or otherwise representing their services to the public, counselors identify their credentials in an accurate manner that is not false, misleading, deceptive, or fraudulent.

In establishing a private practice in counseling, Enrico places advertisements in the yellow pages and the newspaper and mails announcements to local professionals. The advertisements give Enrico's name, address, and telephone number and accurately state that he has a master's degree in counseling (which he received from a fully accredited state university) and is licensed as a professional counselor in the state.

C.3.b. Testimonials

Counselors who use testimonials do not solicit them from current clients nor former clients nor any other persons who may be vulnerable to undue influence.

Glenda, a consultant, conducts a workshop for teachers and asks participants to evaluate the content and presentation style. Feedback is positive, and she decides to create a promotional flyer and market the workshop to other school districts. She secures the permission of some of the teachers to include a few of their comments from the evaluation form in her flyer. The comments are included in an appropriate way to give potential consumers an idea of the focus and format of the workshop.

C.3.c. Statements by Others

Counselors make reasonable efforts to ensure that statements made by others about them or the profession of counseling are accurate.

Luanne is a licensed professional counselor in private practice. She is sometimes mistakenly labeled as a psychologist by prospective clients and members of the community. Whenever this occurs, Luanne carefully explains her credentials to clarify the distinction.

C.3.d. Recruiting Through Employment

Counselors do not use their places of employment or institutional affiliation to recruit or gain clients, supervisees, or consultees for their private practices.

Lupe, a licensed counselor with a private practice, also teaches two counseling courses in a master's degree program at a state university. In her teaching, she draws from her years of experience in working with individuals, couples, and families in her private practice. Whenever she uses clinical cases as examples in class, she is careful to disguise details to protect her former or current clients. Lupe takes care to avoid using her role as an instructor to promote her practice, either directly or indirectly. She is well respected as an instructor and at times students have approached her requesting personal counseling. Lupe declines to accept any student as a counseling client because she does not want to engage in a dual relationship with students and she does not want to use her classroom as a way to recruit clients. She does, however, have a pool of professional counselors that she uses as referral resources.

C.3.e. Products and Training Advertisements

Counselors who develop products related to their profession or conduct workshops or training events ensure that the advertisements concerning these products or events are accurate and disclose adequate information for consumers to make informed choices. *(See C.6.d.)*

James is a counselor who conducts parent effectiveness training workshops, using training materials that he has developed. In his promotional material, he includes the purpose, content, and format of the training, along with a description of the materials that are required reading for the participants. He is careful to clarify that the cost of all required materials is included in the workshop fee.

C.3.f. Promoting to Those Served

Counselors do not use counseling, teaching, training, or supervisory relationships to promote their products or training events in a manner that is deceptive or would exert undue influence on individuals who may be vulnerable. However, counselor educators may adopt textbooks they have authored for instructional purposes.

Raynette, a counselor educator, teaches a multicultural counseling course. The required textbook is one that she has coauthored. She provides students with articles written by others, invites guest speakers to class, and presents a variety of viewpoints so that students receive a balanced perspective.

C.4. Professional Qualifications

C.4.a. Accurate Representation

Counselors claim or imply only professional qualifications actually completed and correct any known misrepresentations of their qualifications by others. Counselors truthfully represent the qualifications of their professional colleagues. Counselors clearly distinguish between paid and volunteer work experience and accurately describe their continuing education and specialized training. *(See C.2.a.)*

Tanya is a counselor who holds a master's degree. She acquires licensure in her state and also seeks specialized additional training and receives certification as a chemical dependency counselor. A continuing education program at a university hires her to conduct a weekend workshop on drug abuse prevention with adolescents. The promotional flyer designed by the continuing education program incorrectly refers to Tanya as "Dr." Fortunately, Tanya asked to see the flyer prior to mailing so that she could give her comments. She immediately informs the program that she does not have a doctoral degree and asks them to change this before mailing the flyer.

C.4.b. Credentials

Counselors claim only licenses or certifications that are current and in good standing.

Edna has a part-time private practice in counseling. She has earned licenses as a professional counselor and a clinical social worker. She has allowed her license as a social worker to lapse. Her business cards state that she is both a licensed counselor and a social worker. Edna destroys these cards and orders new ones that advertise only her LPC status.

C.4.c. Educational Degrees

Counselors clearly differentiate between earned and honorary degrees.

Wilma earned a doctorate in counseling psychology from a CACREP-approved program in a private university. She later became an assistant professor, teaching counseling courses in a graduate program. She is very active in community work. After years of setting up programs in the community and serving as a liaison person between the university where she was teaching and various community agencies, she was granted an honorary doctorate in humane letters by this university. In her résumé she describes her education and lists her undergraduate and graduate degrees. She also lists that she was granted an honorary doctorate.

C.4.d. Implying Doctoral-Level Competence

Counselors clearly state their highest earned degree in counseling or closely related field. Counselors do not imply doctoral-level competence when only possessing a master's degree in counseling or a related field by referring to themselves as "Dr." in a counseling context when their doctorate is not in counseling or a related field.

Jim is a practicing dentist who is also licensed as a counselor. He has had specialized training in hypnosis. Jim has two sets of business cards, one for his counseling practice and one for his dental practice. His business card for counseling announces only his master's degree in counseling and his state license.

C.4.e. Program Accreditation Status

Counselors clearly state the accreditation status of their degree programs at the time the degree was earned.

Vanessa, who recently earned a master's degree in a CACREP-accredited counseling program, is now applying for a position as a counselor in a community agency. On her résumé she lists her degree, the name of the university, and the fact that the program is CACREP-accredited.

C.4.f. Professional Membership

Counselors clearly differentiate between current, active memberships and former memberships in associations. Members of the American Counseling Association must clearly differentiate between professional membership, which implies the possession of at least a master's degree in counseling, and regular membership, which is open to individuals whose interests and activities are consistent with those of ACA but are not qualified for professional membership.

Celeste is a special education teacher. She earned her master's degree in counseling several years ago and maintains her professional membership in ACA, but she has decided that she would rather remain in the classroom. She does some occasional consulting and decides to have some business cards printed. On her cards, she describes herself as a "Teacher and Consultant." She does not include mention of her ACA membership to avoid any possibility of giving readers the impression that she is a practicing counselor. However, in her résumé she lists memberships in ACA as well as other organizations in which she holds membership.

C.5. Nondiscrimination

Counselors do not condone or engage in discrimination based on age, culture, disability, ethnicity, race, religion/spirituality, gender, gender identity, sexual orientation, marital status/partnership, language preference, socioeconomic status, or any basis proscribed by law. Counselors do not discriminate against clients, students, employees, supervisees, or research participants in a manner that has a negative impact on these persons.

Lori is a 29-year-old counselor who has worked for 3 years on an inpatient unit of a psychiatric hospital. She has received very positive annual evaluations from the unit director, a fact she attributes largely to the positive mentoring she has received from Marie. Marie, who is in her early 60s, has been a counselor on the same unit for more than a decade. When the unit director is promoted, he recommends the 29-year-old Lori to succeed him in that position. Lori believes that Marie is better qualified to become unit director, and that the only reason Marie was not recommended was her age. Lori explains her concern to the hospital administrator, who agrees to reopen the search to fill the position and to interview Marie along with other qualified candidates.

C.6. Public Responsibility

C.6.a. Sexual Harassment

Counselors do not engage in or condone sexual harassment. Sexual harassment is defined as sexual solicitation, physical advances, or verbal or nonverbal conduct that is sexual in nature, that occurs in connection with professional activities or roles, and that either

1. is unwelcome, is offensive, or creates a hostile workplace or learning environment, and counselors know or are told this; or
2. is sufficiently severe or intense to be perceived as harassment to a reasonable person in the context in which the behavior occurred.

Sexual harassment can consist of a single intense or severe act or multiple persistent or pervasive acts.

Miguel is cofacilitating a daylong personal growth group for young adults. As the group progresses through its morning session, Miguel notices that his female cofacilitator is being flirtatious with a male group member and hugs him in a way that seems inappropriate during breaks. At the first opportunity, Miguel confronts the cofacilitator and explains his objections to her behavior. The cofacilitator ceases her unprofessional behavior.

C.6.b. Reports to Third Parties

Counselors are accurate, honest, and objective in reporting their professional activities and judgments to appropriate third parties, including courts, health insurance companies, those who are the recipients of evaluation reports, and others. *(See B.3., E.4.)*

Steve receives a court-ordered subpoena for all his records concerning a client. His case notes of early sessions reveal that his initial diagnosis was inaccurate. The notes also show that both the diagnosis and treatment plan were later revised to address more accurately the client's concerns and needs.

Although Steve is somewhat embarrassed that officers of the court will be reading his records and will see his early error, he submits the records to the court in their entirety as required.

C.6.c. Media Presentations

When counselors provide advice or comment by means of public lectures, demonstrations, radio or television programs, prerecorded tapes, technology-based applications, printed articles, mailed material, or other media, they take reasonable precautions to ensure that

1. the statements are based on appropriate professional counseling literature and practice,
2. the statements are otherwise consistent with the *ACA Code of Ethics*, and
3. the recipients of the information are not encouraged to infer that a professional counseling relationship has been established.

Irene, a counselor in private practice, has accepted an invitation from a radio station to talk about one of her popular self-help books on combating depression. During her talk, Irene emphasizes that her general suggestions are not to be taken as a substitute for counseling. She avoids giving simplistic solutions for people suffering from depression.

C.6.d. Exploitation of Others

Counselors do not exploit others in their professional relationships. *(See C.3.e.)*

Sharon is a mental health counselor in private practice. Her client, Suzie, informs her that she can no longer afford to come for counseling because she has unexpectedly lost her job. Suzie proposes to Sharon that she work for Sharon as a nanny, which would allow her to continue her counseling and pay her bills as well. Sharon is looking for a nanny for her young child but, after thinking through the matter, explains to Suzie that she cannot hire her as a nanny. Sharon agrees, instead, to see Suzie on a pro bono basis for a month while Suzie is looking for a job.

C.6.e. Scientific Bases for Treatment Modalities

Counselors use techniques/procedures/modalities that are grounded in theory and/or have an empirical or scientific foundation. Counselors who do not must define the techniques/procedures as "unproven" or "developing" and explain the potential risks and ethical considerations of using such techniques/procedures and take steps to protect clients from possible harm. *(See A.4.a., E.5.c., E.5.d.)*

Hannah attends a weekend workshop on an innovative, body-oriented therapy. Because the workshop is experiential and aimed at personal growth for the participants, Hannah leaves with new insights into how she prevents herself from expressing some painful emotions. Although she benefits from her experience at this workshop, she refrains from introducing this innovative technique in the weekly group counseling sessions she conducts. She is aware of its lack of proven efficacy with the population with whom she is working in her groups. She also realizes that she would need far more supervised training before she uses this body-oriented approach.

C.7. Responsibility to Other Professionals

C.7.a. Personal Public Statements

When making personal statements in a public context, counselors clarify that they are speaking from their personal perspectives and that they are not speaking on behalf of all counselors or the profession.

Boyd, a public offender counselor, attends a community meeting designed to deal with the problem of gang violence on the streets. Boyd is a well-known and respected member of the community. When he gives his input on the issues being discussed, he emphasizes that these are his personal views and that he is not representing the counseling profession.

Section D

Relationships With Other Professionals

Study and Discussion Guide

- **Interdisciplinary Team Work:** If you were a member of a treatment team in an institution or agency that included a psychologist, psychiatrist, clinical social worker, and psychiatric nurse, what kind of professional relationship would you want to have with them? What are some steps you could take to establish and maintain such a relationship?
- **Defining Roles:** What problems have you encountered, or do you anticipate that you might encounter, in defining your professional role to your employer? What might you do if your employer expected you to perform functions that you viewed as incompatible with your role?
- **Discrimination:** If you became aware that another professional in your work setting was discriminating against individuals based on their religion, what might you say or do? What if it were discrimination based on sexual orientation?
- **Exploitive Relationships:** If you became aware that a colleague was engaging in exploitive behavior toward his or her supervisees, what might you do?
- **Consultation:** What do you tell clients about the possibility that you will seek consultation with other professionals to discuss their case? What kind of understanding might you want to have with your clients?

Section D

Relationships With Other Professionals

Introduction

Professional counselors recognize that the quality of their interactions with colleagues can influence the quality of services provided to clients. They work to become knowledgeable about colleagues within and outside the field of counseling. Counselors develop positive working relationships and systems of communication with colleagues to enhance services to clients.

D.1. Relationships With Colleagues, Employers, and Employees

D.1.a. Different Approaches

Counselors are respectful of approaches to counseling services that differ from their own. Counselors are respectful of traditions and practices of other professional groups with which they work.

Gayle is a counseling psychologist who teaches in an interdisciplinary human services program at a university. Her primary theoretical orientation is Gestalt therapy. She teaches an introductory course for undergraduate students who may eventually choose careers as counselors, social workers, school psychologists, or marriage and family therapists. In her classes she includes perspectives from all of these disciplines and demonstrates a respectful attitude toward a variety of helping professions. Gayle also presents basic concepts from the psychoanalytic, humanistic, cognitive-behavioral, and systemic orientations.

D.1.b. Forming Relationships
Counselors work to develop and strengthen interdisciplinary relations with colleagues from other disciplines to best serve clients.

Anthony, a licensed counselor, is the director of an agency-based community program. He is committed to having a group meeting of the professional staff on a weekly basis. These sessions give the team members an opportunity to talk about how their work in the agency is affecting them personally, and how they might better manage the stresses associated with their work. On this team are a social worker, nurse, clinical psychologist, recreational therapist, and counselor. The team members are able to identify ways that they can work with each other collaboratively and how they can enhance the treatment program to best meet the needs of the clients.

D.1.c. Interdisciplinary Team Work
Counselors who are members of interdisciplinary teams delivering multifaceted services to clients keep the focus on how to best serve the clients. They participate in and contribute to decisions that affect the well-being of clients by drawing on the perspectives, values, and experiences of the counseling profession and those of colleagues from other disciplines. *(See A.1.a.)*

Members of a treatment team in a psychiatric hospital meet on a regular basis to share perspectives on client care. At each meeting, on a rotational basis, a different team member is in charge of structuring the agenda and facilitating the meeting. As a group, these professionals identify program needs and what they can do to improve conditions for both those being served and for the team members.

D.1.d. Confidentiality
When counselors are required by law, institutional policy, or extraordinary circumstances to serve in more than one role in judicial or administrative proceedings, they clarify role expectations and the parameters of confidentiality with their colleagues. *(See B.1.c., B.1.d., B.2.c., B.2.d., B.3.b.)*

Jeffrey is a member of the clinical staff and is also the program director of a community health center. In addition to his clinical duties providing direct services to individuals and families, he also participates in hiring and evaluating other members of the treatment team. Jeffrey is a clinical colleague, but he is also expected to conduct regular evaluations of others on the team. He strives to clearly state what is expected of him in his roles of providing clinical services and evaluating others in the professional staff. He has also clarified with his colleagues the parameters of confidentiality.

D.1.e. Establishing Professional and Ethical Obligations

Counselors who are members of interdisciplinary teams clarify professional and ethical obligations of the team as a whole and of its individual members. When a team decision raises ethical concerns, counselors first attempt to resolve the concern within the team. If they cannot reach resolution among team members, counselors pursue other avenues to address their concerns consistent with client well-being.

On a particular treatment team, a decision was made to provide an initial *DSM-IV* diagnosis at the first meeting with a client. This decision was the result of some pressure from the agency director, who made it clear that establishing a diagnosis and formulating a treatment plan were required by the HMO. On ethical grounds, some of the professional staff objected to the pressure to formulate a diagnosis and specific treatment plan at the initial session. Others on the staff did not share the same ethical concerns and believed some policies could not be changed. Because the team did not have a unified view of this policy that affected practice, they asked for time to discuss their concerns with the agency director.

D.1.f. Personnel Selection and Assignment

Counselors select competent staff and assign responsibilities compatible with their skills and experiences.

Martha opened her private practice office a year ago, and her practice has grown to the point where she needs to hire a full-time receptionist/clerical assistant. She advertises the position and interviews an applicant who has had considerable experience working as a receptionist for a group of medical doctors. This applicant has a good grasp of office procedures and understands the importance of maintaining patient confidentiality. Her references are excellent, and she is very amenable to further training and supervision. Martha hires the applicant.

D.1.g. Employer Policies

The acceptance of employment in an agency or institution implies that counselors are in agreement with its general policies and principles. Counselors strive to reach agreement with employers as to acceptable standards of conduct that allow for changes in institutional policy conducive to the growth and development of clients.

Vaughn is employed as a counselor in a residential facility for juvenile offenders. The new director of the facility institutes a policy that involves administering what Vaughn sees as harsh punishments to residents who break the rules. Vaughn consults with the director about his ethical opposition to such methods. The director agrees to call a meeting of all staff counselors to discuss the policy.

D.1.h. Negative Conditions

Counselors alert their employers of inappropriate policies and practices. They attempt to effect changes in such policies or procedures through constructive action within the organization. When such policies are potentially disruptive or damaging to clients or may limit the effectiveness of services provided and change cannot be effected, counselors take appropriate further action. Such action may include referral to appropriate certification, accreditation, or state licensure organizations, or voluntary termination of employment.

An employment counselor finds that so much of her time is needed to contact prospective employers and get information about job openings that she doesn't have enough time to update the files on the qualifications and interests of clients. The counselor informs her supervisor of this concern, and the supervisor agrees to hire an additional clerical staff person.

D.1.i. Protection From Punitive Action

Counselors take care not to harass or dismiss an employee who has acted in a responsible and ethical manner to expose inappropriate employer policies or practices.

At a meeting Marquita raises objections to the fact that a weekly support group for the professional staff has been terminated at the agency due to budget cuts. Marquita states the reasons for her concerns and suggests other alternatives because so many of the staff highly valued this support group. Her supervisor takes measures to see that Marquita will not be subjected to retaliation because of her vocal opposition to a decision that was made at the administrative level.

D.2. Consultation

D.2.a. Consultant Competency

Counselors take reasonable steps to ensure that they have the appropriate resources and competencies when providing consultation services. Counselors provide appropriate referral resources when requested or needed. *(See C.2.a.)*

Chandra is a professor who is offered a position as a consultant to a research project. She is told that her role will be to help with the statistical analysis of the data for the study. She asks to meet with the researchers to define further the parameters of her role. During this meeting, it becomes clear that she will be expected to provide technical help with a particular computerized statistical package in which she does not have expertise. She declines the consultant position and suggests the names of other well-qualified consultants.

D.2.b. Understanding Consultees

When providing consultation, counselors attempt to develop with their consultees a clear understanding of problem definition, goals for change, and predicted consequences of interventions selected.

Nicole, a school district guidance coordinator, is hired by a neighboring school district to mediate a conflict between counselors and faculty. Faculty representatives tell Nicole that they want the counselors to "get out of their offices and do something other than generate paperwork." Counselors tell her that the faculty needs to be educated about the counselor's role. Nicole goes to the principal to be certain that she has a clear idea of her task and the principal's full support. Receiving affirmation, she calls a meeting of the principal, the faculty representatives, and the counselors to outline goals and define the problems they will be working to solve.

D.2.c. Consultant Goals

The consulting relationship is one in which consultee adaptability and growth toward self-direction are consistently encouraged and cultivated.

Ramona is hired as a consultant to a mental health agency. She is asked to help set up an outreach center. She offers illustrations of approaches taken by other agencies and involves the staff in designing the new center. She encourages them to assume responsibility for implementing the design, and she remains available for consultation as they open the new center.

D.2.d. Informed Consent in Consultation

When providing consultation, counselors have an obligation to review, in writing and verbally, the rights and responsibilities of both counselors and consultees. Counselors use clear and understandable language to inform all parties involved about the purpose of the services to be provided, relevant costs, potential risks and benefits, and the limits of confidentiality. Working in conjunction with the consultee, counselors attempt to develop a clear definition of the problem, goals for change, and predicted consequences of interventions that are culturally responsive and appropriate to the needs of consultees. *(See A.2.a., A.2.b.)*

Deanna is hired by a private psychiatric hospital to provide stress-management training for the staff who work there. She informs the staff that she will be expected to provide the director of the hospital with feedback about what they find stressful about working in the facility. She lets the staff know that, although she will provide the director with information about sources of stress, she will take care to protect the identities of specific individuals.

Section E

Evaluation, Assessment, and Interpretation

Study and Discussion Guide

- **Competence:** How can you determine whether you are competent to use a particular assessment instrument?
- **Informed Consent:** Prior to using assessment with clients, how might you explain in clear and specific language the nature and purposes of the assessment? In what ways do you attempt to involve your clients in the assessment process?
- **Administering Assessments:** What factors do you need to consider when you are planning to administer an assessment to a client or a group of clients to ensure that the assessment is properly administered?
- **Diagnosis:** What ethical issues are involved in making a diagnosis? What are your own views about the role of diagnosis in counseling?
- **Cultural Sensitivity:** In making a diagnosis, what attention will you give to the cultural and environmental variables that might pertain to a client's concerns? What role do you think clients' socioeconomic and cultural experiences have in helping you to understand their problems?
- **Assessment and Testing:** When might you make use of assessment instruments as a part of the counseling process? What factors do you need to take into account in selecting, administering, scoring, and interpreting tests? What are the ethical considerations in testing diverse client populations?
- **Forensic Evaluation:** What do you see as the counselor's role in forensic evaluation (evaluation for legal proceedings)? If you were to conduct a forensic evaluation, how could you avoid conflicts between your role as a forensic evaluator and your role as a counselor?

Section E

Evaluation, Assessment, and Interpretation

Introduction

Counselors use assessment instruments as one component of the counseling process, taking into account the client personal and cultural context. Counselors promote the well-being of individual clients or groups of clients by developing and using appropriate educational, psychological, and career assessment instruments.

E.1. General

E.1.a. Assessment

The primary purpose of educational, psychological, and career assessment is to provide measurements that are valid and reliable in either comparative or absolute terms. These include, but are not limited to, measurements of ability, personality, interest, intelligence, achievement, and performance. Counselors recognize the need to interpret the statements in this section as applying to both quantitative and qualitative assessments.

> Melody, a private practitioner, administers a personality test to one of her clients. The instrument has been extensively field-tested and found to be reliable and valid. She carefully explains the purpose of the test and how the results will be used in the therapeutic process.

E.1.b. Client Welfare

Counselors do not misuse assessment results and interpretations, and they take reasonable steps to prevent others from misusing the information these techniques provide. They respect the client's right to know the results, the interpretations made, and the bases for counselors' conclusions and recommendations.

> Nancy is a high school counselor. A week before the administration of achievement tests to the sophomore class, she visits classrooms to explain the purpose of this test series. When the results become available, she meets with each sophomore to interpret the results. She sends the parents a letter that provides information about how test scores should be interpreted and puts a copy of this letter in the mailbox of each sophomore teacher.

E.2. Competence to Use and Interpret Assessment Instruments

E.2.a. Limits of Competence

Counselors utilize only those testing and assessment services for which they have been trained and are competent. Counselors using technology-assisted test interpretations are trained in the construct being measured and the specific instrument being used prior to using its technology-based application. Counselors take reasonable measures to ensure the proper use of psychological and career assessment techniques by persons under their supervision. *(See A.12.)*

> The director of a mental health agency asks Luz, an LPC employed at the agency, to administer the MMPI-II to a client. Luz is not trained in the administration and interpretation of this newer version of the test. She explains this to the director, and they agree that another counselor who recently received the training will administer the test.

E.2.b. Appropriate Use

Counselors are responsible for the appropriate application, scoring, interpretation, and use of assessment instruments relevant to the needs of the client, whether they score and interpret such assessments themselves or use technology or other services.

William, a client in career counseling, wants to become a nurse. He has some doubt, however, about whether this is really the right field for him. The counselor administers a vocational interest test. The results do not support his interest in the nursing field. The counselor explains that although the test shouldn't be the only factor in his decision, the results do indicate that William's interests are different from those of a recent sample of men who are in the nursing profession.

E.2.c. Decisions Based on Results

Counselors responsible for decisions involving individuals or policies that are based on assessment results have a thorough understanding of educational, psychological, and career measurement, including validation criteria, assessment research, and guidelines for assessment development and use.

Sherlene is a school counselor who frequently serves on admission, review, and dismissal (ARD) committees. An ARD committee evaluates a wide range of information, including test data, and then decides if a child qualifies for special education services. Sherlene has a thorough understanding of testing and measurement. She is able to help other committee members see the test results in proper perspective and use them in making wise decisions.

E.3. Informed Consent in Assessment

E.3.a. Explanation to Clients

Prior to assessment, counselors explain the nature and purposes of assessment and the specific use of results by potential recipients. The explanation will be given in the language of the client (or other legally authorized person on behalf of the client), unless an explicit exception has been agreed upon in advance. Counselors consider the client's personal or cultural context, the level of the client's understanding of the results, and the impact of the results on the client. *(See A.2., A.12.g., F.1.c.)*

Two community college counselors work to develop a computer program to assist entering students choose the most appropriate freshman English course. They want to design the software so that students can complete the program without assistance. Over a period of 2 years, the program is pilot tested, and validation studies are conducted. The counselors also enlist the cooperation of the Disability Services Office on campus to field-test the program to ensure that it is accessible to students with visual impairments. When the program is completed, the manual carefully describes how to interpret and use the results in language that the students can understand. During the first two semesters of use, the counselors meet individually with student users of the program to ensure that the students understand how to use it properly.

E.3.b. Recipients of Results

Counselors consider the examinee's welfare, explicit understandings, and prior agreements in determining who receives the assessment results. Counselors include accurate and appropriate interpretations with any release of individual or group assessment results. *(See B.2.c., B.5.)*

Meg develops a computer application designed to help individuals identify their life stressors. In discussing results with clients who have completed the test, she carefully describes how to interpret results and other factors that might suggest the need for further counseling for stress management.

E.4. Release of Data to Qualified Professionals

Counselors release assessment data in which the client is identified only with the consent of the client or the client's legal representative. Such data are released only to persons recognized by counselors as qualified to interpret the data. *(See B.1., B.3., B.6.b.)*

Craig, a licensed counselor, specializes in the assessment and counseling of children. He administers a projective test to a 7-year-old child who refuses to speak. The results indicate an unusual pattern, and the counselor is unsure how to best interpret this. With the written consent of the child's parents, he reviews the test protocol with a professor who is an expert in child assessment and requests the professor's assistance in understanding how to interpret the child's results.

E.5. Diagnosis of Mental Disorders

E.5.a. Proper Diagnosis

Counselors take special care to provide proper diagnosis of mental disorders. Assessment techniques (including personal interview) used to determine client care (e.g., locus of treatment, type of treatment, or recommended follow-up) are carefully selected and appropriately used.

Mel is an intake counselor in a psychiatric hospital. Each time a new patient is admitted, Mel is responsible for formulating an initial diagnosis and suggesting an appropriate course of treatment. Although he generally assigns a tentative diagnosis at the conclusion of the intake interview, he schedules further sessions with each client so that he can ensure an accurate diagnosis. He collaborates with the client's treatment team to formulate a treatment plan.

E.5.b. Cultural Sensitivity

Counselors recognize that culture affects the manner in which clients' problems are defined. Clients' socioeconomic and cultural experiences are considered when diagnosing mental disorders. *(See A.2.c.)*

Sean is a counselor who works in a culturally and racially diverse school. As a certified special education counselor, he is responsible for diagnosing students who may need to be placed in special education classes. He proceeds cautiously, taking into consideration each student's cultural context while formulating his diagnoses.

E.5.c. Historical and Social Prejudices in the Diagnosis of Pathology

Counselors recognize historical and social prejudices in the misdiagnosis and pathologizing of certain individuals and groups and the role of mental health professionals in perpetuating these prejudices through diagnosis and treatment.

Chandrelle comes for counseling at a community agency located in an urban, low-income neighborhood. During her intake session, Chandrelle tells Sally, her counselor, that she is having difficulty sleeping, has lost weight, feels tired most of the time, and is experiencing feelings of helplessness and hopelessness. Chandrelle has a full-time job at minimum wage and is raising three children on her own. She has sought counseling twice before for similar symptoms, and was given a diagnosis of Major Depressive Disorder, Recurrent. She was referred for antidepressant medication that, according to Chandrelle, helped her through the "rough times." Sally recognizes that Chandrelle is describing symptoms of depression, but she also recognizes that women are more likely than men to be diagnosed with depression and that the economically disadvantaged are more likely to be given severe diagnoses. Sally engages Chandrelle in developing an overall treatment plan that includes counselor advocacy to help Chandrelle deal with environmental conditions that are contributing to (and to some extent causing) her depression.

E.5.d. Refraining From Diagnosis

Counselors may refrain from making and/or reporting a diagnosis if they believe it would cause harm to the client or others.

Sidney is a counselor who works in a for-profit substance abuse treatment facility. The facility offers inpatient treatment, day treatment, and aftercare services. The marketing director asks Sidney to meet with and conduct an assessment of Jeremiah, a potential client. The director tells Sidney that the census is low on the inpatient unit right now and that Jeremiah's health insurance will pay for inpatient treatment if Jeremiah is diagnosed with a substance dependence disorder. Sidney meets with Jeremiah and determines that Jeremiah suffers from social anxiety and drinks only to self-medicate when he attends large social gatherings. Sidney refrains from diagnosing a substance dependence disorder and refers Jeremiah to an anxiety disorders clinic.

E.6. Instrument Selection

E.6.a. Appropriateness of Instruments

Counselors carefully consider the validity, reliability, psychometric limitations, and appropriateness of instruments when selecting assessments.

The manager of an employment agency asks her counseling staff for advice on the purchase of an attractive new test of manual dexterity. The counselors evaluate the test manual and advise against purchasing the test because there is limited evidence that the test is valid.

E.6.b. Referral Information

If a client is referred to a third party for assessment, the counselor provides specific referral questions and sufficient objective data about the client to ensure that appropriate assessment instruments are utilized. *(See A.9.b., B.3.)*

Nora is a marriage and family counselor who has been counseling Janine and Jeff, a young couple who are having marital difficulties. Generally, they have brought their 2-year-old child with them to the counseling sessions. As counseling progresses, it becomes apparent to Nora that a major source of stress in the couple's marriage is their fear that their child may have a developmental disability. Due to this fear, the couple has avoided having the child tested. After exploring these fears, Janine and Jeff agree that the child should be tested, and with their permission, Nora arranges for the child to be assessed by a specialist in early childhood developmental disorders. Nora provides the specialist with objective information about the child, clearly indicating what information is based on her own observations and what information has been reported by the parents.

E.6.c. Culturally Diverse Populations

Counselors are cautious when selecting assessments for culturally diverse populations to avoid the use of instruments that lack appropriate psychometric properties for the client population. *(See A.2.c., E.5.b.)*

Faculty of a graduate counseling program meet to discuss tests to be used in selection of candidates for admission to the program. They talk about the Miller's Analogy Test and realize that it may not be suitable for some candidates because it is a highly verbal test, which may not fairly represent the skills of all candidates. They decide not to use this test and to search for alternative assessment strategies that measure a broader range of abilities.

E.7. Conditions of Assessment Administration

(See A.12.b, A.12.d.)

E.7.a. Administration Conditions

Counselors administer assessments under the same conditions that were established in their standardization. When assessments are not administered under standard conditions, as may be necessary to accommodate clients with disabilities, or when unusual behavior or irregularities occur during the administration, those conditions are noted in interpretation, and the results may be designated as invalid or of questionable validity.

During the administration of a standardized test to the juniors in a high school, a malfunction in the timer causes the time to be 7 minutes short for a subtest. The problem is discovered a week later when the timer is used again. The principal is reluctant to report the matter to the national testing center, but the counselor insists that it be reported, pointing out how this could adversely affect the total test results. After discussing the matter, they agree that they will follow the instructions of the national testing center regarding how to explain the problem to the students who were tested, as well as to their parents, and how to caution them about interpreting the results.

E.7.b. Technological Administration

Counselors ensure that administration programs function properly and provide clients with accurate results when technological or other electronic methods are used for assessment administration.

Kyle, a counselor at a vocational-technical college, plans to use a computer-administered-and-scored test with a client. He goes through the entire test-taking and scoring process himself to ensure that the computer program works properly.

E.7.c. Unsupervised Assessments

Unless the assessment instrument is designed, intended, and validated for self-administration and/or scoring, counselors do not permit inadequately supervised use.

> Leticia, an elementary school counselor, is administering a timed, individually administered test designed to detect learning disabilities. She takes precautions to prevent interruptions during the testing session so as not to disturb the child's concentration or invalidate the test results.

E.7.d. Disclosure of Favorable Conditions

Prior to administration of assessments, conditions that produce most favorable assessment results are made known to the examinee.

> Grady, a high school senior, is scheduled to take a college entrance examination. The counselor learns that Grady is upset over the recent death of his grandmother. It is possible for seniors to take the examination at a later date in the fall, so the counselor suggests to Grady that he postpone taking the examination, explaining that the results could be influenced by his emotional state.

E.8. Multicultural Issues/Diversity in Assessment

Counselors use with caution assessment techniques that were normed on populations other than that of the client. Counselors recognize the effects of age, color, culture, disability, ethnic group, gender, race, language preference, religion, spirituality, sexual orientation, and socioeconomic status on test administration and interpretation, and place test results in proper perspective with other relevant factors. *(See A.2.c., E.5.b.)*

> Gregorio, a Mexican American transfer student, is recommended for a low-ability class placement based on his poor performance on a mental ability test. The school counselor learns that Mexican Americans are not represented in the norm group for the test and that Gregorio has always performed well academically. The counselor puts together a variety of more appropriate measures to use as a basis for placement.

E.9. Scoring and Interpretation of Assessments

E.9.a. Reporting

In reporting assessment results, counselors indicate reservations that exist regarding validity or reliability due to circumstances of the assessment or the inappropriateness of the norms for the person tested.

> Corwin is a high school student who has a learning disability. He is disappointed with his low score on the social sciences subtest of a scholastic aptitude test. Corwin places great faith in the test results and says that he will give up his plans to become a history teacher. The counselor explains that the test results may have been affected by the learning disability and helps Corwin explore a range of factors that could have a bearing on his career plans.

E.9.b. Research Instruments

Counselors exercise caution when interpreting the results of research instruments not having sufficient technical data to support respondent results. The specific purposes for the use of such instruments are stated explicitly to the examinee.

Francois is the director of testing at a community college. He has been contacted by a testing company that wants to use college freshmen as part of the item analysis group. Francois agrees to help and explains to student volunteers that they are participating in the development of this test and that they won't be able to get meaningful information from the results.

E.9.c. Assessment Services

Counselors who provide assessment scoring and interpretation services to support the assessment process confirm the validity of such interpretations. They accurately describe the purpose, norms, validity, reliability, and applications of the procedures and any special qualifications applicable to their use. The public offering of an automated test interpretations service is considered a professional-to-professional consultation. The formal responsibility of the consultant is to the consultee, but the ultimate and overriding responsibility is to the client. *(See D.2.)*

Valerie, an LPC in private practice, is hired as a consultant to a large department store. She is asked to do something to determine which job applicants are prone to tardiness and absenteeism due to hypochondriacal tendencies (calling in sick). Valerie proposes a correlational study comparing results from instruments that measure hypochondriacal tendencies with actual employee promptness and attendance over a 10-month period. She secures written agreement from the consultee that any data collected from actual employees will be kept confidential and will not be shared with the consultee. Valerie explains that until and unless sufficient correlation can be found between actual employee performance and test data, no applicant's test result can be considered relevant to potential problems of tardiness and absenteeism.

E.10. Assessment Security

Counselors maintain the integrity and security of tests and other assessment techniques consistent with legal and contractual obligations. Counselors do not appropriate, reproduce, or modify published assessments or parts thereof without acknowledgment and permission from the publisher.

A provision for test security is that no test booklets are to be taken out of the testing room by anyone. One of the proctors starts to leave the room with a test booklet. The counselor reminds him of the rule and has him leave the test booklet in the room.

E.11. Obsolete Assessments and Outdated Results

Counselors do not use data or results from assessments that are obsolete or outdated for the current purpose. Counselors make every effort to prevent the misuse of obsolete measures and assessment data by others.

Harriet is hired as a counselor in a university admissions office. She notices that Graduate Record Exam (GRE) results are routinely used as a criterion for admission to graduate programs without giving consideration to the date of the testing. She calls to the attention of her director that results more than 10 years old should not be used for this purpose, and the director agrees to make the needed change in procedures.

E.12. Assessment Construction

Counselors use established scientific procedures, relevant standards, and current professional knowledge for assessment design in the development, publication, and utilization of educational and psychological assessment techniques.

Ramon is a counselor educator who has specialized knowledge in test construction. As he is designing a new assessment instrument, he takes specific steps to reduce bias against certain cultural groups that may be assessed using the instrument once it is developed. He makes use of current professional knowledge and also has other experts evaluate the instrument.

E.13. Forensic Evaluation: Evaluation for Legal Proceedings

E.13.a. Primary Obligations

When providing forensic evaluations, the primary obligation of counselors is to produce objective findings that can be substantiated based on information and techniques appropriate to the evaluation, which may include examination of the individual and/or review of records. Counselors are entitled to form professional opinions based on their professional knowledge and expertise that can be supported by the data gathered in evaluations. Counselors will define the limits of their reports or testimony, especially when an examination of the individual has not been conducted.

Olivia is a counselor who conducts court-ordered child custody evaluations. She has been asked to evaluate 6-year-old Tiffany, who is the subject of a custody dispute. Tiffany currently lives with her mother and her mother's live-in boyfriend and stays with her father every other weekend. Both parents have made allegations of physical abuse: the father has accused the mother's boyfriend, and the mother has accused the father. Olivia holds a series of counseling sessions with Tiffany, using age-appropriate play therapy techniques. Olivia also conducts individual interviews with all three adults involved in the dispute and visits both homes. When she writes her report, she states her professional opinion based on data collected throughout her evaluation.

E.13.b. Consent for Evaluation

Individuals being evaluated are informed in writing that the relationship is for the purposes of an evaluation and is not counseling in nature, and entities or individuals who will receive the evaluation report are identified. Written consent to be evaluated is obtained from those being evaluated unless a court orders evaluations to be conducted without the written consent of individuals being evaluated. When children or vulnerable adults are being evaluated, informed written consent is obtained from a parent or guardian.

Harry, age 22, has made a court appearance after being arrested for driving under the influence of alcohol. The court has referred Harry for drug and alcohol screening and assessment. Samuel, the counselor who receives Harry's case, is informed that his report will be considered as a factor in determining Harry's sentence. When Samuel meets with Harry, he explains that he will be making a report to the judge and clarifies what types of information the report will include. He obtains Harry's written consent to conduct the assessment.

E.13.c. Client Evaluation Prohibited

Counselors do not evaluate individuals for forensic purposes they currently counsel or individuals they have counseled in the past. Counselors do not accept as counseling clients individuals they are evaluating or individuals they have evaluated in the past for forensic purposes.

Quiana, a marriage and family counselor, receives a telephone call from Annie, a former client whom Quiana had seen with her husband in couples counseling a year ago. Annie states that she and her husband have initiated divorce proceedings and are embroiled in a custody dispute over their children. Annie's attorney has advised her to obtain an evaluation of her fitness as a parent. Because Quiana already knows what a dedicated and caring parent she is, Annie would like Quiana to conduct the evaluation. Quiana declines and explains her reasons for doing so.

E.13.d. Avoid Potentially Harmful Relationships

Counselors who provide forensic evaluations avoid potentially harmful professional or personal relationships with family members, romantic partners, and close friends of individuals they are evaluating or have evaluated in the past.

Lawrence is a counselor employed by the juvenile court system. He recently completed six court-mandated counseling sessions with Amanda, a 15-year-old who had been apprehended for shoplifting. He receives an e-mail message from Amanda's parents, thanking him for making a fair report to the court and offering to take him out to dinner as a token of their appreciation. Lawrence declines the offer and explains his reasons to the parents.

Section F

Supervision, Training, and Teaching

Study and Discussion Guide

- **Counselor Supervision Competence:** How can clinical supervisors acquire and maintain competence if they have not had a course in supervision? How can supervisors acquire knowledge and skills that will enable them to address diversity issues with their supervisees?
- **Counselor Educators and Trainers:** How can appropriate relationship boundaries between counselor educators and students be determined? What ethical, professional, and social relationship boundaries between educators and students do you see as important? Can you think of examples of nonprofessional interactions between educators and students that could be beneficial?
- **Informed Consent in Supervision:** As a supervisee, what kind of information would you most want to know at the outset of supervision? How do you think informed consent can best be accomplished in supervisory relationships?
- **Counseling for Students and Supervisees:** What do you see as the rationale for prohibiting counselor educators or supervisors from serving as counselors to students or supervisees? What is your opinion about the ethics of supervisors or counselor educators entering into counseling relationships with former supervisees or students?
- **Teaching Ethics:** How do you think ethical issues could best be infused throughout a counseling program?
- **Orientation to a Program:** As a student, what would you want to know prior to admission about the program to which you are applying? What kinds of information do students need to be provided with at the beginning of their training programs?
- **Self-Growth Experiences:** What role should therapeutic experiences play in a graduate counseling program? Should these experiences be a basic part of the program or merely recommended? Do you see any problems in combining experiential training experiences with didactic course work? What guidelines might you like to see regarding students' levels of self-disclosure?
- **Promoting Diversity Competence:** Counselor educators and supervisors are ethically bound to actively infuse multicultural competency into their training and supervision practices. How do you think this can best be done?

Section F

Supervision, Training, and Teaching

Introduction

Counselors aspire to foster meaningful and respectful professional relationships and to maintain appropriate boundaries with supervisees and students. Counselors have theoretical and pedagogical foundations for their work and aim to be fair, accurate, and honest in their assessments of counselors-in-training.

F.1. Counselor Supervision and Client Welfare

F.1.a. Client Welfare

A primary obligation of counseling supervisors is to monitor the services provided by other counselors or counselors-in-training. Counseling supervisors monitor client welfare and supervisee clinical performance and professional development. To fulfill these obligations, supervisors meet regularly with supervisees to review case notes, samples of clinical work, or live observations. Supervisees have a responsibility to understand and follow the *ACA Code of Ethics.*

Greta conducts weekly supervision meetings with a small group of counselors-in-training. She expects them to bring up any problems they are facing in their field placements and helps them develop alternative strategies when they are having difficulties. The supervisees are expected to bring samples of their clinical work for discussion. Supervision sessions also focus on supervisees' self-awareness, especially of countertransference issues that might interfere with effective counseling.

F.1.b. Counselor Credentials

Counseling supervisors work to ensure that clients are aware of the qualifications of the supervisees who render services to the clients. *(See A.2.b.)*

Shelley, a counseling supervisor, requires all of her supervisees to inform their clients that they are interns and to discuss with clients their qualifications to provide the services they will render.

F.1.c. Informed Consent and Client Rights

Supervisors make supervisees aware of client rights including the protection of client privacy and confidentiality in the counseling relationship. Supervisees provide clients with professional disclosure information and inform them of how the supervision process influences the limits of confidentiality. Supervisees make clients aware of who will have access to records of the counseling relationship and how these records will be used. *(See A.2.b., B.1.d.)*

Sayuri requires her supervisees to develop a written informed consent document to give their clients and discuss with them at the beginning of the counseling relationship. The contents of this document include a summary of the supervisee's education and training, disclosure of the trainee status of the supervisee along with the implications for confidentiality, and a statement pertaining to regular meetings with a supervisor. After the supervisees have written their informed consent documents, they role-play to demonstrate how they would verbally address key topics of the consent process. Supervisees are given opportunities to discuss any concerns about implementing the informed consent process.

F.2. Counselor Supervision Competence

F.2.a. Supervisor Preparation

Prior to offering clinical supervision services, counselors are trained in supervision methods and techniques. Counselors who offer clinical supervision services regularly pursue continuing education activities including both counseling and supervision topics and skills. *(See C.2.a., C.2.f.)*

Diane, a counselor educator, supervises doctoral students who serve as practicum supervisors to master's level students. She teaches a supervision course that the doctoral students must take before they function as supervisors. In addition, she meets with these doctoral students each week in a small group. In these meetings, the students discuss what they are learning, and Diane helps them with any problems they encounter in providing supervision. Diane herself attends workshops and keeps up to date by reading textbooks and journal articles on clinical supervision.

F.2.b. Multicultural Issues/Diversity in Supervision

Counseling supervisors are aware of and address the role of multiculturalism/ diversity in the supervisory relationship.

As a counseling supervisor, Norman is aware that the range of differences between him and his supervisees may affect their working relationship. As a way to promote a discussion of salient aspects of diversity, Norman has a section on dealing with diversity in the supervisory relationship in the informed consent materials he uses as part of the orientation process with all supervisees. He encourages his supervisees to discuss any aspect of diversity that is important to them. In addition to addressing the role of diversity in his relationship with each of his supervisees, which he models, he asks his supervisees to discuss in their supervisory sessions how they deal with diversity in their relationships with their clients. He encourages students to focus on those aspects of diversity that are especially challenging for them. Norman does not provide simplistic solutions when his supervisees face challenges in dealing with diversity. Instead, he asks them to state how they are addressing issues and how they evaluate what they are doing.

F.3. Supervisory Relationships

F.3.a. Relationship Boundaries With Supervisees

Counseling supervisors clearly define and maintain ethical professional, personal, and social relationships with their supervisees. Counseling supervisors avoid nonprofessional relationships with current supervisees. If supervisors must assume other professional roles (e.g., clinical and administrative supervisor, instructor) with supervisees, they work to minimize potential conflicts and explain to supervisees the expectations and responsibilities associated with each role. They do not engage in any form of nonprofessional interaction that may compromise the supervisory relationship.

The supervisors in a training program recognize that they play multiple roles in the supervisory relationship. As part of their informed consent process with all supervisees, they summarize in writing the various roles they may play, such as teacher, mentor, consultant, adviser, and evaluator. They discuss these roles with supervisees at an orientation session and invite questions and dialogue. The supervisors also explain the importance of establishing appropriate boundaries and provide examples of both appropriate and inappropriate nonprofessional interactions.

F.3.b. Sexual Relationships

Sexual or romantic interactions or relationships with current supervisees are prohibited.

Monica, a counseling supervisor, gives all of her supervisees written informed consent materials to educate them about the process of supervision, including the rights and responsibilities of both supervisor and supervisee. A short section is devoted to boundary issues in general as they apply to the supervisory relationship. It specifically mentions nonprofessional relationships and how these might be addressed in supervisory sessions. A specific clause states that sexual relationships are prohibited in the supervisory relationship. Monica reviews this material with her supervisees and encourages them to ask questions about their relationship with her.

F.3.c. Sexual Harassment

Counseling supervisors do not condone or subject supervisees to sexual harassment. *(See C.6.a.)*

Sylvia, a counselor supervisor, includes in the supervision agreement she gives all new supervisees a written statement pertaining to sexual harassment. She specifically references the standards in the *ACA Code of Ethics* that address sexual harassment. During her initial meeting with new supervisees, Sylvia discusses these standards to ensure that the supervisees understand what may constitute sexual harassment and encourages them to discuss their perceptions of harassment.

F.3.d. Close Relatives and Friends

Counseling supervisors avoid accepting close relatives, romantic partners, or friends as supervisees.

Herb is a faculty member in a counselor education program in a small private college, and he is also the sole clinical supervisor in this program. His cousin Teresa enrolled in the program at the college where Herb teaches. The college is located in a small town, and the nearest counselor education program is in a city that is a 3-hour drive away. Herb explains to Teresa that ethically he cannot accept close relatives as supervisees. Herb makes arrangements with a licensed counselor in the community, who supervises trainees in a community agency, to function as her supervisor. This arrangement is made in collaboration with the chair of the department, who is willing to work closely with Teresa's supervisor and monitor the process.

F.3.e. Potentially Beneficial Relationships

Counseling supervisors are aware of the power differential in their relationships with supervisees. If they believe nonprofessional relationships with a supervisee may be potentially beneficial to the supervisee, they take precautions similar to those taken by counselors when working with clients. Examples of potentially beneficial interactions or relationships include attending a formal ceremony; hospital visits; providing support during a stressful event; or mutual membership in a professional association, organization, or community. Counseling supervisors engage in open discussions with supervisees when they consider entering into relationships with them outside of their roles as clinical and/or administrative supervisors. Before engaging in nonprofessional relationships, supervisors discuss with supervisees and document the rationale for such interactions, potential benefits or drawbacks, and anticipated consequences for the supervisee. Supervisors clarify the specific nature and limitations of the additional role(s) they will have with the supervisee.

Barry is a young clinical supervisor who finds that his personal interests and preferences often match those of his supervisees more closely than those of his colleagues. Living in a relatively small town, Barry frequently encounters his supervisees in social situations and in situations outside the supervisory setting. He realizes that it is not always possible to avoid nonprofessional relationships with some of his supervisees. He believes the best way to deal with many of these situations is to keep the channels of communication open. By doing this, Barry thinks that if conflicts or boundary concerns arise, they can be addressed by the supervisor, supervisee, and colleagues.

F.4. Supervisor Responsibilities

F.4.a. Informed Consent for Supervision

Supervisors are responsible for incorporating into their supervision the principles of informed consent and participation. Supervisors inform supervisees of the policies and procedures to which they are to adhere and the mechanisms for due process appeal of individual supervisory actions.

As a part of the orientation process for counselor interns in a counselor education program, students have a group meeting with all the supervisors before they begin their field placements. At this time, students are given a written contract between the supervisor and supervisee that spells out the scope and expectations of supervision. This contract is designed to assist the supervisor and supervisee in establishing clear expectations about the supervisory sessions, the relationship, and the evaluation process. The written informed consent materials describe how regular feedback and evaluation will be provided. Policies and procedures for conducting ongoing evaluations are described, along with the appeals process. At this orientation meeting, supervisors go over all parts of the contract as a way to ensure informed consent. Students are given opportunities to ask questions about these written materials and about how supervision works. In addition to this general meeting, each supervisor again discusses this document with each of his or her supervisees at the initial supervisory session, and both the supervisor and supervisee sign this contract. The aim is to ensure that supervisees become active participants in the supervisory process and understand what is expected of them and what they can expect of their supervisor.

F.4.b. Emergencies and Absences

Supervisors establish and communicate to supervisees procedures for contacting them or, in their absence, alternative on-call supervisors to assist in handling crises.

As a part of the supervision contract, Betty lists all the ways that her supervisees can contact her, and she also provides names of colleagues who have agreed to assist the supervisees in case she cannot be reached.

F.4.c. Standards for Supervisees

Supervisors make their supervisees aware of professional and ethical standards and legal responsibilities. Supervisors of postdegree counselors encourage these counselors to adhere to professional standards of practice. *(See C.1.)*

Robin provides group supervision to students who are engaged in their first fieldwork placement. At the first meeting with the group, she gives them a copy of the *ACA Code of Ethics*. She asks them to read it and select the areas that are of most concern to them as beginning supervisees. She allocates the second meeting strictly for discussion of these codes and ethical issues. She lets them know that if they have concerns pertaining to ethical or legal issues at any time, they should bring them into the group supervisory sessions.

F.4.d. Termination of the Supervisory Relationship

Supervisors or supervisees have the right to terminate the supervisory relationship with adequate notice. Reasons for withdrawal are provided to the other party. When cultural, clinical, or professional issues are crucial to the viability of the supervisory relationship, both parties make efforts to resolve differences. When termination is warranted, supervisors make appropriate referrals to possible alternative supervisors.

Warren is a counselor intern who tells Wilma, his supervisor, that he wants to be assigned to a different supervisor because of some major personality differences that he thinks are negatively affecting their working relationship. Wilma appreciates the fact that Warren has told her of his desire to terminate their relationship and begin with a new supervisor. Before terminating, Wilma and Warren discuss the strains in their interpersonal relationship to see if they can improve their relationship, but to no avail. With Warren's permission, Wilma arranges for another faculty member to join them in a discussion about their relationship or to discuss an alternative supervisor. After this collaboration, it is decided that Warren will be assigned another supervisor.

F.5. Counseling Supervision Evaluation, Remediation, and Endorsement

F.5.a. Evaluation

Supervisors document and provide supervisees with ongoing performance appraisal and evaluation feedback and schedule periodic formal evaluative sessions throughout the supervisory relationship.

Elizabeth meets with each of her supervisees three times during the semester for her written performance appraisal on a form that all supervisees are given at the outset of the supervision process. Elizabeth asks her supervisees to evaluate themselves on this form and to bring it with them to each of these scheduled evaluation sessions. Elizabeth goes over each of the categories in which the supervisees have rated themselves, and then shares her ratings on each of the dimensions. They compare ratings and discuss both strengths and areas needing further work. Any differences between the supervisor's and the supervisees' ratings are discussed at this session. Supervisees are asked to develop a plan for building on their strengths and for attending to any areas needing remediation. At this time, Elizabeth asks her supervisees to share any feedback they have about her as a supervisor, especially the degree to which they are getting what they want from supervision and any aspects of their supervision they might want to change.

F.5.b. Limitations

Through ongoing evaluation and appraisal, supervisors are aware of the limitations of supervisees that might impede performance. Supervisors assist supervisees in securing remedial assistance when needed. They recommend dismissal from training programs, applied counseling settings, or state or voluntary professional credentialing processes when those supervisees are unable to provide competent professional services. Supervisors seek consultation and document their decisions to dismiss or refer supervisees for assistance. They ensure that supervisees are aware of options available to them to address such decisions. *(See C.2.g.)*

Rachel, a counselor educator, observes a graduate student, Ken, as he counsels clients in his first practicum. She becomes concerned about his lack of counseling skills. Despite feedback, Ken fails to improve. He maintains rigid control of the interview while displaying anger in the form of sarcasm. In response to suggestions from Rachel that he explore his anger by seeking personal counseling, Ken becomes defensive and refuses to consider the idea. Rachel, after informing Ken of her intentions, asks two other clinical supervisors to observe his counseling sessions. They agree that his counseling skills are deficient, and in consultation with Ken, they develop a written plan for remediation that is signed by all parties.

F.5.c. Counseling for Supervisees

If supervisees request counseling, supervisors provide them with acceptable referrals. Counselors do not provide counseling services to supervisees. Supervisors address interpersonal competencies in terms of the impact of these issues on clients, the supervisory relationship, and professional functioning. *(See F.3.a.)*

Denise, a practicum student, demonstrates excellent counseling skills during the first half of the semester. After spring break, however, her supervisor notices that she is struggling to attend to clients and seems preoccupied during sessions. The supervisor shares his observations with Denise, who reveals that her husband asked for a divorce a short time ago. The supervisor and Denise talk about how her impending divorce is likely to affect her work with her clients, especially her counseling with couples. Denise asks the supervisor to counsel her through this difficult time. The supervisor explains that he cannot serve as her counselor. He provides her with the names of several referrals.

F.5.d. Endorsement

Supervisors endorse supervisees for certification, licensure, employment, or completion of an academic or training program only when they believe supervisees are qualified for the endorsement. Regardless of qualifications, supervisors do not endorse supervisees whom they believe to be impaired in any way that would interfere with the performance of the duties associated with the endorsement.

Although Steve earned high grades in his academic courses, certain personality patterns are interfering with his ability to form good relationships with the staff and his clients at the agency where he is doing his fieldwork. The campus supervisor meets with Steve and the field supervisor to identify specific areas of concern. The three of them develop an action plan aimed at modifying some of Steve's behaviors. They plan to meet periodically to evaluate how the plan is working. The campus supervisor makes it clear to Steve that, although he will be supported in his efforts to successfully complete the program, it is essential that he remediate the interpersonal areas of concern before he will be allowed to continue into his second semester of fieldwork.

F.6. Responsibilities of Counselor Educators

F.6.a. Counselor Educators

Counselor educators who are responsible for developing, implementing, and supervising educational programs are skilled as teachers and practitioners. They are knowledgeable regarding the ethical, legal, and regulatory aspects of the profession, are skilled in applying that knowledge, and make students and supervisees aware of their responsibilities. Counselor educators conduct counselor education and training programs in an ethical manner and serve as role models for professional behavior. *(See C.1., C.2.a., C.2.c.)*

Ellen teaches a variety of courses including practicum, family therapy, counseling techniques, and multicultural counseling. As a member of the counseling department, she is partly responsible for the admission of students to the program, and she participates in the process of evaluating students for retention at various points in the program. In all of her classes, she combines experiential and didactic components. She strives to make theory come alive by focusing on practical applications. Because of her approach to teaching, she learns a good deal about her students' values, attitudes, and life experiences. For example, in her family therapy class, her students explore how their family-of-origin experiences influence them today. In her multicultural class, she challenges students to examine their cultural biases and prejudices and how these might affect their work with culturally diverse populations. To model professional behavior, Ellen explains to her students her basis for evaluation in teaching her courses and her role in serving on the admissions and retention committee. She is aware of the differential in power and clarifies how she functions in various roles.

F.6.b. Infusing Multicultural Issues/Diversity

Counselor educators infuse material related to multiculturalism/diversity into all courses and workshops for the development of professional counselors.

Patricia regularly offers continuing education workshops to mental health professionals on clinical supervision. In her written workshop materials, sections are devoted to issues of diversity as they pertain to supervision. In her daylong workshops, Patricia gives participants several opportunities to form small discussion groups to identify areas of concern to them, with a special focus on diversity issues. She initiates role-playing situations when participants identify an area of cultural difference with their supervisees that has caused them to struggle.

F.6.c. Integration of Study and Practice

Counselor educators establish education and training programs that integrate academic study and supervised practice.

The faculty who teach in a master's degree program in counseling hold a retreat to assess their program's balance between didactic and experiential learning. They identify the components in required courses that provide students with opportunities for supervised practice and conclude that their students need more skill-building opportunities before they enter practicum and internship. They make a commitment that full-time faculty will teach the introductory core courses and will infuse role-play and other opportunities to translate theory into practice. They also decide to add to the curriculum an advanced counseling techniques course, with emphasis on supervised practice, that students will take after completing the theories course.

F.6.d. Teaching Ethics

Counselor educators make students and supervisees aware of the ethical responsibilities and standards of the profession and the ethical responsibilities of students to the profession. Counselor educators infuse ethical considerations throughout the curriculum. *(See C.1.)*

During the introductory course in a counselor education program, class time is devoted to studying the *ACA Code of Ethics.* A formal ethics course is also required, and specialized applications of ethics are addressed in other courses such as research methods, psychometric procedures, group process, multicultural counseling, diagnosis and treatment planning, and practicum. Finally, during their internships, students meet weekly with their supervisors in a small group format to discuss cases and explore any problems they might be encountering in their field placements. At the initial meeting, the supervisors ask supervisees to carefully review the *ACA Code of Ethics.* They encourage supervisees to bring to the weekly meetings any concerns they have, especially as they apply to ethical concerns they are confronting at their field placements.

F.6.e. Peer Relationships

Counselor educators make every effort to ensure that the rights of peers are not compromised when students or supervisees lead counseling groups or provide clinical supervision. Counselor educators take steps to ensure that students and supervisees understand they have the same ethical obligations as counselor educators, trainers, and supervisors.

As one component of their practicum in group counseling, the graduate students colead a self-exploration course in the undergraduate program. The groups they lead are supervised by an instructor with whom they meet weekly for group supervision. The supervisor emphasizes the importance of ethical and professional behavior and makes time in the group supervision sessions to discuss any challenging situations they are facing in facilitating their groups. Ethical issues such as informed consent, confidentiality, and appropriate use of techniques are discussed regularly at the weekly meetings.

F.6.f. Innovative Theories and Techniques

When counselor educators teach counseling techniques/procedures that are innovative, without an empirical foundation, or without a well-grounded theoretical foundation, they define the counseling techniques/procedures as "unproven" or "developing" and explain to students the potential risks and ethical considerations of using such techniques/procedures.

In teaching her graduate course on counseling theories and techniques, Bernadine talks to her students about "evidence-based treatments." She explains that empirically supported techniques fit well with behavioral and cognitive-behavioral approaches, but that some theories of counseling do not stress an empirical foundation for techniques. She encourages her students to think about the rationale for any technique they employ and suggests that they have clear therapeutic purposes for the techniques they use even if the techniques are not empirically supported. Bernadine also tells her students that it is sound practice to talk with their clients about potential risks of any clearly innovative techniques they use and to secure client permission.

F.6.g. Field Placements

Counselor educators develop clear policies within their training programs regarding field placement and other clinical experiences. Counselor educators provide clearly stated roles and responsibilities for the student or supervisee, the site supervisor, and the program supervisor. They confirm that site supervisors are qualified to provide supervision and inform site supervisors of their professional and ethical responsibilities in this role.

A professor in the counseling department is appointed field placement director. She meets with all field supervisors to determine their qualifications and willingness to supervise practicum students properly. She meets with the students when they begin their placements and clearly defines their roles and responsibilities. The students then meet with their field supervisors to develop a contract outlining goals, objectives, and strategies. The director periodically visits the sites to ensure that supervisors and students are adhering to the contract and are functioning in an ethical and professional manner.

F.6.h. Professional Disclosure

Before initiating counseling services, counselors-in-training disclose their status as students and explain how this status affects the limits of confidentiality. Counselor educators ensure that the clients at field placements are aware of the services rendered and the qualifications of the students and supervisees rendering those services. Students and supervisees obtain client permission before they use any information concerning the counseling relationship in the training process. *(See A.2.b.)*

It came to the attention of the faculty that one fieldwork placement site was asking their trainees not to reveal that they were students, but simply to say that they were a part of the agency's treatment staff. Once the faculty person in charge of field placement became aware of the practice, he informed the agency that they would need to change this practice immediately and correct any misimpressions held by clients, or the university would no longer place students there. He then contacted by mail all the agencies where student trainees were placed and asked them to ensure that all those who receive services from the agencies be informed accurately of the backgrounds of those who were counselor trainees. He also clarified with all the agencies the importance of developing a written policy that would clearly inform clients that trainees meet regularly with a fieldwork supervisor and a supervisor at the university, along with the possible limitations of confidentiality.

F.7. Student Welfare

F.7.a. Orientation

Counselor educators recognize that orientation is a developmental process that continues throughout the educational and clinical training of students. Counseling faculty provide prospective students with information about the counselor education program's expectations:

1. The type and level of skill and knowledge acquisition required for successful completion of the training
2. Program training goals, objectives, and mission, and subject matter to be covered
3. Bases for evaluation
4. Training components that encourage self-growth or self-disclosure as part of the training process
5. The type of supervision settings and requirements of the sites for required clinical field experiences
6. Student and supervisee evaluation and dismissal policies and procedures
7. Up-to-date employment prospects for graduates

Prospective students who indicate an interest in applying to a counseling program are provided with an informational pamphlet that describes the philosophy of the program; admission, retention, and dismissal policies and procedures; skill and knowledge acquisition required for graduation; and the curriculum. A section details evaluation procedures and identifies training components that include self-growth and self-disclosure as being separate from graded components. A section pertains to informed consent involving experiential learning in components of courses such as group counseling, practicum, and other courses where family-of-origin issues are likely to be explored. The pamphlet describes the required field experiences and explains the program's criteria for selecting sites and site supervisors. At the end of the pamphlet, results of a recent follow-up study of graduates are summarized to give readers information about their employment prospects after graduation. Students who apply for admission are asked to view a videotape, created by the program faculty and students, that provides similar information.

F.7.b. Self-Growth Experiences

Counselor education programs delineate requirements for self-disclosure or self-growth experiences in their admission and program materials. Counselor educators use professional judgment when designing training experiences they conduct that require student and supervisee self-growth or self-disclosure. Students and supervisees are made aware of the ramifications their self-disclosure may have when counselors whose primary role as teacher, trainer, or supervisor requires acting on ethical obligations to the profession. Evaluative components of experiential training experiences explicitly delineate predetermined academic standards that are separate and do not depend on the student's level of self-disclosure. Counselor educators may require trainees to seek professional help to address any personal concerns that may be affecting their competency.

Jane is a counselor educator who teaches the introductory counseling skills course. A significant portion of the course is devoted to having students learn and practice basic counseling skills, working in dyads and videotaping their work. At the beginning of the semester, Jane thoroughly explains to students that she will be reviewing the videotapes with them, with a focus on the skill development of the student who is in the counselor role. She clarifies that she will not be evaluating the self-disclosures of the student in the client role, and that she will keep these disclosures confidential. She does alert students, however, that her ethical obligations to the profession require her to act in certain circumstances, such as hearing a student client reveal information that might lead her to believe that there was a danger to the student or to others. She also reiterates the grading criteria as outlined in her syllabus, including the fact that students are not graded on their performance in the client role.

F.8. Student Responsibilities

F.8.a. Standards for Students

Counselors-in-training have a responsibility to understand and follow the *ACA Code of Ethics* and adhere to applicable laws, regulatory policies, and rules and policies governing professional staff behavior at the agency or placement setting. Students have the same obligation to clients as those required of professional counselors. *(See C.1., H.1.)*

Madelyn is about to begin her internship in counseling. She carefully reviews the *ACA Code of Ethics* before she reports to her internship site. She reviews with her site supervisor her ethical obligations as they pertain to her internship work. Over the course of the semester, Madelyn brings into her supervision sessions any ethical dilemmas she encounters.

F.8.b. Impairment

Counselors-in-training refrain from offering or providing counseling services when their physical, mental, or emotional problems are likely to harm a client or others. They are alert to the signs of impairment, seek assistance for problems, and notify their program supervisors when they are aware that they are unable to effectively provide services. In addition, they seek appropriate professional services for themselves to remediate the problems that are interfering with their ability to provide services to others. *(See A.1., C.2.d., C.2.g.)*

Adriane is serving her internship working with hospice patients. Adriane has been experiencing a great deal of stress balancing her regular work schedule with her course work at the university and her internship. She has been having personal difficulties in dealing with people who are dying and is finding it a challenge to maintain objectivity. Adriane learns that her mother has been diagnosed with pancreatic cancer and probably has about 2 months to live. Now that she is confronted with her mother's illness and impending death, Adriane is highly anxious, finds it difficult to stay focused on her studies, and is constantly upset at her internship site. She realizes that she needs to take action for the sake of her clients and her own psychological and physical health. She talks to her clinical supervisor about the difficulties she is experiencing, and he helps Adriane find a counselor to deal with her personal crisis and its effect on her personally, in her internship work, and in her studies. She arranges to take an "incomplete" in most of her courses, and her supervisor works with her to terminate her internship placement for this semester.

F.9. Evaluation and Remediation of Students

F.9.a. Evaluation

Counselors clearly state to students, prior to and throughout the training program, the levels of competency expected, appraisal methods, and timing of evaluations for both didactic and clinical competencies. Counselor educators provide students with ongoing performance appraisal and evaluation feedback throughout the training program.

Students are informed before they enter a counseling program that they will be expected to acquire competency in group work, and that although experiential learning in this skill area will be required, self-disclosure will not be graded. A full-time faculty member teaches the didactic component of the group counseling course, and her syllabus clearly indicates the grading requirements. An adjunct professor teaches the experiential component, which involves the students leading a small group in which they explore some of their own personal concerns. The adjunct professor supervises these groups and offers feedback but does not evaluate (grade) students on their performance as group members or leaders or on their level of self-disclosure in the groups.

F.9.b. Limitations

Counselor educators, throughout ongoing evaluation and appraisal, are aware of and address the inability of some students to achieve counseling competencies that might impede performance. Counselor educators

1. assist students in securing remedial assistance when needed,
2. seek professional consultation and document their decision to dismiss or refer students for assistance, and
3. ensure that students have recourse in a timely manner to address decisions to require them to seek assistance or to dismiss them, and

4. provide students with due process according to institutional policies and procedures. *(See C.2.g.)*

In evaluating students, the counseling faculty is aware of the importance of giving students feedback on their clinical skills and interpersonal characteristics that influence their ability to function effectively as counselors-in-training. The faculty has developed a rating form for the evaluation of students' personal and professional competencies. Areas that are evaluated include counseling skills, professional responsibility, and personal responsibility. Each student is assessed at candidacy, prior to internship, and at the end of each semester of the two-semester internship. Students are aware of the Personal and Professional Competencies form when they enter the program and are made aware of the fact that they will be regularly evaluated on these competencies. If certain competencies have not been met, faculty advisers assist them in designing action plans to remediate the situation. Students understand that unmet competencies will need to be met before they finish the program. At the orientation session prior to admission to the program, students are informed that action will be taken, including possible dismissal from the program, if they demonstrate dysfunctional interpersonal behavior or serious unresolved conflicts. Students are given specific, written information about the policies and procedures for dismissing students for nonacademic reasons, as well as policies pertaining to appeals and due process procedures. Students are also informed that dismissal from a program is a last resort.

F.9.c. Counseling for Students

If students request counseling or if counseling services are required as part of a remediation process, counselor educators provide acceptable referrals.

Ben, a student, approaches Sarah, one of his counseling professors. Ben says that he would like to talk with her about his lack of self-confidence and doubts about becoming a counselor. Sarah sees Ben during an office hour and explores with him how his doubts are getting in the way and may be negatively affecting his performance in his courses. At the end of the discussion, Ben expresses his gratitude and asks Sarah if he could come in for weekly sessions to work on his problems. He tells her that he really trusts her and that this one session has helped him gain a focus. Sarah lets Ben know that she appreciates his desire to get counseling for his personal problems but that she cannot ethically be his professor and counselor at the same time. She discusses the resources available at the university counseling center and encourages him to take advantage of these counseling services.

F.10. Roles and Relationships Between Counselor Educators and Students

F.10.a. Sexual or Romantic Relationships

Sexual or romantic interactions or relationships with current students are prohibited.

Mark is a middle-aged professor in a counseling program. He has recently gone through a painful divorce. He feels emotionally vulnerable and finds himself attracted to one of his students. He seeks personal counseling to deal with his feelings and is very careful to maintain appropriate professional boundaries with this student and all other students.

F.10.b. Sexual Harassment

Counselor educators do not condone or subject students to sexual harassment. *(See C.6.a.)*

Students receive a handbook at their orientation session prior to admission to the program. It explicitly addresses sexual harassment and includes a statement that such behavior is not condoned in the program. Examples are given of what is meant by sexual harassment. In addition, the handbook provides the name and telephone number of the office on campus that students can contact if they believe that they are being subjected to sexual harassment.

F.10.c. Relationships With Former Students

Counselor educators are aware of the power differential in the relationship between faculty and students. Faculty members foster open discussions with former students when considering engaging in a social, sexual, or other intimate relationship. Faculty members discuss with the former student how their former relationship may affect the change in relationship.

Nobu is a counselor educator in a doctoral program. He served as the chair of the dissertation committee of one of his former students, Judith. Three years after Judith graduated from the program, she is hired in this same program. Judith and Nobu will be teaching in the same program, and both are interested in developing a social relationship. They talk about how their former student–professor relationship might influence their roles as colleagues in the same department and how their intended social relationship might affect their professional work together.

F.10.d. Nonprofessional Relationships

Counselor educators avoid nonprofessional or ongoing professional relationships with students in which there is a risk of potential harm to the student or that may compromise the training experience or grades assigned. In addition, counselor educators do not accept any form of professional services, fees, commissions, reimbursement, or remuneration from a site for student or supervisee placement.

Ruth, a counselor educator, makes it a practice to mentor doctoral students by coauthoring journal articles and copresenting at state and regional conferences with them. When this occurs, they frequently meet for lunch to discuss writing projects or prepare for presentations. At conferences, they also attend many of the same conference-related social functions. Ruth discusses with students, prior to forming a mentoring relationship, the potential benefits and risks of such a relationship. She clearly states her expectations about division of work when they are involved in writing projects, and she follows ACA guidelines regarding credit for coauthorship. Before agreeing to copresent or coauthor with students, Ruth discusses how this relationship might affect other aspects of their involvement in the program. If a student has reservations about any aspect of a potential mentoring relationship and such reservations cannot be resolved to their mutual satisfaction, such a relationship is not initiated.

F.10.e. Counseling Services

Counselor educators do not serve as counselors to current students unless this is a brief role associated with a training experience.

Virginia teaches a practicum course and other courses that involve experiential activities. She often conducts live demonstrations in class with students who volunteer to become "clients" for couples counseling, individual counseling, and group counseling. Generally, she prefers that student "clients" discuss genuine concerns they have. At times, she also asks students to role-play a difficult client to demonstrate her approach to working with this situation. Students consistently have given feedback that they find these live demonstrations to be helpful, both personally and for learning how to apply counseling techniques. In Virginia's courses, students often identify some personal concerns that they would like to explore, either during the course or once the course is completed. Virginia makes it clear that she does not provide counseling for any current student and that she does not accept former students as clients. She informs students about various resources available to students for personal counseling, both on campus and within the community.

F.10.f. Potentially Beneficial Relationships

Counselor educators are aware of the power differential in the relationship between faculty and students. If they believe a nonprofessional relationship with a student may be potentially beneficial to the student, they take precautions similar to those taken by counselors when working with clients. Examples of potentially beneficial interactions or relationships include, but are not limited to, attending a formal ceremony; hospital visits; providing support during a stressful event; or mutual membership in a professional association, organization, or community. Counselor educators engage in open discussions with students when they consider entering into relationships with students outside of their roles as teachers and supervisors. They discuss with students the rationale for such interactions, the potential benefits and drawbacks, and the anticipated consequences for the student. Educators clarify the specific nature and limitations of the additional role(s) they will have with the student prior to engaging in a nonprofessional relationship. Nonprofessional relationships with students should be time-limited and initiated with student consent.

The faculty of a counselor education program holds a weekend residential retreat in a mountain setting, which is about a 2-hour drive from campus. This retreat involves the faculty, all incoming students to the program, and selected doctoral students. The purposes of this retreat are to help new students get acquainted with one another, explore their career interests, learn about the program, and examine their personal characteristics that could either help or hinder them as future counselors. New students participate in a number of small groups that are facilitated by doctoral students, who are supervised by different faculty members. When students are in their groups, faculty members take advantage of this time to talk about how they can work effectively as a team during the upcoming academic year. There are many opportunities for informal time including hikes, recreational activities, and interactional games. These informal activities provide new students, advanced students, and faculty with time together to build trust. Students are informed prior to admission to the program that attendance at this weekend retreat is required, and former students describe at an orientation session what the retreat experience was like for them.

F.11. Multicultural/Diversity Competence in Counselor Education and Training Programs

F.11.a. Faculty Diversity

Counselor educators are committed to recruiting and retaining a diverse faculty.

A counseling department announces an opening for a faculty position. The department actively recruits qualified candidates representing a variety of cultural and ethnic backgrounds. The faculty meet to discuss how to assist all tenure track professors toward tenure and promotion. Tenured professors volunteer to assist their colleagues, especially in preparing their research and writing agendas.

F.11.b. Student Diversity

Counselor educators actively attempt to recruit and retain a diverse student body. Counselor educators demonstrate commitment to multicultural/diversity competence by recognizing and valuing diverse cultures and types of abilities students bring to the training experience. Counselor educators provide appropriate accommodations that enhance and support diverse student well-being and academic performance.

The faculty in a counselor education program make it a regular practice to speak in community college classes to inform students about their program. They also speak in selected psychology, social work, sociology, and human services undergraduate classes in their university for the purpose of informing students about the graduate program in counseling. Former students representing diverse backgrounds join the professors in making these presentations to classes for recruitment of potential students. Once students are admitted to the program, they are assigned an adviser who works closely with them to locate any resources on campus they might need to successfully navigate through the program.

F.11.c. Multicultural/Diversity Competence

Counselor educators actively infuse multicultural/diversity competency in their training and supervision practices. They actively train students to gain awareness, knowledge, and skills in the competencies of multicultural practice. Counselor educators include case examples, role-plays, discussion questions, and other classroom activities that promote and represent various cultural perspectives.

Faculty participate in a weekend faculty and student retreat. They spend time exploring ways to effectively infuse diversity perspectives into all aspects of the program. During this weekend retreat, the faculty members each talk about what they are doing to infuse multicultural competencies into their courses. They share the content of their courses, the ways they use community resources, and their methods for incorporating multicultural awareness, knowledge, and skills. They also examine how they can assess students to increase their level of multicultural competence in the various categories.

Section G

Research and Publication

Study and Discussion Guide

- **Research Responsibilities:** If you were designing a research project to assess the effectiveness of counseling with clients, what ethical considerations might guide your project?
- **Informed Consent:** What might you want to tell clients who were participating in a research study designed to test counseling outcomes? What steps might you take to obtain informed consent?
- **Reporting Results:** What steps do you need to take in reporting results to ensure that you give accurate information and minimize misleading results?
- **Publication:** If you were preparing and submitting a journal article for publication, what ethical considerations might you need to address? What issues might you need to take into account if you had a coauthor?

Section G

Research and Publication

Introduction

Counselors who conduct research are encouraged to contribute to the knowledge base of the profession and promote a clearer understanding of the conditions that lead to a healthy and more just society. Counselors support efforts of researchers by participating fully and willingly whenever possible. Counselors minimize bias and respect diversity in designing and implementing research programs.

G.1. Research Responsibilities

G.1.a. Use of Human Research Participants

Counselors plan, design, conduct, and report research in a manner that is consistent with pertinent ethical principles, federal and state laws, host institutional regulations, and scientific standards governing research with human research participants.

Joanne is a counselor educator who is conducting a research study. Her research protocol requires that participants remain engaged for an extended period of time, and for some this experience may be very fatiguing and frustrating. She arranges the procedure so that there is a brief rest period at the end of each hour if the participant desires one. At the recommendation of the university's Institutional Review Board (IRB), she adds ample time to confer with participants after they finish to offer support, answer questions, and provide information about the study.

G.1.b. Deviation From Standard Practices

Counselors seek consultation and observe stringent safeguards to protect the rights of research participants when a research problem suggests a deviation from standard or acceptable practices.

Christine, a counselor educator, is conducting research to assess the impact of certain techniques on establishing trust and developing cohesion in group counseling. She questions whether one of the techniques she wants to use is consistent with standard practices. Before implementing the technique, she seeks peer consultation and obtains approval from the Institutional Review Board at her university.

G.1.c. Independent Researchers

When independent researchers do not have access to an Institutional Review Board (IRB), they should consult with researchers who are familiar with IRB procedures to provide appropriate safeguards.

Ellis is an LPC who practices in a community agency. He designs a research study to compare the effects of two techniques for treating panic disorder. Because his agency does not have a mechanism for reviewing research protocols, he contacts the faculty member who chairs the Institutional Review Board at his local university and asks her to carefully review his protocol.

G.1.d. Precautions to Avoid Injury

Counselors who conduct research with human participants are responsible for the welfare of participants throughout the research process and should take reasonable precautions to avoid causing injurious psychological, emotional, physical, or social effects to participants.

Winston, the director of a community mental health agency, wants to study the personality traits and presenting symptoms of clients seeking services. All clients are asked to complete an extensive test battery as part of the intake procedure. Clients who complete the battery are given a full explanation of the purpose of the testing and are carefully monitored to ensure that they experience no adverse effects.

G.1.e. Principal Researcher Responsibility

The ultimate responsibility for ethical research practice lies with the principal researcher. All others involved in the research activities share ethical obligations and responsibility for their own actions.

The administrators of a school district grant permission to a researcher from the local university to study the impact of parental divorce on achievement test scores of elementary school children. The researcher has secured approval to conduct the study from her university's Institutional Review Board. The study requires the assistance of the school counselors on each campus. Before agreeing to help, the school counselors read the proposal carefully to be sure the study falls within ethical guidelines and that their student clients' rights are protected.

G.1.f. Minimal Interference

Counselors take reasonable precautions to avoid causing disruptions in the lives of research participants that could be caused by their involvement in research.

Irma is a counselor in a college residence hall. She wants to study social communication among roommates. The most rigorous design for the purpose of this investigation would require splitting certain roommates and temporarily reassigning them to other rooms. Irma decides to create a design that will not disrupt students' social relationships because the ratio of expected benefit to risk does not justify the more rigorous design.

G.1.g. Multicultural/Diversity Considerations in Research

When appropriate to research goals, counselors are sensitive to incorporating research procedures that take into account cultural considerations. They seek consultation when appropriate.

Latoya is a doctoral student who is required to conduct a research study as part of her qualitative research course. Her proposed study involves working with older persons in an inpatient facility. Because Latoya is committed to respecting the rights of the participants in her study and because she wants to do quality research, she consults with a professor who is nationally recognized as an expert on counseling older persons. The expert suggests several minor changes in the design of the study, and Latoya incorporates them.

G.2. Rights of Research Participants

(See A.2, A.7.)

G.2.a. Informed Consent in Research

Individuals have the right to consent to become research participants. In seeking consent, counselors use language that

1. accurately explains the purpose and procedures to be followed,
2. identifies any procedures that are experimental or relatively untried,
3. describes any attendant discomforts and risks,
4. describes any benefits or changes in individuals or organizations that might be reasonably expected,
5. discloses appropriate alternative procedures that would be advantageous for participants,
6. offers to answer any inquiries concerning the procedures,
7. describes any limitations on confidentiality,
8. describes the format and potential target audiences for dissemination of research findings, and
9. instructs participants that they are free to withdraw their consent and to discontinue participation in the project at any time without penalty.

Melissa, a counselor educator, obtains two groups of student volunteers as participants for an experiment in group process. She carefully explains the study's purpose and procedures, potential risks and benefits, and limitations that the group format places on confidentiality. She explains that there are no alternative procedures for the study, but that participants are free to drop out of the experiment without penalty at any time. Melissa explains that she plans to disseminate her research findings at a professional conference on group work and hopes to publish an article describing the study in a professional journal. She assures potential participants that their identities will be disguised in both formats.

G.2.b. Deception

Counselors do not conduct research involving deception unless alternative procedures are not feasible and the prospective value of the research justifies the deception. If such deception has the potential to cause physical or emotional harm to research participants, the research is not conducted, regardless of prospective value. When the methodological requirements of a study necessitate concealment or deception, the investigator explains the reasons for this action as soon as possible during the debriefing.

A group of master's students volunteer to participate in a simulated counseling interview. Although the purpose of the experiment is to study participants' reactions to the interviewer, the students believe that it is the content of the interview that is under investigation. After completing the dependent measures, the investigator informs the participants of the true purpose of the study and the reason for the deception. An opportunity is provided for participants to debrief with a counselor if they wish to do so.

G.2.c. Student/Supervisee Participation

Researchers who involve students or supervisees in research make clear to them that the decision regarding whether or not to participate in research activities does not affect one's academic standing or supervisory relationship. Students or supervisees who choose not to participate in educational research are provided with an appropriate alternative to fulfill their academic or clinical requirements.

Damien, a professor who teaches a course in group dynamics, designs a study to investigate students' behavior in small task-oriented groups. His students would be suitable participants for the study. Damien offers them the opportunity to participate in the task groups and explains that their participation is strictly voluntary. He further explains that their decision to participate or not will not affect their grade in the course.

G.2.d. Client Participation

Counselors conducting research involving clients make clear in the informed consent process that clients are free to choose whether or not to participate in research activities. Counselors take necessary precautions to protect clients from adverse consequences of declining or withdrawing from participation.

Mary Lou, a practicing counselor, wants to study the depth of self-disclosure that occurs in a therapy group. Because the experience of participating in such a group can be emotionally intense, Mary Lou decides that only volunteer participants will be used. All potential participants will be informed of the nature of the experiment and the potential risks. As additional precautions, Mary Lou will screen each volunteer for sufficient ego strength and emotional stability and will offer the option of individual counseling with another counselor to those who withdraw from the group.

G.2.e. Confidentiality of Information

Information obtained about research participants during the course of an investigation is confidential. When the possibility exists that others may obtain access to such information, ethical research practice requires that the possibility, together with the plans for protecting confidentiality, be explained to participants as a part of the procedure for obtaining informed consent.

Kimberly, a doctoral student, plans to review client files as part of her research project investigating the content of session notes. Counselors who have agreed to participate in the project are instructed to use pseudonyms or false initials for clients when writing the records. They are also instructed to explain to clients the nature and purpose of the research, the procedures for protecting their confidentiality, and the possibility that they might inadvertently include the client's name in the records. Clients are assured that only the researcher, who shares the counselor's ethic of confidentiality, will see the records. The records of only those clients who have given their informed consent are used in the research study.

G.2.f. Persons Not Capable of Giving Informed Consent

When a person is not capable of giving informed consent, counselors provide an appropriate explanation to, obtain agreement for participation from, and obtain the appropriate consent of a legally authorized person.

Phil, a doctoral student, plans to conduct research with first graders. After obtaining permission from the principal to conduct the study, he explains the research procedures to the children's parents and obtains their written consent. He provides the children with an explanation about the project in language they can comprehend and obtains their assent.

G.2.g. Commitments to Participants

Counselors take reasonable measures to honor all commitments to research participants. *(See A.2.c.)*

Lorna is a counselor educator who teaches the introduction to counseling course. Some of the students in her class volunteer to participate in a study that involves their completing a paper-and-pencil inventory of attitudes toward ethical behaviors. Lorna tells the participants that when the study is completed she will provide them with a summary of the results. After she analyzes the data, she gives each student a description of her findings and conclusions.

G.2.h. Explanations After Data Collection

After data are collected, counselors provide participants with full clarification of the nature of the study to remove any misconceptions participants might have regarding the research. Where scientific or human values justify delaying or withholding information, counselors take reasonable measures to avoid causing harm.

Abe, a counselor educator, conducts a research study using undergraduate students in a human services program as volunteer subjects. He provides participants with general information about the nature and purpose of the study. After the study is completed, he conducts a debriefing session to fully explain the study and correct any possible misperceptions that participants may have held.

G.2.i. Informing Sponsors

Counselors inform sponsors, institutions, and publication channels regarding research procedures and outcomes. Counselors ensure that appropriate bodies and authorities are given pertinent information and acknowledgment.

The director of a community mental health agency gives permission to Hal, a graduate student, to conduct a research study on how agency counselors determine which clients to refer to a psychiatrist for evaluation for psychotropic medication. When Hal completes his study, he provides the director with a description of his procedures, findings, and conclusions. Hal submits a manuscript describing his study to a professional journal for publication consideration. In the manuscript, he acknowledges the assistance of the agency and the director in making the study possible.

G.2.j. Disposal of Research Documents and Records

Within a reasonable period of time following the completion of a research project or study, counselors take steps to destroy records or documents (audio, video, digital, and written) containing confidential data or information that identifies research participants. When records are of an artistic nature, researchers obtain participant consent with regard to handling of such records or documents. *(See B.4.a., B.4.g.)*

Carolyn, a doctoral student, is conducting a qualitative research study for her dissertation. She conducts two rounds of audiotaped interviews with her participants. She keeps the audiotapes in a locked file cabinet in a secure location. When she transcribes the interviews, she assigns pseudonyms to the participants to protect their confidentiality in written documents. When she has no further use for the audiotapes, she destroys them.

G.3. Relationships With Research Participants (When Research Involves Intensive or Extended Interactions)

G.3.a. Nonprofessional Relationships

Nonprofessional relationships with research participants should be avoided.

Jade, a doctoral student, calls for volunteers to participate in a focus group she plans to conduct. The group will be composed of master's-level counseling students. One of the students who volunteers to participate is Lydia, a friend whom Jade has known for several years. Jade explains to Lydia that she will not be selected to participate in the focus group because they already have another, nonprofessional relationship.

G.3.b. Relationships With Research Participants
Sexual or romantic counselor–research participant interactions or relationships with current research participants are prohibited.

Crystal is a counselor educator who is conducting a longitudinal study of the career paths of beginning faculty members. Joe, one of the participants in Crystal's study, expresses his attraction to her and asks her out on a date. Crystal declines, explaining that a romantic relationship between them is not possible while they have a researcher–participant relationship.

G.3.c. Sexual Harassment and Research Participants
Researchers do not condone or subject research participants to sexual harassment.

Shannon, a doctoral student, is a member of a research team that is observing the group process as it unfolds in an undergraduate class. During the class break, Shannon overhears Louis, a fellow member of the research team, make sexually suggestive comments to one of the undergraduates. The undergraduate student seems very uncomfortable with Louis's remarks. Shannon takes Louis aside and tells him that she will not condone sexual harassment of a research participant and that he must cease this behavior.

G.3.d. Potentially Beneficial Interactions
When a nonprofessional interaction between the researcher and the research participant may be potentially beneficial, the researcher must document, prior to the interaction (when feasible), the rationale for such an interaction, the potential benefit, and anticipated consequences for the research participant. Such interactions should be initiated with appropriate consent of the research participant. Where unintentional harm occurs to the research participant due to the nonprofessional interaction, the researcher must show evidence of an attempt to remedy such harm.

Althea, a counselor educator, is conducting a qualitative research study that involves three rounds of individual interviews with selected participants. After the second round of interviews is completed, Althea receives an e-mail message from one of the participants requesting to postpone her third interview for a couple of weeks due to a death in her family. Althea calls the participant to express her condolences and to reschedule the interview. She also sends a sympathy card to the participant. Althea documents her actions and reactions in the reflective journal she is keeping as part of her study.

G.4. Reporting Results

G.4.a. Accurate Results
Counselors plan, conduct, and report research accurately. They provide thorough discussions of the limitations of their data and alternative hypotheses.

Counselors do not engage in misleading or fraudulent research, distort data, misrepresent data, or deliberately bias their results. They explicitly mention all variables and conditions known to the investigator that may have affected the outcome of a study or the interpretation of data. They describe the extent to which results are applicable for diverse populations.

> Becky is a researcher who is well known for espousing a particular theoretical position. She conducts an experiment that only partially supports her point of view. In the discussion section of her report on the experiment, Becky interprets the data first in light of their support of her favored theory, then in light of support for an opposing theory. She states that the choice of interpretation may depend on the reader's own theoretical orientation. She urges readers to consider the applicability of either interpretation to working with the diverse client populations they serve.

G.4.b. Obligation to Report Unfavorable Results
Counselors report the results of any research of professional value. Results that reflect unfavorably on institutions, programs, services, prevailing opinions, or vested interests are not withheld.

> Yi, a high school counselor, conducts a study to determine whether seniors have engaged in unprotected sex. The administration in this district takes particular pride in the sex education program that has been offered to middle school students for the past 7 years. The results of Yi's study show that an unexpectedly high number of students appear to be oblivious to the threat of sexually transmitted diseases. The results are made available in a pamphlet to other counselors, to students, and to parents. The administration decides to revise the sex education curriculum to reemphasize the prevention of sexually transmitted diseases.

G.4.c. Reporting Errors
If counselors discover significant errors in their published research, they take reasonable steps to correct such errors in a correction erratum, or through other appropriate publication means.

> The guidance director and a counselor in a school system collaborate on a research study investigating school dropout rates. The guidance director summarizes the data on the past year's dropouts and publishes the results in a report to the school board. The counselor learns that some schools have included summer dropouts in their reports whereas others have not. The counselor tells the guidance director about this discrepancy. They revise the data analysis and submit a corrected report to the school board.

G.4.d. Identity of Participants
Counselors who supply data, aid in the research of another person, report research results, or make original data available take due care to disguise the identity of respective participants in the absence of specific authorization from the participants to do otherwise. In situations where participants self-identify their involvement in research studies, researchers take active steps to ensure that data are adapted/changed to protect the identity and welfare of all parties and that discussion of results does not cause harm to participants.

Tara plans to submit an article for publication in a state journal. The article will be based on a workshop she conducted at the state's annual professional counselors' conference. The manuscript contains direct quotes from some of the workshop participants. Even though Tara has used pseudonyms to disguise participant identities, she realizes that some readers of the journal may know who attended the workshop. She sends each participant a copy of the proposed article and asks for feedback to ensure that they are comfortable with its content. She obtains the written permission of each participant before submitting the article to the journal.

G.4.e. Replication Studies

Counselors are obligated to make available sufficient original research data to qualified professionals who may wish to replicate the study.

A counselor education department has a policy that all theses and dissertations completed by students in that department must include sufficient information so that another investigator might be able to perform a different analysis or replicate the study. The data must be presented in a way that protects the anonymity of individual participants.

G.5. Publication

G.5.a. Recognizing Contributions

When conducting and reporting research, counselors are familiar with and give recognition to previous work on the topic, observe copyright laws, and give full credit to those to whom credit is due.

Horst, a counselor educator, replicates a study that was terminated by the death of the original researcher. In reporting this investigation, Horst acknowledges the original researcher as author of the hypothesis and design of the study.

G.5.b. Plagiarism

Counselors do not plagiarize; that is, they do not present another person's work as their own work.

Maurice, a doctoral student, is writing the literature review for his dissertation. Working meticulously, he provides accurate citations for the sources of the material. He is careful to avoid any inferences that he is the author of work that others have produced.

G.5.c. Review/Republication of Data or Ideas

Counselors fully acknowledge and make editorial reviewers aware of prior publication of ideas or data where such ideas or data are submitted for review or publication.

Corinne, a counselor educator, submits a manuscript to a professional journal for publication consideration. In the manuscript and in her cover letter to the journal editor, Corinne acknowledges that a portion of the material is based on an article that she has published previously.

G.5.d. Contributors

Counselors give credit through joint authorship, acknowledgment, footnote statements, or other appropriate means to those who have contributed significantly to research or concept development in accordance with such contributions. The principal contributor is listed first, and minor technical or professional contributions are acknowledged in notes or introductory statements.

Three counselor educators write an article that describes a study they have conducted on the effectiveness of brief solution-focused therapy. In the manuscript they submit for publication, all three counselor educators are listed as coauthors. The order of presentation of their names is determined by the relative contribution of each of them to the project. In a footnote, they acknowledge the assistance of a statistician who helped them interpret a portion of the data.

G.5.e. Agreement of Contributors
Counselors who conduct joint research with colleagues or students/ supervisees establish agreements in advance regarding allocation of tasks, publication credit, and types of acknowledgment that will be received.

Aidan, a counselor educator, plans to conduct a research study that involves interviewing counselor supervisors and their supervisees. Aidan enlists the assistance of three doctoral students to conduct the interviews, using an interview protocol he has developed. He meets with the doctoral students before the project begins. At this meeting, clear agreement is reached regarding the allocation of tasks, timelines for completion, and methods for proceeding. It is agreed that Aidan will be listed first as senior author on the manuscript that will be submitted for publication and that students' names will follow in alphabetical order.

G.5.f. Student Research
For articles that are substantially based on students' course papers, projects, dissertations or theses, and on which students have been the primary contributors, they are listed as principal authors.

Charles, a doctoral student, works together with his major professor to write an article based on Charles's dissertation. When the article is submitted for publication, Charles's name is listed first as principal author, and the professor's name is listed second.

G.5.g. Duplicate Submission
Counselors submit manuscripts for consideration to only one journal at a time. Manuscripts that are published in whole or in substantial part in another journal or published work are not submitted for publication without acknowledgment and permission from the previous publication.

Sylvia, a counselor educator, draws heavily on a published journal article on adolescent development in a chapter of a book she is writing. She contacts the journal's publisher and obtains permission to reproduce tables from the journal article in the book chapter. She acknowledges the author of the journal article in appropriate citations throughout the chapter.

G.5.h. Professional Review

Counselors who review material submitted for publication, research, or other scholarly purposes respect the confidentiality and proprietary rights of those who submitted it. Counselors use care to make publication decisions based on valid and defensible standards. Counselors review article submissions in a timely manner and based on their scope and competency in research methodologies. Counselors who serve as reviewers at the request of editors or publishers make every effort to only review materials that are within their scope of competency and use care to avoid personal biases.

> Irvin, a counselor educator, serves on the editorial board of a professional journal. All manuscripts are subjected to blind review; that is, the editorial board members do not know the identity of authors of manuscripts. Irvin receives a manuscript that is of great interest to him because he is scheduled to present a workshop in 2 weeks on the very topic addressed in the manuscript. Although he believes that his workshop presentation could be strengthened by including material from the manuscript, he realizes that it would be unethical for him to appropriate the material. He reviews the manuscript promptly and returns it to the journal editor.

Section H

Resolving Ethical Issues

Study and Discussion Guide

- **Ethical Responsibilities:** What ethical responsibilities do you have when you become aware of the unethical behavior of a colleague?
- **Informal Resolution:** If you had reasonable cause to believe that another professional was violating an ethical standard, how might you try (at least initially) to resolve the issue informally?
- **Consultation:** When might you seek consultation regarding a suspected ethical violation by another professional?
- **Steps in Resolving Ethical Dilemmas:** What are some ways you can use the *ACA Code of Ethics* to assist you in resolving ethical dilemmas? If you were confronted with a difficult ethical issue, what steps might you take in resolving the problem?
- **Conflict Between Ethics and Law:** If you were faced with a situation wherein you believed there was a conflict between the ethical and the legal course of action, what would you do?

Section H

Resolving Ethical Issues

Introduction

Counselors behave in a legal, ethical, and moral manner in the conduct of their professional work. They are aware that client protection and trust in the profession depend on a high level of professional conduct. They hold other counselors to the same standards and are willing to take appropriate action to ensure that these standards are upheld.

Counselors strive to resolve ethical dilemmas with direct and open communication among all parties involved and seek consultation with colleagues and supervisors when necessary. Counselors incorporate ethical practice into their daily professional work. They engage in ongoing professional development regarding current topics in ethical and legal issues in counseling.

H.1. Standards and the Law

(See F.9.a.)

H.1.a. Knowledge

Counselors understand the *ACA Code of Ethics* and other applicable ethics codes from other professional organizations or from certification and licensure bodies of which they are members. Lack of knowledge or misunderstanding of an ethical responsibility is not a defense against a charge of unethical conduct.

Karen is a professional member of ACA and is a licensed professional counselor in the state where she practices. She specializes in sex education and therapy, and she is a member of the American Association of Sex Educators, Counselors, and Therapists (AASECT). When the revised 2005 *ACA Code of Ethics* is published, she reads the document carefully to ensure that she understands it. She reviews the codes of ethics of AASECT and her state licensure body and compares their standards to those of ACA. She discovers that, according to the *ACA Code of Ethics,* counselors are expected to contribute a portion of their activity to pro bono service. Although the other two codes do not mention pro bono work, Karen decides to offer a series of free educational seminars for parents on how to talk to their teenagers about sex.

H.1.b. Conflicts Between Ethics and Laws

If ethical responsibilities conflict with law, regulations, or other governing legal authority, counselors make known their commitment to the *ACA Code of Ethics* and take steps to resolve the conflict. If the conflict cannot be resolved by such means, counselors may adhere to the requirements of law, regulations, or other governing legal authority.

In his private practice, Scott frequently counsels clients who are HIV positive. Although he has not encountered a situation where he deemed it necessary to breach a client's confidentiality due to a client's unwillingness to share his or her HIV status with a partner, Scott wonders about the practical applications of ACA's standard pertaining to contagious, life-threatening diseases. In the state where Scott practices, there is no legislation that allows professionals to notify third parties by informing them directly. He has been advised by legal experts that reporting clients who refuse to inform a partner of their HIV status could expose him to a malpractice action and could result in the loss of his license to practice. Scott is concerned about this issue because he sees it as a potential conflict between what is ethical and what is legal. Scott addresses both the legal and ethical dimensions of maintaining confidentiality of one's HIV status in his informed consent document. He also gives his informed consent document to an attorney for legal review.

H.2. Suspected Violations

H.2.a. Ethical Behavior Expected

Counselors expect colleagues to adhere to the *ACA Code of Ethics.* When counselors possess knowledge that raises doubts as to whether another counselor is acting in an ethical manner, they take appropriate action. *(See H.2.b., H.2.c.)*

An employment service supervisor is concerned that a new counselor, who has said that he likes a challenge, is spending more and more time with a few difficult-to-place clients to the exclusion of others seeking counseling. The supervisor confers with the counselor, who redistributes his time more equitably for a few weeks. Then, once again the counselor begins to focus on just a few challenging clients. The supervisor, uncertain what to do at this point, consults with another supervisor at a different agency.

H.2.b. Informal Resolution

When counselors have reason to believe that another counselor is violating or has violated an ethical standard, they attempt first to resolve the issue informally with the other counselor if feasible, provided such action does not violate confidentiality rights that may be involved.

Pat, a counselor in private practice, meets Eugene at a local professional association meeting. As they converse, they discover a shared professional interest in learning more about hypnotherapy. Pat offers to send Eugene a copy of some materials. Eugene hands her one of his new business cards. Later Pat reads the card and realizes that it contains misleading information about the services that Eugene is qualified to offer. She calls Eugene and expresses her concerns. Eugene agrees to destroy his business cards immediately and obtain a new set that advertises accurately.

H.2.c. Reporting Ethical Violations

If an apparent violation has substantially harmed or is likely to substantially harm a person or organization and is not appropriate for informal resolution or is not resolved properly, counselors take further action appropriate to the situation. Such action might include referral to state or national committees on professional ethics, voluntary national certification bodies, state licensing boards, or to the appropriate institutional authorities. This standard does not apply when an intervention would violate confidentiality rights or when counselors have been retained to review the work of another counselor whose professional conduct is in question.

Toni learns that an ACA member, Enoch, who teaches psychology part-time at a local community college, has been recruiting his students as clients for his private practice. She calls Enoch and attempts to express her concern, but he refuses to discuss it with her. Toni then informs him that she will set up a time to talk to the chair of the psychology department about his behavior. Enoch still says he will not discuss the issue with her. Toni then arranges to meet with the department chair to discuss her concerns about Enoch's behavior.

H.2.d. Consultation

When uncertain as to whether a particular situation or course of action may be in violation of the *ACA Code of Ethics,* counselors consult with other counselors who are knowledgeable about ethics and the *ACA Code of Ethics,* with colleagues, or with appropriate authorities.

Xavier is a counselor for a private rehabilitation counseling service. The director of the service has instituted a new set of record-keeping procedures, and Xavier questions whether the procedures are ethical. He calls and consults with his former ethics professor. He also calls a colleague who served for many years on the ethics committee of the state rehabilitation counseling association.

H.2.e. Organization Conflicts

If the demands of an organization with which counselors are affiliated pose a conflict with the *ACA Code of Ethics*, counselors specify the nature of such conflicts and express to their supervisors or other responsible officials their commitment to the *ACA Code of Ethics*. When possible, counselors work toward change within the organization to allow full adherence to the *ACA Code of Ethics*. In doing so, they address any confidentiality issues.

Nguyen, an LPC who works in an agency, determines after consultation that the new record-keeping procedures developed by the agency director violate ethical standards. He takes his concerns to the director, pointing out the ethical standards in question and describing the results of his consultations. The director agrees to appoint a committee to review the procedures and modify them if necessary and asks Nguyen to serve on the committee.

H.2.f. Unwarranted Complaints

Counselors do not initiate, participate in, or encourage the filing of ethics complaints that are made with reckless disregard or willful ignorance of facts that would disprove the allegation.

Alan is a counselor educator at a state university. He consults with Vicky, who works at a private university in the same city, about his anger at his department chair who is an ACA member. Alan says he believes that the department chair is unethical, and he is considering filing a complaint with the ACA Ethics Committee. It is apparent to Vicky that Alan's anger has nothing to do with the department chair's ethical conduct, although it may be justified for other reasons. She shares her perception of the situation with Alan and encourages him to take appropriate action rather than file an unwarranted complaint.

H.2.g. Unfair Discrimination Against Complainants and Respondents

Counselors do not deny persons employment, advancement, admission to academic or other programs, tenure, or promotion based solely upon their having made or their being the subject of an ethics complaint. This does not preclude taking action based upon the outcome of such proceedings or considering other appropriate information.

Gretchen is a counselor educator who teaches group counseling courses in a master's program in counseling. One of her students filed a complaint with the ACA Ethics Committee because of his objection to being required to participate in an experiential group as part of the group course. The student also complained about his grade of "B," stating he thought the instructor downgraded him for not engaging in meaningful self-disclosure. In her written response to the Ethics Committee, Gretchen emphasizes the measures she took to inform students about expectations of the course from the first day. Her course outline stated that students were not graded on the experiential aspect of the course but were graded on other bases such as papers and tests. When Gretchen came up for review for tenure and promotion, the chair of the counseling department did not consider the information pertaining to her being the subject of an ethics complaint.

H.3. Cooperation With Ethics Committees

Counselors assist in the process of enforcing the *ACA Code of Ethics.* Counselors cooperate with investigations, proceedings, and requirements of the ACA Ethics Committee or ethics committees of other duly constituted associations or boards having jurisdiction over those charged with a violation. Counselors are familiar with the *ACA Policies and Procedures for Processing Complaints of Ethical Violations* and use it as a reference for assisting in the enforcement of the *ACA Code of Ethics.*

Candace is shocked to learn that a former client has filed a complaint against her with the ACA Ethics Committee. Although Candace firmly believes the complaint is unjustified, she takes the matter seriously. She reads the *ACA Policies and Procedures for Processing Complaints of Ethical Violations,* consults with an attorney, and writes a response that gives the fullest possible description of the events in question. She submits documentation to support her response.

Part IV

Issues and Case Studies

Part IV presents 10 chapters highlighting key ethical issues that counselors encounter in their work. We wrote some of these chapters, and experts on particular topics contributed others. The chapters address the following issues:

- Client rights and informed consent
- Ethical issues in multicultural counseling
- Confidentiality
- Competence
- Working with multiple clients
- Counseling minor clients
- Avoiding detrimental multiple relationships
- Working with clients who may harm themselves
- Counselor education and supervision
- The relationship between law and ethics

Each chapter is followed by two case studies in which counselors confront ethical dilemmas related to the issues discussed and make decisions—sometimes wisely, sometimes unwisely. The case studies are more detailed than the vignettes in Part III and more illustrative of the complex realities of actual practice. These are not actual cases from the Ethics Committee files, which are confidential, but they have been written by professionals who are particularly knowledgeable about ethics, many of whom are current or former members of the Ethics Committee. Contributors provided both the case study and the case analysis, which explains how the *Code of Ethics* might be used to help the counselor solve the dilemma and ways in which the counselor's actions complied with or violated the *Code. ACA Code of Ethics* (2005) section numbers are provided to enable you to easily find more specific information on a topic under discussion. To the extent possible, these cases are representative of the types of cases actually encountered by the Ethics Committee and by practitioners in the field.

As we noted in the introduction, formal complaints to the ACA Ethics Committee rarely allege a single violation of the *Code of Ethics*. Rather, cases typically involve claims of violation of multiple standards and involve multiple ethical issues. In this respect, the case studies presented here are also quite realistic as each one raises a number of considerations that need to be studied in light of more than one standard. We invite readers to grapple with the complexities of the cases and to discuss and debate the issues they raise.

Chapter 1

Client Rights and Informed Consent

Gerald Corey and Barbara Herlihy

The counseling relationship is founded on trust, which is a deeply personal experience that defines the counseling relationship and provides a context for the therapeutic process (Pope & Vasquez, 1998). One of the best ways to build trusting relationships with clients is to respect their many rights and to inform them of their choices. Clients have the right to receive the information they need to become active participants in the therapeutic relationship (Corey, Corey, & Callanan, 2007).

Informed consent is perhaps the most basic right of clients in counseling: Clients have a right to know what they are getting into when they come for counseling (Remley & Herlihy, 2005). The process of securing clients' informed consent begins when the counseling relationship is initiated and continues throughout the relationship. Standard A.2.a. of the *ACA Code of Ethics* specifies that "clients have the freedom to choose whether to enter into or remain in a counseling relationship." To make this decision, they need adequate information about the counseling process and the counselor.

The *Code* specifies the types of information counselors need to provide to clients, including the purposes, goals, techniques, procedures, limitations, potential risks, and benefits of services; the counselor's qualifications, credentials, and experience; how services will be continued if the counselor dies or becomes incapacitated; the implications of diagnosis; the intended use of tests and reports; and fees and billing arrangements. Clients also have the right to know the limits of confidentiality, to obtain clear information about their case records, to participate in their ongoing counseling plans, and to refuse any recommended services or modality change and be advised of the consequences of doing so. Other factors that may affect the client's decision to enter the therapeutic relationship are the responsibilities of the counselor and of the client, legal and ethical parameters that could define the relationship, and the approximate duration of the counseling relationship.

Obviously, informed consent is not a simple procedure. The challenge for counselors is to strike a balance between giving clients too much or too little information (Corey et al., 2007). Too much information can be overwhelming, but it is too late to disclose information after a problem has already arisen. It seems to us that counselors may err in either direction, depending on the setting in which they work. For example, in inpatient psychiatric facilities, clients are often required to sign an array of consent documents before being admitted to the hospital. However, they are likely to be under great stress and may have diminished capacity to make well-considered decisions at this time. Conversely, in the school setting, some counselors give only the briefest explanation of such elements of informed consent as the limits of confidentiality or the purposes and potential uses of tests.

Of course, the types and amount of information, as well as the style of presentation, are governed by many factors. Some of these include legal requirements (such as due process), system policies and procedures (many agencies and institutions have standard forms), the capacity of clients to understand the information, and whether the client is an adult or a minor. It is important to provide clients with opportunities to ask questions, and information should be provided in language that is understandable to them. Counselors are obligated to "communicate information in ways that are both developmentally and culturally appropriate" (A.2.c.). Counselors need to use clear and understandable language when they discuss issues pertaining to informed consent. It is important for counselors to take the cultural implications of informed consent procedures into account and to adjust their practices accordingly.

In addition to following the letter of the *Code of Ethics,* counselors will do well to consider the spirit that underlies the informed consent guidelines in deciding what to tell their clients. Clients should be provided with enough information to enable them to make wise choices. This includes choosing whether to enter into counseling, selecting their counselor, and making choices about their treatment plan.

Clients need to be active participants in the therapeutic relationship, yet they are often unaware of their rights. In addition, they may not have given any thought to their own responsibilities in solving their problems. In seeking the expertise of a professional, they may unquestioningly accept whatever their counselor suggests, without realizing that the success of this relationship depends largely on their own investment in the process. Providing clients with information about what to expect from the counseling process can demystify the process and ensure that clients become active partners in defining the counseling relationship.

It is important to address clients' expectations of the counseling process. Clients often ask how long counseling will last. Although counselors cannot give a specific amount of time, we can address clients' concerns and provide appropriate information. Clients are sometimes unaware that they are likely to experience uncomfortable emotions associated with counseling, and they may harbor expectations of quick relief and happiness.

Putting informed consent information in writing is a good method to help ensure client understanding. Clients can take this information home and bring to the following session any questions or concerns they may have. Counselors in all settings are now required under the provisions of the Health Insurance Portability and Accountability Act (HIPAA), which went into effect in 2003, to provide clients with written disclosure statements or informed consent documents.

With these guidelines in mind, we now turn to two case studies that illustrate informed consent decisions in actual practice. The counselors in the cases work in very different settings—one in a community counseling center and the other in a rehabilitation agency—yet they each discover how difficult it can be to keep the client's welfare foremost when dealing with complex issues of informed consent.

Case Study 1

Fully Informed Consent?

Karen Doboval

Susan called a community counseling center seeking counseling for her daughter Leah, a 15-year-old 10th grader. Susan's concerns about Leah included poor academic achievement during the current school year and defiant behavior at home. Leah lives with her mother, her father, and one younger brother who is 11 years old. Until the current school year, Leah had been an above average student.

An appointment was made for Susan and Leah, who were both present during the intake session with Carmen, the counselor. Carmen presented the standard "declaration of practices and procedures" document used by the counseling center. Because Leah is a minor, Carmen explained the benefits of maintaining Leah's confidentiality while also explaining Susan's right as the parent to know about the counseling process. Susan and Leah both agreed that the counselor would share only general information with Susan, and that Leah was free to discuss any aspects of the counseling process with her mother. Carmen explained the limitations to confidentiality, including (in general terms) potential harm to self or others. Carmen asked Susan and Leah if they had any questions, and then asked them both to verify that they understood the provisions of the informed consent document. Carmen asked them each to sign the document, and she gave them a copy to take with them for future reference.

Carmen began seeing Leah on a weekly basis. As counseling progressed, Leah disclosed that she felt as if her mother was trying to control her, and she resented what she considered to be her mother's excessive involvement in her life. In today's session, Leah revealed that she is secretly dating a boy named John who is 18 years old, and that her mother is not aware of her relationship with John. She stated that her mother does not approve of her dating. Leah added that she was considering having sex with John. In further exploring this issue, Carmen explained that counselors have a legal obligation to report situations that involve a minor having a sexual relationship with a legal adult, and that John, at age 18, was considered an adult. Leah was adamant in insisting that Carmen not tell her mother about anything she had revealed about her relationship with John. She thought for a minute and then told Carmen she had a solution to the problem. She stated, "Well, if I do decide to have sex with John, I just won't tell you about it. Then you won't have to talk to my mother."

Questions for Thought and Discussion

1. If you were in the counselor's place, what would you do now?
2. Do you think Carmen has an ethical or legal obligation, at this point, to inform the mother of her 15-year-old daughter's dating relationship with an 18-year-old?
3. What do you foresee as possible consequences if Carmen decides to keep Leah's revelations in confidence and the mother later finds out that Leah was dating (and perhaps having sex with) a young man who is a legal adult?
4. What do you think the consequences might be if Carmen does decide that Leah's mother must be informed?

Analysis

It is difficult to fault the counselor's informed consent procedures in this case. It appears that the counselor addressed issues of informed consent quite conscientiously. She provided both the minor client and the mother with a written document, verbally reviewed the document with them, asked them to verify their understanding, and gave them a copy to take home. These procedures are consistent with Standard A.2.a. in the *ACA Code of Ethics.*

The counselor did explain the limitations of confidentiality, as required by Standards A.2.b. and B.2.a., when she told the client and the mother that she would need to breach confidentiality if she knew of potential harm to self or others. It does not appear that the counselor discussed the specific example of statutory rape (a minor having a sexual relationship with an adult, whether consensual or nonconsensual). It is impossible to foresee and discuss with clients, at the outset of the counseling relationship, every conceivable circumstance that might require a breach of confidentiality. Could the counselor reasonably have foreseen this situation?

Informed consent is a complex process that becomes even more complex when clients are minor children. The *Code of Ethics* states that when counseling minors, counselors seek the assent of clients and include them in the decision making process as appropriate. There is a delicate balance between minor clients' rights to confidentiality and their parents' rights to be informed. This is addressed in Standard A.2.d., which states that "counselors recognize the need to balance the ethical rights of clients to make choices, their capacity to give consent or assent to receive services, and parental or familial legal rights and responsibilities to protect these clients and make decisions on their behalf." How the balancing of minor client and parental rights is handled will vary to some degree depending on the age of the minor client. At age 15, the client in this case is an adolescent, not a young child. If the client were 12 or 13 years old, the counselor's decision might seem more clear-cut.

In working with this teenager, the counselor may have several conflicting therapeutic goals. The counselor will want to preserve the counseling relationship so that the issue of becoming sexually active can be further explored with the client. Meeting this goal may not be possible if the counselor insists on involving the mother at this point in time. If the mother is informed against the client's wishes, there is a very good chance that the counseling relationship will be irreparably damaged. At the same time, the counselor will want to protect this minor client from any harm that could potentially result from her entering into a sexual relationship with an adult male.

From a legal standpoint, the counselor could be putting herself at risk if she keeps the client's confidence. There could be repercussions if the mother were to later discover that her daughter had been having sex with the boyfriend and had told her counselor that she was considering doing so. The counselor will need to carefully consider the therapeutic, ethical, and legal ramifications of any decision she makes. Because the risk of harm does not appear to be immediate, perhaps the counselor's best course of action is to postpone (for now) the decision about informing the mother. That would give the counselor the opportunity to continue to explore with the client a range of issues involved in having a dating (and potentially sexual) relationship with an 18-year-old boyfriend.

The best solution in this situation probably would be for the minor client to come to her own decision to tell her mother about her relationship with the boyfriend. The counselor could facilitate this outcome by securing the client's permission to include the mother in some ensuing counseling sessions. Resolving the larger relationship and communication problems between mother and daughter would open the door for the daughter to reveal the dating relationship to her mother. The counselor can find some support for proceeding in this manner by consulting the *Code of Ethics,* which advises counselors to enlist the support, involvement, and understanding of others in the client's world, including family members, when appropriate and with client consent (A.1.d.). The *Code* also urges counselors to work to establish "collaborative relationships with parents/guardians to best serve clients" (B.5.b.).

Questions for Further Reflection

1. Do informed consent procedures need to be specifically tailored when working with children and adolescent clients? If so, what are some of the issues that need to be directly addressed?
2. Does the age of a minor client make a difference with respect to the counselor's obligations to parents? If so, in what ways?
3. What criteria should counselors use to determine a minor client's capacity to assent to counseling?

Case Study 2

Pressures From All Sides: A Rehabilitation Counselor's Dilemma

Mary Ellen Young

Kate was delighted to be hired as a vocational rehabilitation counselor by the Metropolitan Rehabilitation Company immediately after she graduated from her master's degree program in rehabilitation counseling. A client named Brad was one of her first referrals.

Brad had been a construction worker all his life. He started working at the age of 16, helping on a construction site near his home. He was raised by a single mother, and the money he earned helped pay the bills and support his younger siblings. By the time Brad was 17, he had dropped out of high school and was working full time. He did not regret leaving school because his grades had never been very good and the money really helped. He also liked the other men he worked with and appreciated the fact that they were willing to teach him the trade. He particularly liked doing structural work on tall buildings as they were going up. By the time Brad was 20, he was a skilled worker with a formal apprenticeship behind him. He met and married Pam, and they had two children.

Brad was on the job when a rope broke, causing him to fall from a scaffolding 20 feet above the ground. He hit his head and sustained an injury to his spinal cord that resulted in incomplete paraplegia, or partial paralysis of his lower extremities. After being treated in a trauma center, Brad was sent to a rehabilitation hospital where he learned to use a wheelchair. His major concern was whether he would walk again. After several months of physical therapy, he was able to walk a short distance using two canes. However, he was sent home with his wheelchair for primary mobility. His doctor documented that he had a mild brain injury with some short-term memory loss. He was trained to use a memory notebook as a compensation strategy.

While Brad was still in the hospital, he received a letter from an attorney who stated that he should be informed of his rights to recover damages because of his employer's negligence. Brad hired this attorney to represent him should the need arise. Because his injury was job related, Brad qualified for worker's compensation to cover his medical expenses and wage loss. At the suggestion of the hospital social worker, he also applied for Social Security Disability Insurance. This could eventually provide additional income and qualify him for Medicare. Following his discharge from the rehabilitation hospital, Kate visited Brad at home, informing him that the insurance company had hired her company to help him return to work.

After her initial interview with Brad, Kate received a series of phone calls. The first was from the attorney whom Brad had hired. The attorney told Kate that Brad was too disabled to pursue employment at this time and that Kate should not contact him again. The second call was from the claims adjuster who told her that she should get Brad back into sedentary work with the construction firm as soon as possible to minimize the long-term costs to the insurance company.

The third call was from Brad's wife, Pam, who expressed concern that Brad not be forced into going back to work too soon. His income from his construction job had been good when he was working, but periods of employment had been interspersed with periods of unemployment and limited income. Pam thought that because of the severity of Brad's injury, he should continue to draw benefits that could provide a steady income to the family. She also expressed her concerns about medical expenses unrelated to the injury as well as other family medical expenses should Brad not be covered by medical insurance in the future.

Finally, Brad called and tearfully told her that he did not want to spend the rest of his life as a cripple and that he wanted to get back to work as soon as possible. Unsure what to do next, Kate spoke with her supervisor. The supervisor reminded her that Brad's insurance carrier did a lot of work with their company and suggested that she work with the employer to get him back to work as soon as possible, at least on a part-time basis.

Questions for Thought and Discussion

1. If you were in Kate's place, how would you deal with the apparently conflicting desires and needs of all the parties involved in Brad's case?
2. How can Kate keep the welfare of her client foremost, when so many competing demands are being made on her?
3. Who should decide what is in Brad's best interest?
4. What are the elements of informed consent that Kate needs to be concerned with in working with Brad?

Analysis

The practice of vocational counseling in a situation such as a worker's compensation injury is fraught with ethical challenges. In this case, the client's employer, the insurance company, the attorney, and even the counselor's employer may all have a financial stake in Brad's outcome, that is, in whether he will return to work. The decisions that Brad makes will also have far-reaching effects on the family's financial resources and plans for the future. A counselor, particularly a newly trained counselor, may have difficulty keeping the client's best interest at the forefront of the counseling process. The revised *Code of Professional Ethics for Rehabilitation Counselors* (Commission on Rehabilitation Counselor Certification [CRCC], 2002) states that the "primary obligation of rehabilitation counselors will be to their clients" (A.1.a.). Kate's role will include advocating for Brad to remove systemic barriers that might inhibit his continuing recovery and rehabilitation (*ACA Code of Ethics,* A.6.a.). Kate will need to keep these obligations in mind as she negotiates the minefield of a potentially litigious situation.

Whether Brad returns to work or when he returns depends on many factors including the course of his medical recovery, his transferable skills, his ability and willingness to explore new vocational areas and obtain additional training, and his overall ability to cope with this traumatic life event. Pressure to return to work as soon as possible will come from many directions. Brad himself is eager to get back to work, and both Kate's employer and the insurance company paying Kate's employer support this goal, although their motivations are different. However, a system of compensation and benefits exists so that Brad and his family will not be financially devastated by this work-related injury. His wife's concern about his returning to work too soon is valid, and Brad's attorney is acting on his behalf to obtain the highest possible financial compensation for his injury. The *ACA Code of Ethics* states that counselors "assist in the placement of clients in positions that are consistent with the interest, culture, and the welfare of clients, employers, and/or the public" (A.1.e.). Involving Brad's wife in the counseling process as a "positive resource" may also be recommended and is supported by Standard A.1.d.

Rehabilitation is usually funded by a service delivery system, and numerous parties may be involved in both the process and the outcome of rehabilitation counseling services. Payers for services (whether the state rehabilitation agency, an insurance carrier, or an employer) usually require extensive reporting to establish accountability for money expended to help the client's return to work or for other positive vocational outcomes. Such information is needed to document the favorable cost-benefit ratio of the program and to justify continuation of services. However, this system creates a potential ethical dilemma for the counselor because there are additional limits to confidentiality beyond those in a traditional counseling relationship. Brad has a right to full disclosure from Kate about what the counseling process will entail and an explanation of the limits of confidentiality; he also has a right to refuse any recommended service and to be advised of the consequences of that refusal (A.2.b., B.1.d.). Kate must inform him that it is her responsibility to report his progress to the insurance company and to do so accurately and objectively (C.6.b.).

Finally, Kate must be particularly concerned about her supervisor's response to her questions about the dilemma. Her continued employment with Metropolitan Rehabilitation Company implies that she is in agreement with her employer's policies. According to the *Code of Ethics,* counselors should alert their employers to conditions that may be potentially damaging (D.1.h.). Kate will need to establish a dialogue with her supervisor to resolve these issues. If the supervisor continues to pressure her to act in an unethical manner, she may need to notify "appropriate certification . . . or state licensure organizations" and/or seek employment elsewhere (D.1.h.).

Questions for Further Reflection

1. When counselors work in complex systems with multiple and competing demands (such as rehabilitation companies, hospitals, schools, business and industry, or agencies), how can they ensure that they are keeping their clients' welfare foremost?
2. When working in complex systems, how can counselors serve as advocates for their clients?
3. How is the advocate role different in this situation from the traditional counselor role, and what problems or ethical dilemmas might arise when serving as a client advocate?

Chapter 2

Ethical Issues in Multicultural Counseling

Courtland C. Lee

Contemporary counseling practice is greatly influenced by the new realities that have been promulgated by changing demographics. Projections of the United States population into the 21st century indicate that by the year 2050 the non-Hispanic White population will decrease to 50% of the total population; 25% of the population will be Hispanic; 15% Black; 1% American Indian, Eskimo, and Aleut; and 9% Asian and Pacific Islander (U.S. Bureau of the Census, 2004). Three contributing factors to the shift in population distribution are higher birth rates of people of color, increased immigration from non-European parts of the world, and higher White mortality rates as more of this population enters old age. Significantly, people of color are now the fastest growing portion of the U.S. labor force (Bureau of Labor Statistics, 2004). Moreover, by 2020 most school-age children attending public schools will come from diverse cultural, ethnic, and/or racial backgrounds (National Center for Educational Statistics, 1997).

These changing demographics of American society make it imperative that counselors become culturally responsive in their practice. Broadly conceptualized, multicultural counseling considers the personality dynamics and cultural backgrounds of both counselor and client in creating a therapeutic environment in which these two individuals can purposefully interact. Multicultural counselors consider the cultural background and individual experiences of diverse clients and how their psychosocial needs might be identified and met through counseling (Lee & Ramsey, 2006; Sue & Sue, 2003).

Counselors must examine their practice to ensure that it is culturally responsive. A major part of such introspection involves close scrutiny of the ethical standards that guide practice. Scholars have written extensively on ethical standards as they relate to counseling across cultures (Delgado-Romero, 2003; Durodoye, 2006; LaFromboise, Foster & James, 1996; Lee & Kurilla, 1997; Pack-Brown & Williams, 2003; Ridley, Liddle, Hill & Li, 2001; Sue, 1996). The literature suggests that counselors who are culturally responsive increase their chances of practicing in an ethical fashion with diverse client groups. Counselors who are not aware of cultural dynamics and their impact on client development risk engaging in unethical conduct.

Ethical standards establish principles that define ethical behavior and best practice designed to guide counseling. The *ACA Code of Ethics* (2005) provides such principles. In a multicultural society such standards have implications for cross-cultural counselor–client interactions. Counselors have an ethical responsibility to meet the needs of diverse clients within the context of a multicultural society (Delgado-Romero, 2003; Durodoye, 2006; LaFromboise et al., 1996; Lee & Kurilla, 1997; Pack-Brown & Williams, 2003; Ridley et al., 2001; Sue, 1996).

Given the dynamics of culture that may affect counseling, the issue of client welfare warrants examination with respect to the potential harm that may occur when these dynamics are not taken into consideration. Ethically counselors are obligated to protect clients from potential harm or prevent harm when possible (beneficence), but they are equally responsible for not inflicting harm upon clients (nonmaleficence). There can be little doubt that potential harm can be inflicted when counselors do not effectively address the dynamics of culture in counseling interactions.

Counselors must address the challenges of diversity in a manner that is both culturally responsive and ethically responsible. Counselors should aspire to the following with respect to behavior that is culturally responsive (ACA, 2005):

- Recognize diversity and embrace a cross-cultural approach in support of the worth, dignity, potential, and uniqueness of people within their social and cultural contexts.
- Actively attempt to understand the diverse cultural backgrounds of clients.
- Explore your own cultural identity and how it affects your values and beliefs about the counseling process.
- Recognize that support networks hold various meanings in the lives of clients from diverse cultural backgrounds and consider enlisting the support, understanding, and involvement of meaningful others as positive resources, when appropriate.
- Take responsibility for communicating information in ways that are culturally appropriate. In addition, consider the cultural implications of informed consent procedures, and where possible adjust practices accordingly.
- Have an awareness of your own values, attitudes, beliefs, and behaviors and how these apply in a diverse society. Avoid imposing your own values on clients.
- Understand the challenges of accepting gifts from clients, recognizing that in some cultures small gifts are a token of respect and show gratitude.
- Communicate with clients about the parameters of confidentiality in a culturally competent manner. Respect differing cultural views toward disclosure of information, and understand that some clients will not expect confidentiality to be upheld in traditional ways.
- Practice in a nondiscriminatory manner.
- Recognize that culture affects the manner in which clients' problems are defined. Consider clients' socioeconomic and cultural experiences when diagnosing mental disorders.

- Use caution when selecting assessments for culturally diverse populations to avoid inappropriate assessments that may be outside socialized behavioral or cognitive patterns.
- Recognize the effects of various aspects of culture on test administration and interpretation.
- Be aware of and address the role that cultural issues play in the supervisory relationship.
- Make every effort to infuse material related to human diversity into all courses and/or workshops that are designed to promote the development of professional counselors.
- Minimize bias and respect diversity in designing and implementing research programs.

Inherent in these aspirational ethical behaviors is the notion that necessary precautions have been taken by counselors to ensure that their cultural value judgments and biases do not enter into the counseling relationship, and further, that they are consciously aware of any cultural biases and prejudices they may have. Traditional counseling practice reflects the values of the dominant European American culture (Lee, 2006; Sue & Sue, 2003), and the potential for disregarding or misunderstanding the importance of the values and beliefs of culturally diverse clients is great. Thus it is highly probable that the welfare of culturally diverse clients may be at risk even though counselors' actions are well intended.

Questionable or unethical conduct with clients from culturally diverse backgrounds is often due to a lack of multicultural literacy on the part of counselors. However, cultural ignorance should be no excuse for unethical counseling practice. Providing counseling services to culturally diverse clients if you are not competent to do so should be considered unethical practice.

To effectively engage in ethical practice across cultures, counselors must participate in an ongoing professional development process. The focus of this process should be the development and upgrading of skills to intervene effectively in the lives of clients from a variety of cultural backgrounds. To become culturally responsive, counselors must become fully aware of their own cultural heritage, examine possible biases that may interfere with helping effectiveness, gain knowledge about the history and culture of diverse groups of people, and develop culturally responsive skills. Counselors who engage in ethical practice with culturally diverse clients have an awareness of their own cultural assumptions, values, and biases. They also have developed an understanding of the worldviews of culturally diverse clients, and they have acquired culturally appropriate intervention strategies and techniques (Lee & Chuang, 2005). The first case study in this chapter illustrates what can happen when a counselor lacks such awareness and understanding.

Ethical practice requires counselors to promote respect for human dignity and diversity. Ethical conduct in a multicultural context is predicated on a recognition of diversity and a full embrace of a cross-cultural approach in support of the worth, dignity, potential, and uniqueness of people within their social and cultural contexts (ACA, 2005). This should be readily apparent in counselor awareness of and sensitivity to unique cultural realities and their relationship to optimal human development. Counselors who practice without such awareness and sensitivity run the danger of engaging in unethical conduct as is illustrated in the second case study. Ignorance of cultural dynamics can be no excuse for unethical practice.

Case Study 3

Allison: The Case of the Well-Meaning Feminist

Courtland C. Lee

Allison, a 28-year-old, White, first-year doctoral student is doing a practicum at a community agency in a predominantly Latino neighborhood in a large urban area. The agency offers comprehensive counseling services including career counseling. One of Allison's clients is Carmen, a 19-year-old Latina. Carmen and her family moved from Puerto Rico when she was 10 years old. Carmen is single, lives with her parents, and attends a nearby community college.

Allison has been counseling Carmen for several sessions on career options that Carmen might pursue after she obtains her associate's degree. In one of these sessions, Allison reviewed with Carmen the results of an interest inventory that she had recently completed that suggested a number of career options Carmen might consider pursuing. After each option was presented, Carmen would reflect on it and then say, "That sounds like it might be a good job, but I need to check with Popi to see what he thinks about it." After reviewing several options, Allison asked Carmen who Popi was and why his opinion was so important to her. Carmen stated that Popi was her father and that she needed to seek his guidance and permission prior to entering a career. When Allison heard this, it aroused her feminist sensibilities and she responded that Carmen was a woman now and did not need her father, or any man for that matter, giving her permission to live her life and pursue a career.

Allison believed Carmen was in a highly dysfunctional enmeshed family situation, and she wanted to explore strategies that would help Carmen break free of her father's seemingly oppressive grip and allow her to assert her independence as a woman. For the next counseling session, Allison brought several books on women's issues for Carmen to read. She also engaged Carmen in a discussion about what it means to be a woman in contemporary American society. Allison's goal was to get Carmen to begin to assert her independence from her family, in particular her father. Allison attempted to stress to Carmen that the decision to pursue a career was hers alone. She could certainly listen to her father's advice, but as a modern American woman, Carmen did not need her father's permission to pursue a career. This session ended with Allison attempting to get Carmen to think of ways that she could move out of her father's house. Carmen did not return for further counseling after this session.

Questions for Thought and Discussion

1. If you were Allison's practicum supervisor, what would you want her to understand about the cultural dynamics that appear to underlie Carmen's case?
2. As a supervisor, how could you help Allison process her own cultural values, which appear to block effective counseling with Carmen?
3. What steps would you suggest Allison might take to enhance her awareness, knowledge, and skills and become a more culturally responsive counselor?
4. How do you handle situations in which aspects of a client's worldview or specific cultural practices "push your cultural buttons" as a counselor?
5. What comprises ethical practice when there is a conflict of culture between counselors and their clients?

Analysis

It is obvious that Allison and Carmen make meaning for their lives within two different cultural contexts. At the core of the relationship dynamics between this counselor and her client are cultural differences with respect to individualism versus collectivism and gender-role socialization. For Carmen, the dynamics of this case center on some important aspects of Latino culture. The first of these is the cultural dynamic of *familismo,* the collective loyalty to one's family or group (Lopez-Baez, 2006; Vasquez, 1994). The second is *machismo,* the essence of which is a man's sense of family honor and his responsibility to provide for and protect his family (Arredondo, 1991). The third dynamic is *marianismo,* in essence, the female counterpart to *machismo,* which delineates certain responsibilities for women within the family structure (Arredondo, 1991).

Carmen possesses a collectivistic worldview wherein her interconnectedness with her family is very important in shaping her values and behavior. It is apparent that within her kinship system hierarchical relationships in the family are to be respected. Carmen's father plays a significant role in the family, and his place as head of the family is to be respected. As head of the family, Carmen's father has an important responsibility to his unmarried daughter. This responsibility includes providing guidance to her as she plans for the future. Carmen's reciprocal duty and obligation is to honor her father by ensuring that he plays an important role in her career decision making.

In contrast to this is Allison's worldview, which centers on the concept of individualism. She perceives male and female socialization dynamics as androgynous in nature. Implied in her counseling approach with Carmen are the Western or Eurocentric cultural concepts that individuals are the building blocks of society, that dependent relationships are to be discouraged, and that there should be minimal differentiation in the socialization of men and women.

Allison seemingly meant well in her work with Carmen, but her actions border on unethical behavior. Allison attempted to impose her cultural values on Carmen by trying to persuade her to remove her father from her career decision-making process. Allison goes even further with this imposition when she attempts to share the women's literature with Carmen and engages her in a discussion about asserting her independence from her family.

In practicum supervision it would be important to point out to Allison the ethically questionable nature of key aspects of her counseling relationship with Carmen. In particular, Allison should be referred to Standard A.4.b. of the *ACA Code of Ethics,* which states that "counselors are aware of their own values, attitudes, beliefs, and behaviors and avoid imposing values that are inconsistent with counseling goals." In addition, it would be important to discuss with Allison Standard A.1.d, which states that "counselors recognize that support networks hold various meanings in the lives of clients and consider enlisting the support, understanding, and involvement of others (e.g., religious/spiritual/community leaders, family members, friends) as positive resources, when appropriate, with client consent." Finally, Allison should be encouraged to reflect on the aspirational Introduction to Section A, which states that "counselors actively attempt to understand the diverse cultural backgrounds of the clients they serve," and goes on to state that "counselors also explore their own cultural identities and how these affect their values and beliefs about the counseling process."

A review of the *Code of Ethics* during the supervision process should help Allison see that a more culturally responsive and, ultimately, ethical course of action with Carmen would have been to work within the parameters of her culture and help her to consider ways to effectively incorporate her father's input into the career decision-making process. Allison must begin to understand that distinct cultural differences between her and her clients are just that, differences, and are not necessarily deficiencies or pathological deviations. Even though it might severely challenge a counselor's cultural sensitivities, ethical practice demands that counselors respect the cultural dynamics that form clients' worldviews. It is important for Allison to learn that her cultural values cannot be imposed on clients who hold different cultural values. She must come to realize that a culturally responsive and ethical counseling relationship is predicated on a counselor possessing the awareness, knowledge, and skills to meet clients where they are in terms of their unique social and cultural context.

Questions for Further Reflection

1. How can counselors ensure that multicultural competence and literacy are demonstrated in both their personal and professional lives?
2. Multicultural counseling competence has become synonymous with a social justice perspective. How do you see these two concepts being linked?

Case Study 4

Strengths or Limitations? Acknowledging Multicultural Competencies in Counselor Supervision

Beth A. Durodoye

Dr. Rebecca Aten is an assistant professor of counselor education at a thriving and culturally diverse university in California. This semester she is supervising a master's-level practicum class held in the department's on-site counseling clinic. There are six students in the class, five of whom are White, as is Dr. Aten, and one who is of Mexican heritage. The Latina student, Miriam Hernandez, is bilingual in Spanish and English.

After viewing 15 minutes of one session for each supervisee in the class, Dr. Aten feels confident that all the students should be able to perform to her level of expectation in their work with clients from the community. The outcome of this initial basic skills assessment includes a decision by Dr. Aten to route minority clientele solely to Miriam; her rationale is that Miriam "can understand them better with her culturally diverse background." One of Miriam's clients, Alberto Garcia, speaks only Spanish. Dr. Aten, unaware of any Spanish-speaking counselors or services in the surrounding community, decides that Miriam can be of assistance to this client because of her language skills. Because Dr. Aten does not speak Spanish, she requests that Miriam verbally translate the highlights of her sessions with Mr. Garcia for supervisory purposes. She guides Miriam's work with him based on Miriam's overview. Dr. Aten does not view any of Miriam's tapes because she "wouldn't understand what they are talking about, anyway."

Toward the middle of the semester, Miriam finds that she is not entirely satisfied with her practicum experience. She has noticed that her peers get more attention and supervision time from the professor as they present their cases. Miriam believes that she is left to fend largely for herself. One of her classmates even made a comment, which the professor overhears, that he feels bad that she does not get the chance to work with "regular community clients." Moreover, Miriam is also surprised that the professor seems to get irritated if any mention of race is made within the context of her counseling sessions. Though it seems unbelievable, given that Dr. Aten is the professor and is "supposed to know this already," Miriam sometimes thinks she knows more about working with many of her clients than does her own supervisor. Even so, she finds that she needs more direction in her counseling because she gets stuck, especially with Mr. Garcia. Miriam is hesitant to tell the professor about her difficulties for fear that her lack of knowledge will affect her grade and how she might be perceived.

Dr. Aten, however, is pleased with what she has seen of Miriam's work. Given her own lack of experience working with ethnic minority clients, she believes Miriam is making progress. She does get somewhat frustrated, though, if the topic of race is mentioned in her supervision sessions with Miriam because she sees it as a "crutch" that some of Miriam's clients use to avoid dealing with deeper issues. Luckily, she has noticed that Miriam has stopped talking along these lines and attributes this to Miriam's ability to help her clients "get to the root of their problems." From Miriam's reports, her work with Mr. Garcia seems to be coming along fine. Dr. Aten believes this is a definite indication that she can supervise in situations where she does not know the client's language so long as her supervisee does speak the language. In fact, Dr. Aten believes that things are going so well this semester with Miriam that she is both quick and proud to report to interested colleagues about the diversity represented in her practicum. They encourage her to "keep up the good work."

Questions for Thought and Discussion

1. What ethical standards, if any, do you believe Dr. Aten may have violated?
2. How might you advise Dr. Aten to demonstrate appropriate multicultural practices in her classroom?

Analysis

The issues raised in this case study highlight several standards regarding ethical behavior and responsibility. Standard A.11.b. addresses the inability to assist clients and is relevant to this case. Dr. Aten does not speak Spanish and relies for guidance solely on the interpretation of her bilingual supervisee. Dr. Aten does not realize the amount of information she is missing in this case—information that is necessary to assist both the client and her supervisee. She also does not consider factors that may complicate her supervisee's work such as differences in age, gender, and socioeconomic status. In addition, the supervision process is hindered because of the supervisee's concern for her grade. The end result is that the ability to assist Mr. Garcia is greatly reduced compared to the assistance provided to English-speaking clients being served at the clinic.

As the supervisor for the practicum, Dr. Aten's responsibility is to both her supervisees and their clients. Because appropriate services are not available to Mr. Garcia, termination and referral for this client would be in order. It is incumbent on Dr. Aten to be familiar with and develop a list of Spanish-language services in the surrounding community given the array of needs that may be evidenced by potential clients of the on-site clinic. An available list of services would provide resource material for clients and students as well as referral sources for clients.

A second standard at issue in this case concerns the boundaries of competence (C.2.a.). By her own admission, Dr. Aten is not practicing within her areas of competence. She does not speak Spanish, yet she supervises sessions conducted in Spanish. Perhaps believing that White individuals cannot be effective in working with ethnic minority clients, she assigns them to the ethnic minority counselor in practicum. This diminishes her own supervisory responsibilities in this area and deflects attention from her limits in working with diverse clientele. Issues of race as related to the counselor–client relationship seem to cause Dr. Aten discomfort. She seems unaware that she is pushing away from Miriam and Miriam's clients due to her lack of personal awareness regarding race and ethnicity. She also ignores comments made by a student that indicate some clients may be more highly valued than others and thus misses the opportunity to educate. Despite her lack of cultural competence, Dr. Aten appears to relish the façade of diversity in her class. Dr. Aten needs to be challenged to gain personal awareness about her biases, knowledge about general cultural characteristics, and skills as they pertain to the counselor education and supervision process.

Standard C.5. addresses nondiscrimination, another ethical issue clearly present in this case. The standards of care evidenced for White clients and ethnic minority clients differ in Dr. Aten's practicum, as does the behavior that she demonstrates toward her diverse class of supervisees. This seems to result in a tiered system of instruction, or lack of instruction, based on cultural background. Dr. Aten's behaviors appear to be based on ignorance rather than intentional malice. However, her behaviors, unintentional or not, ultimately have a negative impact on the participants in this practicum experience.

Dr. Aten seems resistant to addressing cultural issues in her supervisory relationships (F.2.b.). As long as her supervisory sessions with students do not include the topic of race or ethnicity, she feels comfortable and relaxed. Her resistance is evident with both the ethnic minority and White students in class. It is clear that Dr. Aten's supervisory relationship with Miriam is much more tentative than is her relationship with the other students in the class. Miriam is experiencing increasing anxiety because she feels hesitant to discuss her cases. Dr. Aten's anxiety in working with Miriam is reduced when Miriam sidesteps racial and ethnic issues.

This relationship is made even more sensitive by the fact that Dr. Aten, the supervisor, is less familiar with cultural issues than is her supervisee. Dr. Aten is unwilling to disclose the limitations of her cultural competence, given her status in the class, and Miriam is unwilling to challenge these views, given her own status.

Dr. Aten also chooses to ignore a comment made by a White student that appears to equate "regular community clients" with White community clients. In varying ways, Dr. Aten is relaying a message to the entire class, intended or not, that cultural issues are insignificant to the supervisory process. Refusing to broach the topic of diversity with her White supervisees, or tentatively broaching the issue with her ethnic minority supervisee, inhibits the personal and professional growth of all of Dr. Aten's students.

Finally, Standard F.11.c., Multicultural/Diversity Competence, seems to lie at the core of the ethical issues in this case. Dr. Aten is neither questioned nor challenged with regard to the depth of her cultural understanding. Pronouncements that she has a Mexican American student in her class, or that a number of ethnic minority clients are being seen in her practicum, are met with accolades. If Dr. Aten were pressed beyond this pretense, she would likely have great difficulty speaking to the specifics of how her practicum infuses multicultural competencies. Classroom activities relating to multiculturalism are obviously inadequate. Efforts have not been made by Dr. Aten to encourage students toward multicultural awareness, knowledge, and appropriate skill interventions. In fact, Dr. Aten seems to have inadvertently structured her class in a way that blocks the promotion and representation of diverse perspectives, making it easier for her to remain in her own academic and personal comfort zones.

Questions for Further Reflection

1. In what ways can counselor education departments and programs be held accountable to multicultural competency standards?
2. What resources should counselor educators have available to them and their students that address multicultural issues specific to their departments and programs?

Chapter 3

Confidentiality

Barbara Herlihy and Gerald Corey

Confidentiality is essential to the counseling relationship. For genuine therapeutic work to occur, clients need to feel free to explore their fears, hopes, fantasies, hurts, and other intimate and private aspects of their lives. They need to know that their counselor is trustworthy and will treat their revelations with respect. The counselor's confidentiality pledge is the cornerstone on which this trust can be built. Counselors are committed to earning this trust by creating a collaborative partnership, establishing and maintaining appropriate boundaries, and respecting the confidentiality and privacy of their clients.

Confidentiality is both one of the most basic of our ethical obligations and, at the same time, one of the most problematic. Professional counselors increasingly confront confidentiality issues created by complex legal requirements, developing technologies, health care service delivery systems (such as health maintenance organizations and preferred provider networks), and a culture that places greater and greater emphasis on the rights of service recipients.

An entire section (Section B) of the *Code of Ethics* is devoted to confidentiality, privileged communication, and privacy. Standard B.1.a. states that counselors must be aware of and sensitive to the cultural meanings of confidentiality and privacy. It is important to remember that not all clients share a Western, individualistic notion of personal privacy. Some clients may want confidential information shared with members of their family or community. Counselors should discuss with clients, at the outset of the relationship, when, what, how, and with whom information can be shared so that any cultural differences can be discovered and procedures can be adjusted.

The *Code of Ethics* states that "counselors do not share confidential information without client consent or without sound legal or ethical justification" (B.1.c.). Some counselors have taken their confidentiality obligation so literally that they believe they should maintain a client's confidentiality even when the client asks them to share information with others. It is important to remember that confidentiality belongs to the *client*, not to the counselor, and may be waived only by the client (or the client's authorized representative).

A new standard in the 2005 *Code* pertaining to counselor advocacy has implications for confidentiality: Counselors are ethically obligated to advocate for their clients by working to remove "potential barriers and obstacles that inhibit access and/or the growth and development of clients" (A.6.a.). Standard A.6.b. reminds counselors that they must "obtain client consent prior to engaging in advocacy efforts on behalf of an identifiable client."

Exceptional Circumstances

The exceptions and limitations to confidentiality need to be discussed with clients when counseling is initiated and throughout the relationship as needed (B.1.d.). Counselors have an obligation to tell clients that what they reveal in the counseling relationship will be kept confidential, *except in certain circumstances.* Confidentiality is not absolute, and other obligations may override the pledge. Some exceptional circumstances include sharing information to provide the best possible services or to protect someone in danger, group or family counseling, counseling minors, and obeying court orders. Conscientious counselors must constantly navigate through a complicated array of exceptions, some legal and others ethical.

Sharing Information to Improve Services to Clients

Sometimes it is permissible to share information with others in the interest of providing the best possible services to clients. Here are some situations in which confidential information may be shared:

- Clerical or other assistants may handle confidential information.
- A counselor may consult with experts or peers.
- A counselor may be working under supervision.
- Other professionals may be involved in coordinating client care.
- Other mental health professionals may request information, and the client may give consent to share.

Clerical assistants and other employees or subordinates of the counselor may handle confidential client information, and there is no ethical problem in their doing so. However, counselors need to be aware that they are responsible for any breach of confidentiality by someone who assists them. This speaks to the importance of training subordinates about confidentiality and carefully monitoring office procedures.

Counselors are certainly encouraged to consult with colleagues or experts when they have questions or concerns about their work with a client. If possible, consultation should be managed without revealing the identity of the client, and the client should be informed beforehand of the counselor's intention to seek consultation.

Supervision raises a different circumstance, one in which the client's identity cannot be concealed. The supervisor needs to have access to client records, may observe an actual counseling session through a one-way mirror, or may review audio- or videotapes of sessions. Again, though, the purpose is to ensure quality service, and the ethical obligation is to inform the client fully that supervision is taking place.

In inpatient settings, treatment teams routinely work together in providing services to clients. In these instances, the benefits of coordinating the efforts of various professionals are obvious, but clients have a right to be informed of the information about them that is being shared, with whom, and for what purposes (B.3.b.).

Finally, confidential information may be shared with other helping professionals who are not members of a treatment team when the client requests it or gives permission. This often occurs when a client (or counselor) moves to a different location and records are sent to a new therapist.

Duty to Protect Clients or Others

Sometimes it is permissible to breach confidentiality in order to protect someone who is in danger. Counselors who suspect abuse or neglect of a child, an older person, a resident of an institution, or others who have limited ability to care for themselves must break confidentiality to help that person. In addition, when the client's condition poses a clear and imminent danger to self or others, the counselor is also required to act.

Some people are dependent on others to intervene on their behalf because they are unable to protect themselves from harm due to their youth or diminished capacity. For this reason, both federal and state laws mandate the reporting of suspected child abuse or neglect, and statutes often include a requirement to protect others who may have diminished capacity to care for themselves such as the frail elderly or developmentally disabled. This reporting obligation is clear and leaves little room for judgment calls by counselors.

Confidentiality "does not apply when disclosure is required to protect clients or identified others from serious and foreseeable harm or when legal requirements demand that confidential information must be revealed" (B.2.a.). A legal duty to warn and protect an identifiable or foreseeable victim may exist when a client threatens violence toward another person or persons. This duty, which arose out of the *Tarasoff* (1974) case in California, has created considerable consternation among helping professionals. The *Tarasoff* precedent has been applied in some states, but there is variation on several dimensions, such as whether a counselor *may* warn or *must* warn, to whom a warning should be given, and under what circumstances. We must disclose when legal requirements demand it, and it is essential that we consult with other professionals when we are uncertain. Counselors must be familiar with their state laws regarding a duty to warn and should not hesitate to consult with an attorney as well as with experts when they are in doubt.

A duty to warn also may exist when a client is suicidal and poses a danger to self. Counselors struggle with the demands of deciding when to take a client's threats or hints seriously enough to report the condition. A difficult and sensitive issue is whether counselors should breach confidentiality when working with terminally ill clients who are considering hastening their own deaths. Ethical issues in working with clients who may be suicidal and in end-of-life decisions are further addressed in Chapter 8.

Mental health professionals have questioned whether an ethical duty to warn may exist when a client is HIV positive or has AIDS and may be putting others at risk. The 2005 *ACA Code of Ethics* contains a revised standard that addresses this matter:

> When clients disclose that they have a disease commonly known to be both communicable and life threatening, counselors may be justified in disclosing information to identifiable third parties, if they are known to be at demonstrable and high risk of contracting the disease. Prior to making a disclosure, counselors confirm that there is such a diagnosis and assess the intent of clients to inform the third parties about their disease or to engage in any behaviors that may be harmful to an identifiable third party. (B.2.b.)

Note that counselors should not take action until they have confirmed the diagnosis and have ascertained that the client has not already informed the third party and does not intend to do so in the immediate future. The first case study in this chapter illustrates some of the dilemmas counselors encounter around this issue.

Situations in Which Confidentiality Cannot Be Guaranteed

In some situations, counselors must clarify that confidentiality cannot be guaranteed. These circumstances include when counseling groups or families, or whenever there are more than two people (counselor and individual client) in the room, and when the client is a minor. The confidentiality pledge is different for counselors working with groups. Although group counselors can make their own promise not to disclose information shared during group sessions, they cannot guarantee the behavior of group members. Group counselors must "clearly explain the importance and parameters of confidentiality for the specific group being entered" (B.4.a.). Also, counselors need to convey to group members the fact that confidentiality cannot be guaranteed. Counselors who work with couples and families also encounter some unique confidentiality dilemmas. Counselors need to clearly define who the client is, discuss the limitations of confidentiality, and seek agreement among all involved parties. Issues that arise when counselors work with multiple clients are further addressed in Chapter 5.

When clients are minor children, their parents or guardians may have rights to certain information. Although from an ethical perspective children should be able to expect confidentiality, their legal rights are more limited. In addition, the counseling process can sometimes be enhanced by including parents or guardians. Counselors are advised to strive to establish collaborative relationships with parents or guardians (B.5.b.). Chapter 6 focuses specifically on ethical issues in working with minor clients.

Court Ordered Disclosures

Counselors, like all citizens, must obey orders given to them by a judge or an official of the court—which creates an exception to our confidentiality pledge. However, when counselors are required to release confidential or privileged information without a client's permission, they are expected to "obtain written, informed consent from the client or take steps to prohibit the disclosure or have it limited as narrowly as possible due to potential harm to the client or counseling relationship" (B.2.c.). When disclosure is required, "only essential information is revealed" (B.2.d.).

Whether a counselor will be able successfully to request in court to withhold information may depend on the privileged communications provisions in the state where the counselor practices. Confidentiality is an *ethical* obligation, whereas privileged communication is a *legal* concept that protects clients from having their confidential communications revealed in court without their permission. Confidential or privileged information should not be shared in a court until an attorney representing the counselor has advised this course of action (Remley & Herlihy, 2005). State laws vary considerably with respect to which mental health professionals' communications are privileged, and under what circumstances. Counselors must know the laws in their own states.

Records

We need to remember that not only are clients' communications confidential but so are their counseling *records*. Standard B.6. sets forth several guidelines for maintaining, storing, transferring, sharing, and disposing of records. This section reminds counselors of their obligation to store records in a secure place and to exercise care when sending records to others by mail or through electronic means. Despite counselors' best efforts, it is possible for the confidentiality of records to be inadvertently breached, particularly when counselors are not aware of the confidentiality implications of new technologies. The second case study in this chapter provides an illustration of just such an occurrence.

Counselors should remember that clients have a legal right to obtain copies of their records. Counselors should write their clinical case notes carefully, always with the assumption that someone else will read them at a later time (Remley & Herlihy, 2005).

Case Study 5

Confidentiality and HIV/AIDS: The Case of Norma

Jorge Garcia

Norma is a 21-year-old college student who immigrated to the United States with her parents from El Salvador when she was 2 years old. She is bicultural in the sense that she proudly identifies herself as a Latina while at the same time having learned the instrumental behaviors that allow her to be effective and successful in the host culture. She speaks English and has been able to advance educationally to the point that she will soon graduate with a bachelor's degree. Socially, she interacts with people from different cultures.

Two years ago Norma started dating a young Latino man about her age, named Javier. They became close very quickly and started spending a lot of time together. Even though she is aware of the need for protection, they have had sex repeatedly without safety precautions. Javier refuses to engage in safe sex, and Norma has not been able to assert herself in this situation. Although he never went to college, Javier finished high school and was able to keep a job for a while. He was fired when he stopped going to work regularly. About a year ago, Norma learned through common friends that Javier has been engaging in antisocial behavior such as dealing drugs and joining groups that commit acts of violence. She has also been the victim of his violent and abusive behavior. Because of his behavior, Norma has been slowly separating herself from Javier, which makes him even angrier. Last semester she attended a workshop about HIV and realized that she could be at great risk, so she was tested for the virus. To her extreme shock, she found out that she was HIV positive; she became so disturbed that she started seeing a counselor at the university. Norma thinks that Javier may have transmitted this disease to her, but she is not entirely sure as she had sexual relations with other people before Javier (sometimes unprotected).

Soon the counselor realized that she had an ethical dilemma because Norma has not disclosed her condition to Javier, even though she did inform her other former partners. Informing Javier would allow him to make a decision about seeking testing and treatment if necessary. The counselor wonders whether she has a duty to warn Javier about the danger of being infected with the HIV virus. The counselor shared with Norma that she might have to disclose Norma's condition to Javier, under her duty to warn, unless Norma agreed to do it herself. Norma replies fearfully that if such information is disclosed to Javier she will be in imminent danger of being attacked by him to the point of fearing for her life. This belief is consistent with the history of Javier's violent behavior as reported by Norma. The counselor realized that this ethical dilemma has suddenly become more complex.

Questions for Thought and Discussion

1. What action(s) do you think the counselor should take in this case?
2. What process of ethical decision making would you use to determine the counselor's best course of action?
3. If this counselor practiced in a state that had a law that mandates disclosure, how would that affect her decision-making process?

Analysis

The ACA ethical standard on contagious, life-threatening diseases (B.2.b.) applies in this case. That is, counselors may be justified in disclosing information to an identified third party if that person is at high risk of contracting the disease by his or her relationship with the client, and if the client has not informed the third party and does not intend to reveal such information in the future.

From a legal perspective, in the 1980s most states embraced strict confidentiality statutes specifying that HIV test results could not be disclosed and that the identity of people testing positive had to be kept confidential. However, states began amending these laws in the 1990s because of concerns about the protection of third parties. Today most states (29) have permissible legislation, without mandated disclosure, that allows professionals to notify third parties by informing them directly or by notifying authorities (e.g., health department). Other states (13) have legislation that is permissible in nature but mandates disclosure to specific parties such as school officials, penal institutions, and blood banks. Only one state has passed legislation mandating disclosure only to a specific party, without permissible provisions.

This case appears straightforward in the sense that Javier has been identified as the third party, he is at high risk, and Norma refuses to disclose this information to him. This is consistent with the requirements for disclosure under Standard B.2.b. It is also compatible with most statutory laws allowing such disclosure. However, such disclosure may be life threatening to Norma.

The dilemma for this counselor involves a conflict between two standards found in the *ACA Code of Ethics*: Standard A.1.a. states that it is the primary responsibility of the counselor to promote the welfare of the client, and Standard B.2.b. permits disclosure of confidential information to protect a third party from a contagious or fatal disease if certain conditions are met. So what should the counselor do in this case when upholding one standard compromises the other?

The ethical principle of nonmaleficence, or avoidance of harm, may come into play here, as use of the ethical standards alone seems insufficient to resolve this case. It is generally accepted that the principle of nonmaleficence supersedes all other principles in the face of an ethical dilemma; however, in this case both possible courses of action are supported by the same principle of "do no harm." The counselor must answer the question, "Is the harm of nondisclosure (for Javier) greater than the harm of disclosure (for Norma)?" If the counselor is able to demonstrate that a greater harm exists for one over the other, then a course of action consistent with that conclusion should be chosen (disclosure or nondisclosure of Norma's condition to Javier).

What if the counselor is unable to decide conclusively who is at greater harm by disclosing or not disclosing in this case? A reasonable course of action might then be to avoid disclosing Norma's condition to Javier directly but to find a way to disclose the information to Javier anonymously. Of course, the counselor would have to weigh the possibility that Javier could find out about Norma's HIV status and react violently against her. Another option would be for the counselor to disclose the information to Javier while taking measures to protect Norma. Again, it is a question of which action would pose more risk to either party. This case illustrates that confidentiality issues can be very complex, particularly when confidentiality standards are in conflict with other standards.

Questions for Further Reflection

1. What resources other than the *ACA Code of Ethics* are available to counselors when they are confronted with ethical dilemmas for which there seems to be no acceptable solution?
2. How might considerations of cultural diversity play a role in cases such as this one?

Case Study 6

An Inadvertent Breach of Confidentiality

Walter Breaux III

Gwen is a master's-level student in her second semester of internship at her university's counseling center. Gwen is doing very well at the center and is feeling confident about her clinical skills as she begins to deal with more complex client issues. Gwen is now working with her first suicidal client and has been commended by her director for her empathy and willingness to challenge herself.

Recently Gwen has missed several weekly supervision sessions with her site supervisor at the counseling center, pleading other commitments. She has told her fellow interns that she gets enough supervision within the counseling program and that the site supervisor, a clinical social worker, does not understand the humanistic aspects of therapy.

As part of her internship duties, Gwen is currently facilitating three self-image groups for undergraduate students. At the end of each group session, Gwen records session notes in her laptop computer and transfers the notes to the counseling center's office computer every Friday. Gwen is required to create session notes for each individual client in the group. She believes that using her laptop for her internship duties helps her save time, as she would have to wait for access to the office computer (which is usually being used by other interns) before entering her notes for each of her 20 clients. Gwen's university supervisor has advised Gwen in the past to be careful to keep her client notes confidential and to transfer them to the office computer daily.

Last week Gwen was ill and saw clients at the counseling center only during the first half of the week. It is now Sunday, and she will be unable to transfer her session notes to the office computer until Monday. After the weekend, Gwen is feeling better and plans to transfer the notes, saved under the file name "confidential," when she reports to the counseling center at 11:00 a.m. on Monday. Adrianne, Gwen's roommate, is working on an advanced degree in business and asks to borrow Gwen's laptop to finish a report that is overdue. Gwen agrees to her roommate's request and, after lightheartedly reminding Adrianne not to break the laptop, leaves to go to the library. Adrianne logs on to the laptop and sees Gwen's "confidential" file on the computer's desktop. Overcome by curiosity, Adrianne double-clicks the file, which opens to reveal 20 session notes labeled by client name. Adrianne recognizes her younger sister's name and opens the session note to find that her sister has been referred for concurrent individual counseling and has been battling with suicidal ideations for the past several weeks after breaking up with her boyfriend. Alarmed at the thought of losing her sister, Adrianne immediately calls her sister and confronts her about what she has just read. At this point, Gwen is unaware that her roommate and her client are sisters and is unaware of their discussion of the session notes.

The client is quite upset by this intrusion of her older sister and contacts the counseling center about the incident first thing Monday morning. It does not take long for the director of the counseling center to make the connections among the client, Gwen, the laptop, and the client's sister. Gwen is called into the counseling center to meet with the director concerning this breach of confidentiality.

Questions for Thought and Discussion

1. If you were the counseling center director, what would say to the student counselor when you meet with her?
2. What action(s) would you take to resolve the problem with the student counselor? with the upset client? with respect to counseling center policies and procedures?
3. Do you think the supervisor has an obligation to take disciplinary action against the supervisee?
4. Would the supervisor need to report the ethical violation to the ACA Ethics Committee (assuming the intern was a student member of ACA)?

Analysis

Standard F.8.a. states that "counselors-in-training have a responsibility to understand and follow the *ACA Code of Ethics.*" This standard also states that "students have the same obligation to clients as those required of professional counselors." Thus, although Gwen is still a student, she is responsible for understanding and complying with the *Code.*

Although Gwen's recent failure to regularly attend the supervision sessions provided by the counseling center is not an unethical behavior, it may have contributed to the incident. The potential for a breach of confidentiality may have been detected at the center if Gwen's site supervisor had been aware (through regular supervision) of how Gwen was handling her client notes. Thus, the incident might have been averted.

Gwen's handling of the session notes was not in compliance with Standard B.6.a., which states that "counselors ensure that records are kept in a secure location and that only authorized persons have access to records." Gwen's use of her personal laptop computer to record client session notes may have seemed like a good idea, yet she failed to secure her clients' confidential information in a manner that would prevent intentional or unintentional access. Gwen's negligence in failing to take adequate security precautions led directly to the breach of confidentiality.

In terms of her clinical skills, Gwen appears to be a good student counselor with potential to become an effective practitioner. However, she does need to learn to take some of her professional responsibilities more seriously. There are several ways that this incident could have been prevented. First, Gwen should have attended all required supervision sessions at the counseling center. Second, the counseling center should have had a policy in place regarding the use of personal laptop computers for professional matters. If the policy allowed the use of laptop computers, Gwen's procedures should have been reviewed and modified by the site supervisor to bring them into line with the center's policy. Finally, Gwen should have secured her laptop and client files with a nondescriptive password system and file labels.

In this case, it appears that both the counseling center director and the student intern have some responsibility for the incident. The center director is responsible for assuring that interns are being appropriately and carefully supervised, and Gwen's poor judgment caused problems for her client, her internship site, and herself.

When the center director meets with Gwen, she will want to ensure that Gwen understands the seriousness of the situation and has an acceptable plan for preventing any future problems. Coming to an informal resolution in this way is in accord with Standard H.2.b. The director would not be obligated to report the violation to the ACA Ethics Committee unless the problem could not be resolved during the meeting (H.2.c.). The resolution might include several steps: a change in Gwen's record-keeping procedures, a promise from Gwen that she will attend all supervision sessions with her site supervisor, a change in counseling center policies and procedures, placing Gwen under more intensive supervision, and meeting with the upset client. The client herself might decide to file a formal complaint against Gwen and the counseling center, and the client should be informed of her right to do so. Whatever the outcome, this counselor intern will have learned a painful lesson.

Questions for Further Reflection

1. When a supervisor discovers that an intern under his or her supervision has violated the confidentiality of a client (even inadvertently), what steps should the supervisor take?
2. What steps do you need to take (regardless of the medium used to store client information) to ensure the security and confidentiality of your clients' records?
3. Student counselors have the same ethical obligations as practicing counselors to maintain client confidentiality. What are some ways that counselors-in-training might unintentionally breach the confidentiality of their fellow students or their clients?

Chapter 4

Competence

Gerald Corey and Barbara Herlihy

Trust is a key element in any discussion of competence because it defines the context in which clients enter into a therapeutic relationship. "When clients put their trust in us as professionals, one of their most fundamental expectations is that we will be competent" (Pope & Vasquez, 1998, p. 59). Clients, as help seekers, place themselves in a vulnerable position, allowing their counselors to hear their most personal secrets and learn about their most private struggles. The trust that clients bestow on counselors is a source of power that must not be abused; clients need to be able to rely on their counselor's competence as a helper.

Counselors have an ethical obligation to "practice only within the boundaries of their competence, based on their education, training, supervised experience, state and national professional credentials, and appropriate professional experience" (C.2.a.). Competence in counseling is difficult to define. Remley and Herlihy (2005) discuss competence as an ethical and legal concept. They point out that competence is not a simple either/or matter; rather, it is a complex concept with many possible levels along a continuum. From an ethical perspective, competence implies that counselors do no harm to clients. Although counselors may not intend to harm their clients, incompetence often is a contributing factor in causing harm to clients. From a legal perspective, counselors who are incompetent can be sued for malpractice and held legally responsible in a court of law.

Counseling is a very broad profession, and counselors work with a wide spectrum of clients and client concerns in very diverse settings that require different skills and competencies. Thus, ethical practice requires counselors to acquire knowledge, personal awareness, sensitivity, and the skills necessary for working with diverse client populations. No professional counselor can be competent in every aspect of potential practice. Appropriate education, training, and experience in working with children do not qualify us to work with older adults; competence in individual counseling does not qualify us to conduct groups or work with families; and expertise in working with clients who suffer from depression does not qualify us to work with clients with borderline personality disorders.

How can boundaries of competence be determined and assessed? Mental health professionals have long struggled with this question, and their efforts have taken varied forms, including the development of standards for training, credentialing, continuing education, and new specialty areas of practice, as well as self-monitoring.

Obviously, training is a basic component in developing competence to counsel. Although graduate students in counselor education programs may be excited about the knowledge and skills they are learning, they must avoid the temptation to counsel others until they are fully qualified to do so. The first case study in this chapter illustrates this point.

Key issues in training include determining who should be selected for admission to counselor education programs and by what selection methods, what should be taught and by which methods, and what procedures should be used to ensure that only competent counselors are graduated from training programs. Ethical issues in training and supervision are more fully addressed in Chapter 9, but one reality particularly germane to the development of competence is that training institutions may vary considerably in the quality of training provided. The Council for Accreditation of Counseling and Related Educational Programs (CACREP, 2001) is one organization that provides national standards for training counselors. CACREP is an independent accrediting body that accredits programs that have undergone a rigorous review. Graduates of CACREP-accredited programs can be reasonably assumed to possess certain competencies. However, many competent counselors are graduates of training programs that are not CACREP-accredited.

Credentials are presumed to be a tangible indicator of accomplishment with implications for assessing the competence of the credential holder. The state licensure movement has been significant in this respect. Licensure assures clients that their counselors have completed minimal educational requirements, have had supervised experience, and have successfully completed an examination or other form of screening. Licensure requirements vary from state to state, however, and the possession of a license does not ensure that practitioners will competently *do* what their credential permits them to do. The second case study in this chapter describes the pitfalls encountered by a counselor opening a private practice, even though he is fully licensed and possesses the appropriate credentials.

Licensure laws typically require that professionals complete continuing education requirements to renew their licenses. Continuing education is also an ethical obligation. Standard C.2.f. states that counselors recognize the need for continuing education to keep abreast of current information and developments, and that they "take steps to maintain competence in the skills they use, are open to new procedures, and keep current with the diverse populations and specific populations with whom they work." As with other means of assessing competence, there are limitations to what continuing education requirements can accomplish. It is difficult to monitor the quality of continuing education offerings or their relevance to a particular counselor's needs. The number of clock hours obtained may have little relationship to how much the counselor has actually learned and integrated into practice.

Without an agreed-upon definition of competence, it is difficult for ethically conscientious counselors to determine exactly where their boundaries of competence lie and to recognize when they are in danger of exceeding them. In the absence of formal criteria for evaluating competence in specific practices or specializations, counselors must carefully assess whether they should accept or continue to work with certain clients or refer them. Consultation with other professionals in these situations is also a prudent and ethically appropriate measure (C.2.e.). While learning skills in new specialty areas, "counselors take steps to ensure the competence of their work and to protect others from possible harm" (C.2.b.). Working under supervision while stretching one's boundaries of competence is perhaps the best way to prevent any harm.

Chapter 2 provides a thorough discussion of ethical issues in multicultural counseling, yet we want to reemphasize here that multicultural competence is essential for counselors who practice in today's diverse society. Although early versions of the *ACA Code of Ethics* did not address multicultural competence as an ethical obligation (Watson, Herlihy, & Pierce, 2006), the need for multicultural awareness, knowledge, and skills is emphasized throughout the current *Code.* The counseling profession has reached consensus that counselors who provide services to clients who are culturally different from them have an ethical duty to be competent to work effectively with these clients.

Because competence is so difficult to define and assess, careful self-monitoring may be the most effective method for counselors to ensure that they are providing the highest quality of services. Counselors are ethically obligated to "monitor their effectiveness as professionals and take steps to improve when necessary" (C.2.d.).

It is incumbent on each of us to strive to maintain self-awareness and to be alert to any signs of burnout or impairment. Counselors' obligations to clients necessitate that they seek assistance for their own problems that are interfering with their professional effectiveness, and that, "if necessary, they limit, suspend, or terminate their professional responsibilities until such time it is determined that they may safely resume their work" (C.2.g.). The importance of maintaining a connectedness with peers cannot be overemphasized in this regard. Peer consultation groups can provide a source of support to counter the loneliness that is often associated with the work of the counselor, especially the private practitioner. Koocher and Keith-Spiegel (1998) have observed that the impaired mental health professional is most typically a professionally isolated individual. Peers can help us see our blind spots, offer new perspectives on ethical and practice issues, and provide us with opportunities to share information about resources and effective therapeutic procedures.

The ultimate answer to maintaining competence most likely lies in our ability to explore our own motives and relationships insightfully. As Koocher and Keith-Spiegel note, this ability is not easily taught and never perfected, yet it is among the most critical to the effective ethical functioning of the professional counselor. Development of competence is an ongoing process that is never really completed.

Case Study 7

Jocelyn's Dilemma: How to Answer a "Calling"

Zarus E. Watson

Jocelyn is a part-time graduate student who has completed 18 credit hours toward her 60-credit master's degree program in mental health counseling. She lives and works in a housing development in an older section of a medium-sized city in the South. The neighborhood is populated largely by African Americans and Hispanic Americans, with smaller groups of White Americans and a more recently arrived population of immigrants from Southeast Asia. Female-headed households predominate and most occupy the lower to working middle economic classes. The housing development and its surrounding neighborhood are in a general state of disrepair, with few actual on-site homeowners. Crime and drug use are increasing problems, especially among the youth, as are persistent issues of domestic violence and an escalating high school dropout rate.

Jocelyn, a 35-year-old Afro/Hispanic American, works as a coordinator for social services at a faith-based community center. She is the oldest of seven children and was reared in a single-parent household (her father died in an accident when she was 12 years old). Jocelyn continues to help her mother and younger siblings at home. The family and the neighbors often hold Jocelyn up as a model for their children to follow. This visibility has intensified since she accepted the coordinator's position at the neighborhood church. Within the community, the church is seen as the keystone of survival and hope. Those who hold prominent positions in it are seen as leaders of the community and are afforded a great deal of respect.

The church offers a number of services that have been made possible through a local government grant including health education, workplace training, reading literacy programs, and a church-brokered program of spiritual advisement. These services, as well as a prayer line, are made available to the community through trained church volunteers. Clients receive services on site at the church or through the spiritual home visitors program, which is the off-site component of the spiritual advisement program.

The pastor of the church and the board of elders have asked Jocelyn to address a growing need among the church congregation and surrounding community. At issue, they believe, is the growing tide of distress emanating from domestic violence and trauma among the population. The pastor, knowing of Jocelyn's enrollment in a mental health counseling graduate program, asks her to train the prayer line staff to take calls that go beyond simple prayer requests.

Jocelyn thinks this is within her scope of competence. She reminds the pastor and the elder board, however, that none of the personnel who work the prayer line are qualified to counsel people regarding their mental health issues. She offers to train them to recognize issues that go beyond the scope of a prayer request and to refer these callers to the pastor.

Several weeks after Jocelyn has implemented the training of prayer line workers in recognition and referral protocols, she receives a call from the pastor, who asks her to meet with him. At the meeting, the pastor commends Jocelyn on her skill in training the prayer line staff. In fact, he states, referrals have roughly tripled in number in only a month's time. He adds, "Normally, I would be overjoyed by this result, but I'm no longer 30 years old. I'm over 70, and I just can't deal with such large numbers of folks needing help." The solution is obvious, asserts the pastor: Jocelyn must take on part of the referral load. He maintains that, with her graduate school training and with the level of trust and respect that she holds in the community, she would be a godsend. "Jocelyn," he states, "your life ministry is to help others to the best of your ability, and I know you will respond with your brethren in mind."

Jocelyn leaves the meeting without giving the pastor a definitive answer to his request. Privately, she muses, "Am I really prepared to counsel people with real issues?" Information gleaned from her course work suggests not. After all, she will need to complete eight additional courses before she will be eligible to begin her supervised fieldwork (practicum) experience. However, she thinks, the pastor does make a compelling point. This is a matter of a "calling" to do God's work. Can it really be compared with work in the secular world? Also, she remembers, clergy are exempt from the requirement to hold licensure as professional counselors in her state. Although she is not clergy, she would be acting under the auspices of the pastor and, in fact, as an extension of him. She thinks, "How could I let down people in pain? These are my neighbors." Besides, she reasons, after seeing them in a therapeutic setting, she can see if there is a need for more extensive treatment and, if so, make a referral. She considers that they may be more willing to accept a referral after having talked with her. She calls the pastor and accepts the charge.

Questions for Thought and Discussion

1. Has Jocelyn exceeded her bounds of competence? If so, in what respects?
2. As you analyze this case, are there any cultural elements that have to be considered? If so, what are they?
3. If you were to advise Jocelyn regarding her boundaries of competence in this matter, what would you suggest to her?

Analysis

This case illustrates the complexity of issues that can be involved in determining one's boundaries of competence. From a legal perspective, Jocelyn is correct when she notes that pastoral counselors generally are exempt from licensure requirements. Thus she probably would not be legally vulnerable to a charge of practicing counseling without a license. However, the ethical question is whether she has the competence to offer the services she has agreed to provide (C.2.). Jocelyn has learned through her graduate course work that she is not adequately prepared at this time to offer *counseling* services to "real" clients. Whether she would be exceeding her boundaries of competence in this position depends on the nature of the services she ultimately offers to the parishioners and community members. The fact that she plans to see them "in a therapeutic setting" and to refer them "if there is a need for more extensive treatment" implies that she intends to provide clinical mental health counseling services, even though the services might be short-term. If this is the case, she will be exceeding the boundaries of her present competence (C.2.a.).

Jocelyn's situation is complicated by the difficulty of distinguishing between counseling and a "calling" or ministry, as there are many similarities between the two vocations. The contextual and cultural aspects of the situation also need to be considered. Jocelyn realizes that many of the potential clients are members of racial or ethnic minority groups and are economically disadvantaged, and that these populations are often reluctant to seek counseling from service providers who do not share their cultural values or live and practice in their communities. Jocelyn is uniquely positioned to be able to serve this population. Not only is she a member of the community and a well-respected role model, her position in the church provides her with ready access to those in need. She could serve effectively as a gateway to counseling services for potential clients who might not otherwise seek services.

The most desirable outcome in this case would be for Jocelyn to be able to answer her "calling" and fulfill her commitment to her community, but to do so without exceeding the limits of her present training. She might work with the pastor to develop proposals for additional grant monies that would fund on-site mental health counseling at the church. In her position as coordinator of social services, she might accept referrals from the prayer line workers while making it clear that the services she personally offers do not include mental health counseling. By developing a repertoire of referral resources, she could serve as a gateway to a variety of needed services for the parishioners and community members. Her referral list could include qualified professional counselors who are culturally competent and who work in the community or in nearby areas. Other referral resources could include advocacy groups and agencies that provide assistance with problems of discrimination, inadequate financial resources, drug abuse, domestic violence, crime prevention, job training, and access to health care services. In this way, Jocelyn could serve at the present time as a vital link between members of her community and social service providers. Later, once she has completed her academic course work and is ready to begin her counseling practicum, perhaps she could arrange to work under the supervision of one of the counselors on her referral list. This would move her closer to her goal of becoming a counselor while at the same time serving her community and answering her calling to do God's work.

Questions for Further Reflection

1. What are the major factors to consider in determining one's boundaries of competence?
2. What differences and similarities do you see in the competencies needed by pastoral counselors and by licensed mental health counselors?

Case Study 8

Ethical Pitfalls in Managed Care

Larry Golden

After completing his master's degree in counseling, Martin worked at the Family Service Center, an agency where he received the 3,000 hours of supervised practice required for licensure in his state. He passed the state board examination and became a licensed professional counselor. Only then, in accordance with state licensing regulations, did Martin hang out his shingle and open his independent private practice.

Martin wanted to provide the best possible counseling services to his clients. He also wanted—and needed—to earn a good living. During the first few months he struggled, unaware of the extent to which managed care had affected the private practice of counseling. He placed ads in the yellow pages of local telephone directories, gave free talks at PTA meetings and to various civic clubs, invited referral sources out to lunch, and attempted several other strategies to build a client base. Very few referrals came.

Martin pursued an opportunity to become a network provider with HealthCo, a managed care company. He accepted the company's $50 per hour payment, although it was considerably less than his usual fee, and agreed to comply with HealthCo's approach to managed care. He was delighted when HealthCo referrals began to come in on a regular basis.

In some respects, Martin was pleased with the services provided by the managed care company. When he ascertained that a client who presented with depression was also suffering from anorexia, he realized that he needed to refer the client because he lacked training and supervised experience with this disorder. He called his HealthCo case manager, who arranged a referral to a psychiatrist in the network who specialized in eating disorders.

However, there were some aspects of the relationship with HealthCo that worried Martin. He was required to get telephone authorizations for client sessions, but it seemed that whenever he called, he was connected to a different case manager who identified him- or herself only by first name. The case managers began the telephone conferences by keying in Martin's client's Social Security number to gain access to the client's computerized file. Before he began to work with HealthCo, Martin had been required to give a diagnosis when completing paperwork for third-party payers, and he was comfortable with giving that information. But these case managers insisted that if they were to *manage*, they needed much more information. They inquired about clients' childhood traumas, marital problems, addictions, and other matters. Martin realized that this questioning was legal because the clients had signed HealthCo's disclosure form. But he wondered, was it ethical? He became concerned about just what happened to the information he disclosed over the telephone.

Soon after these concerns began to emerge, one of Martin's clients ran out of insurance benefits. The case manager suggested that Martin space out the last 3 of the 20 allocated visits over a period of several months or arrange a referral to a community mental health center. Martin didn't feel that these options were acceptable. The client needed weekly sessions, and considerably more than the 3 that remained. He also believed that she needed continuity of care, and that a transfer to a new counselor was not in her best interest. Martin attempted to explain his concerns to the case manager but was unsuccessful in convincing her to alter her decision. Because he could not consider abandoning a client and would not agree to make a referral, he decided, with some resentment toward HealthCo, to continue to see the client pro bono. This interaction caused Martin to wonder what professional credentials HealthCo's case managers possessed. Were they qualified to make decisions about psychotherapy?

Soon thereafter, an 11-year-old boy named Joshua was referred to Martin under the boy's father's company insurance plan administered by HealthCo. Joshua was getting in fights at school. It quickly became clear to Martin that Joshua's parents were in conflict, so Martin recommended marital counseling. However, this particular HealthCo plan didn't cover marital counseling. Martin, beginning to feel frustrated with managed care, saw the parents in counseling and billed the sessions under Joshua's name. He justified his decision to himself by reasoning that, after all, gains in the marital relationship should surely yield benefits for Joshua.

Questions for Thought and Discussion

1. In what respects has Martin's behavior been in compliance with the *Code of Ethics*? Do you see any ways in which he has acted unethically?
2. If Martin had been meeting regularly with a peer consultation group, how might such a group have helped him deal with the ethical and practice issues he encountered?
3. If Martin consulted with you regarding his concerns about HealthCo, what advice might you give him?
4. How can counselors in private practice best deal with managed care companies?
5. Do you believe Martin was competent to open an independent private practice?

Analysis

An ethical issue first arose in this case when Martin ascertained that one of his clients suffered from anorexia. He realized that he would be exceeding the boundaries of his competence if he continued to work with her, and he appropriately arranged a referral to a qualified provider. He acted in accordance with Standard A.11.b., which states that "if counselors determine an inability to be of professional assistance to clients, they avoid entering or continuing counseling relationships" and refer the client, and with Standard C.2.a., which states that "counselors practice only within the boundaries of their competence."

Martin grew concerned about a possible breach of confidentiality via HealthCo's anonymous case managers and potential lapses in the company's computer system. Standard B.3.d. is pertinent here. It states that "counselors disclose information to third-party payers only when clients have authorized such disclosure." As a matter of informed consent, Martin has a duty to inform clients of the limitations of confidentiality that HealthCo may place on him as a provider of counseling services. Martin had a responsibility to ensure that he knew what information about clients he was required to provide *before* he agreed to become a HealthCo provider. It appears that Martin allowed his decision to affiliate with the company to be driven by his frustrations and financial needs, and he may have acted hastily. At this point, Martin needs to resolve his concerns directly with HealthCo and determine whether he can ethically continue to be a network provider. If he decides to continue, he also has a responsibility to ensure that his HealthCo clients are fully informed about the information he will be providing to the company. Ethically, he cannot rely solely on the fact that the clients have signed the company's disclosure form.

Martin began to grow disenchanted with the managed care company's policies and procedures and to have some concerns about the quality of care that he could provide under their aegis. He will be well advised to consider whether he can remain a network provider and continue to adhere to Standard D.1.g.: "The acceptance of employment in an agency or institution implies that counselors are in agreement with its general policies and principles."

It was only with resentment that Martin continued to see a client whose benefits had been exhausted. He acted in accordance with the *Code of Ethics* in refusing to abandon the client (A.11.a) and in agreeing to provide pro bono services (Section A, Introduction). However, he needs to seriously consider whether he will be able to work effectively in this counseling relationship or whether his feelings will interfere with his ability to provide the best services possible.

Martin's decision to see Joshua's parents and bill the sessions under Joshua's name is a serious error. His failure to provide a proper diagnosis is a violation of Standard E.5.a., and his misleading report to the insurance company is a violation of Standard C.6.b. Insurance fraud is a legal as well as an ethical issue. Martin's rationalizations in this case might well be the beginning of an ethical slippery slope for him. He might find it easier and easier to condone dishonest practices in the future. He might have been pleasantly surprised had he discussed his thinking with HealthCo's case manager for Joshua and his family. Managed care companies want to be time efficient and may well have supported Martin's view that helping the parents was the quickest and most effective way to help the son.

The managed care industry confronts the practitioner with some difficult ethical issues. The industry is not inherently unethical, but there are no industrywide ethical standards. Counselors are advised to consult the *ACA Code of Ethics* as well as their state licensure laws when questions arise in working with managed care systems. Counselors as a professional group will also be wise, if we wish to continue to work with managed care companies, to work to persuade them to hire only licensed practitioners as case managers and to develop industrywide standards of ethical practice.

In Martin's case, an overarching question is whether he possessed sufficient competence to establish an independent private practice. Although he was fully qualified according to the requirements in his state, which allowed only licensed counselors to establish independent private practices, he was naive and uninformed about many issues related to managed care.

Questions for Further Reflection

1. To be successful as independent private practitioners, counselors need to have skills and knowledge not only as clinicians but also as businesspersons. How can counselors acquire the business skills and knowledge they need?
2. Are independent private practitioners particularly vulnerable to burnout or impairment? What steps can they take to ensure their competence on an ongoing basis?

Chapter 5

Working With Multiple Clients

Barbara Herlihy and Gerald Corey

Counselors often work with couples, families, and groups in addition to working with individuals. When counselors work with more than one client at a time, some new ethical considerations arise and existing ones become more complicated. Several new standards in the *ACA Code of Ethics* address working with multiple clients, but family counseling and group work are specialized areas. The ACA standards are not truly comprehensive with respect to specific issues that need to be addressed when practitioners work with multiple clients. In addition to the *ACA Code,* counselors who work with families and groups are advised to familiarize themselves with the *AAMFT Code of Ethics* (American Association for Marriage and Family Therapy, 2001), the "Ethical Code for International Association of Marriage and Family Counselors" (IAMFC, 2002), the "Best Practice Guidelines" (Association for Specialists in Group Work [ASGW], 1998), and the "Principles for Diversity-Competent Group Workers" (ASGW, 1999).

Most general ethical obligations apply not only to individual counseling but also to family counseling and group work. We will discuss here only a few issues that have particular relevance to working with multiple clients. These issues include client welfare and protection from harm, informed consent, confidentiality, counselor values, competence, and managing boundaries.

Client Welfare and Protection From Harm

The primary responsibility of counselors is to promote the welfare of the client. When counselors offer individual counseling services, the question, "Who is the client?" does not arise as a precursor to determining what is in the client's best interest. However, this seemingly basic question can be difficult to answer when working with families or groups. As Corey and colleagues (2007) note, when the focus of counseling shifts from the individual to the family system, a new set of ethical questions arises. Whose interests should the counselor serve? To whom does the counselor have primary responsibility—an individual family member who may have originally sought counseling or the family as a whole? Standard A.7. provides some guidance on this issue, stating that "when a counselor agrees to provide counseling services to two or more persons who have a relationship, the counselor clarifies at the outset which person or persons are clients and the nature of the relationships the counselor will have with each involved person." Even when good-faith efforts at clarification are made, role conflicts can develop. When this happens, counselors "clarify, adjust, or withdraw from roles appropriately" (A.7.).

When working with an individual, the counselor may find it helpful to involve the client's family in the counseling process. A systems perspective is reflected in Standard A.1.d., which points to the importance of involving various support networks in the lives of clients. Some of these positive resources include "religious/spiritual/community leaders, family members, and friends." When it is appropriate, and with client consent, counselors can enlist the involvement of these resources in working with a client.

In group work, ensuring client welfare can be particularly difficult because the group counselor has less situational control. Groups can be powerful catalysts for change. This potency, along with the difficulty of monitoring the moment-to-moment experiencing of members, means that groups can be risky. Screening and selection are important ethical considerations because the degree of compatibility of the group members will have a strong impact on the success of the group experience. Standard A.8.a. requires counselors to do their best to "select members whose needs and goals are compatible with goals of the group, who will not impede the group process, and whose well-being will not be jeopardized by the group experience." It is important to remember that not all people can benefit from a group experience, and some can even be harmed by it (Yalom, 2005).

Counselors in a group setting need to "take reasonable precautions to protect clients from physical, emotional, or psychological trauma" (A.8.b.). In the second case study in this chapter, a group counselor implements a questionable intervention that potentially could traumatize two of its members. Difficulties may arise when events that occur during a group's process are therapeutic to one member or to some members but are aversive to others. For example, emotions (including anger, sadness, and pain) are regularly elicited in groups, and facilitating emotionality is one of the most powerful change mechanisms in groups. However, one member's emotional catharsis might be anxiety provoking for another member. Similarly, in family therapy, ethical dilemmas can arise when an intervention that serves one person's best interests comes into conflict with the wishes or needs of another family member.

Informed Consent

Informed consent issues take on new complexity when applied to counseling with families or groups. When working with families, several questions arise: "Who gives consent for the family? Which family members are actively seeking counseling, and who in the family is a reluctant participant? Are there differences among family members in their capacity to understand what the counseling process may involve? How can family counselors adequately address, at the outset, the reality that there may be confrontative interactions during sessions, and how can counselors describe the ways they will deal with these events?" It is not a simple task for counselors to give clear information to individual clients regarding the life changes they might anticipate through therapy; it is a real challenge for family counselors to describe potential changes in family relationships as well as changes that individual family members might make in conjunction with shifts in the system.

Informed consent is particularly important in groups because group counseling involves risks and responsibilities that are not typically part of individual counseling (Welfel, 2006). Scapegoating, undue pressure or coercion, and inappropriate confrontation are among the possible risks for group participants. Securing informed consent is both a pregroup task and an issue that needs to be revisited during the first group session. Potential participants need to have adequate information so that they can decide whether they want to join the group. Thus, counselors need to explain the nature, goals, and purposes of the group; the leader's (and, if applicable, coleader's) qualifications; the group's format, procedures, and rules; and fees and arrangements for payment, if any. Group leaders also should be prepared to assist prospective participants to clarify their personal goals for participating and to discuss ways the group may be congruent or incompatible with their cultural beliefs and values (Corey & Corey, 2006).

Confidentiality

Couples and family counselors have unique confidentiality concerns. A particular issue that often emerges in practice is how to deal with secrets: information one family member may have shared with the counselor during an individual session but has withheld from a spouse or parents or children. According to the *Code of Ethics*, in counseling couples and families, it is essential to "clearly define who is considered 'the client' and discuss expectations and limitations of confidentiality" (B.4.b.). Part of informed consent involves discussing with all parties the parameters of confidentiality.

Questions about the confidentiality of counseling records can also arise. For example, a couple may come for couples counseling and then later seek a divorce. In a child custody dispute, one marital partner may want the counselor to testify about what was discussed in counseling, and the other partner may want the sessions kept confidential. Although the ruling of the court will have to guide the counselor in a particular case, the *Code of Ethics* guideline is that "counselors provide individual clients with only those parts of records that related directly to them and do not include confidential information related to any other client" (B.6.d.).

Group counseling, like couples and family therapy, raises some unique confidentiality issues. Confidentiality is difficult to enforce in group situations, yet it is a key condition for effective group work because it builds trust among the members and fosters the development of cohesion as the group moves through its developmental stages (Herlihy & Flowers, 2006).

Standard B.4.a. provides some guidelines for handling the issue of confidentiality in groups: "In group work, counselors clearly explain the importance and parameters of confidentiality for the specific group being entered." Although counselors are expected to stress the importance of confidentiality and set a norm, they also must inform members about its limits. Members need to understand that the group leader cannot guarantee confidentiality. Leaders can pledge confidentiality on their own part but cannot guarantee the behavior of group members. Also, if members pose a danger to themselves or to others, the counselor would be ethically and legally obliged to breach confidentiality.

The legal concept of privileged communication generally does not apply in a group setting, unless there has been a statutory exception. Therefore, counselors are responsible for informing members of the limits of confidentiality within the group setting, as well as their responsibilities to other group members.

Counselor Values

According to the *Code of Ethics,* "counselors are aware of their own values, attitudes, beliefs, and behaviors and avoid imposing values that are inconsistent with counseling goals" (A.4.b.). This standard also reminds counselors that it is crucial to "respect the diversity of clients, trainees, and research participants." This ethical imperative has some special applications to family and group counseling.

The counselor's values will have a crucial influence on how the counselor works with a couple or family. Of particular relevance are the counselor's personal values pertaining to such issues as marriage and divorce, traditional and nontraditional lifestyles, contraception, abortion, gender roles, extramarital affairs, homosexuality, and child rearing and the discipline of children.

Group counselors, like family therapists, are not value free. Certain values are inherent in the group process, such as self-disclosure, risk taking, learning to be direct and open, choosing for oneself, and increasing awareness and autonomy. It is essential for group counselors to examine their assumptions about human nature and the therapeutic process if they are to avoid imposing their beliefs and values on group members, even in subtle and unintended ways. It is important that counselors remain cognizant that their role is not to impose their own values on a family or a group but to help individual members find their own way and arrive at solutions that work for them.

On a related note, respecting diversity is relevant to both family counseling and group work. It is essential that counselors who work with clients who are culturally different from them take steps to learn about specific cultural values and practices that will affect the course of counseling. For example, striving for autonomy may be an alien concept for certain families or group members, yet an uninformed counselor might influence family members or group participants to strive for independence and assert their autonomy.

Competence

Counselors who want to work with couples and families should be aware that competence in marriage and family therapy involves more than the completion of one or two specialized courses. The American Association for Marriage and Family Therapy has developed academic standards for marriage and family therapists and has also recommended that trainees have supervised experience in working with families, experience in their own family-of-origin work, and personal therapy. Counselors who work with groups can assess their level of training by studying the "Professional Standards for the Training of Group Workers" (ASGW, 2000). These standards describe core skills and knowledge and make recommendations for supervised practice. Although these training standards for family counselors and group workers are helpful, it should be remembered that developing and maintaining competence is a lifelong process.

Competence in group work implies that counselors who lead groups are able to effectively address diversity factors within the various groups they lead. Being a diversity-competent group counselor entails having a general understanding of the diverse cultural backgrounds of the group members so that interventions used are congruent with the worldviews of the participants in the group. The "Principles for Diversity-Competent Group Workers" (ASGW, 1999) addresses diversity issues such as racism, classism, sexism, heterosexism, and ableism with sensitivity and skill and spells out the implications of these principles for awareness of self, knowledge, and skills. In working with groups characterized by diversity, it is essential to have knowledge of the characteristics of different cultural groups as well as within-group differences. Counselors need to be aware of the assumptions they make about ethnic and cultural groups. They are also challenged to adapt their practices to the needs of the members. It is essential that the goals and processes of the group match the cultural values of the members of that group. It is critical that counselors become aware of their potential biases based on age, disability, ethnicity, gender, race, religion, or sexual orientation.

Managing Boundaries

It is crucial for counselors to maintain proper therapeutic boundaries in couples and family counseling. When couples and family counselors mismanage the boundaries of the relationship, inappropriate alliances can be created, and counseling can be rendered ineffective. Boundary issues may arise in couples and family counseling when there is a change from individual to couples or family counseling, or vice versa, and when individual and couples or family counseling are conducted concurrently. Sometimes counselors working with a couple or family may see one family member individually for one or several sessions. At other times, counseling may begin with an individual client and then later may include the client's spouse, partner, or family. Herlihy and Corey (2006) have noted that some counselors may have difficulty sorting out their primary allegiances in these situations. Because confidentiality issues may arise, counselors need to be clear about their policies regarding family secrets and hidden agendas. The first case in this chapter demonstrates the problems that can occur when this issue is not addressed.

Some unique boundary issues that arise when working with groups include socializing among members outside of group time and admitting former individual clients into groups. Group leaders often set ground rules to discourage members from socializing outside of group sessions in an attempt to prevent cliques or subgroups from forming. Despite any rules that might be stated, however, leaders have limited control over interactions that occur among members outside of group. It should also be noted that socializing among group members is not always discouraged and, in fact, may be encouraged in certain types of groups such as substance abuse and support groups. Some counselors see group work as a useful progression to facilitate continuing client growth after individual counseling has been completed. Problems can arise, however, when groups are comprised of some members who have been in individual counseling with the leader and other members who have not. Group members who have been clients in individual counseling might resent having to share the leader, and group members who have not been individual clients might feel jealous of the members who have already established a relationship with the leader.

Case Study 9

A Marriage and Family Counselor Learns a Secret

Mary E. Moline

Diana, a private practitioner, began working with Mrs. Cole, who was referred for counseling by her family doctor. Her doctor had not been able to find any physiological basis for her complaint that on several occasions she had felt as though she were choking and could not breathe. After several sessions, it became apparent to both Diana and the client that these choking symptoms occurred when Mrs. Cole's husband came home from work. Through further exploration, Mrs. Cole came to realize that she felt a great deal of anger that she had not been able to express, and that her relationship with her husband was directly related to her choking. With Mrs. Cole's permission, Mr. Cole was invited for conjoint therapy.

During the first conjoint session, Diana noted that Mr. Cole was not being congruent when he discussed his relationship with his wife. He said that he loved her, but his nonverbal communications and tone of voice indicated otherwise. When Diana asked him if he had any feelings other than love for his wife, he became defensive and said "no." At this point, Diana told Mr. and Mrs. Cole that she wanted to see each of them separately. Concerned that Mr. Cole might become hostile and uncooperative, she neglected to discuss issues pertaining to secrets and how they are handled.

Mr. Cole did come for an individual session, during which he admitted that he had been having an affair for 8 months. He was adamant in stating that he would never reveal the affair to his wife. He also stated that he would deny it if the counselor brought it up in a conjoint session. He urged Diana not to bring up the affair during sessions with Mrs. Cole. He felt certain that his wife would leave him if she knew. He became very emotional when he spoke of their four young children, saying that he was a good father and did not want their lives disrupted. When Diana asked him if he was committed to the marriage, he said that he was, but he wanted very much to have this other relationship. He stated that his goal in counseling was to adjust to balancing two relationships and to reduce his stress, and he requested additional sessions to help him with these goals.

Questions for Thought and Discussion

1. If you were the counselor in this case, how might you deal with Mr. Cole's refusal to disclose his affair in a conjoint session?
2. If you kept his secret, do you think that counseling with this couple would stand much chance of being productive?
3. If Diana were to approach you and ask for help in resolving her dilemma, what might you say to her? What recommendations could you offer regarding how she might proceed?
4. If you were working with a couple, might you be willing to see each of them for individual sessions also? Why or why not?

Analysis

There are many ethical issues to be considered in this case. Perhaps the primary issues are confidentiality, neutrality, and competence. The counselor cannot reveal information given by one family member (Mr. Cole) to another member (Mrs. Cole) without his permission. If the counselor does not reveal this information, however, she might be rendered ineffective as their family therapist. She might transfer her reactions to this secret into their conjoint sessions.

For Diana to be able to reveal the information to Mrs. Cole in an ethical manner, she would have had to make clear *before* treatment began that she did not keep secrets. This should have been part of her informed consent procedure. Sound, ethical practice would have been to make clear to both parties at the outset how she would handle issues of confidentiality (A.2.a., B.4.b.). Because she was ethically remiss and failed to do so, she now finds herself caught in the middle.

Assuming that Diana believes the information about Mr. Cole's secret affair is harmful to the counseling process, she might attempt to encourage Mr. Cole to reveal it himself. Another factor that has not been explored is the possibility that Mr. Cole's lover could be infected with a fatal, communicable disease such as AIDS. If that were the case and safe sex were not being practiced, Diana might be justified in sharing the information with Mrs. Cole (B.2.b.). If this is not the case, however, Diana is now stuck with the secret.

Diana might feel torn by conflicting obligations. Mrs. Cole was her original client, and much progress remains to be made with respect to the choking problem. Because she was referred to the counselor first, any interventions need to be aimed at helping her reduce her incidents of choking. At the same time, it is clear that Mr. Cole feels a great deal of stress, and he wants help. The situation is complicated by the fact that Mr. Cole had a part in the inception of his wife's problem, yet he does not want to be honest about it. Moreover, he now wants the counselor to help him solve his problem of balancing both relationships. Will Diana be able to remain neutral or objective in working with them? According to some experts in the field of family therapy, a neutral position is necessary for a practitioner to work on behalf of both individuals. If Diana sides with one person over another, this will affect her ability to gain trust and will decrease her chances of being helpful. It will be important for Diana to assess her degree of effectiveness in this case. If she believes she cannot serve them effectively as a couple, she will need to withdraw from her position as their counselor and refer them to another therapist (A.11.b.). It might be a good course of action to refer Mr. Cole to one therapist and Mrs. Cole to another.

Given the nature of the ethical dilemma that this counselor has created for herself, it seems appropriate to question her preparedness to work with couples and families. If she is not fully prepared to work from a systemic perspective, she should suspend her work with couples and families until she can receive further, specialized training (C.2.a., C.2.b.).

Questions for Further Reflection

1. What ethical considerations are involved in deciding what would be the most appropriate form of treatment—individual, conjoint, or family therapy?
2. How can counselors assess their own neutrality when working with couples?

Case Study 10

A Group Leader's Questionable Intervention

George T. Williams

Ryan is leading a group of five women and three men who range in age from 24 to 63. The group has contracted to meet for 10 weekly sessions, with each session lasting 1½ hours. The major theme for the group is enhancing intimacy in interpersonal relationships.

During the initial group screening process, each member met individually with Ryan to develop a personal written contract regarding participation in the group. Contracts included each member's assessment of his or her own interpersonal relationships, goals, strategies for improving interpersonal communications and relationships, and the evaluation criteria for determining whether members achieved their personal goals.

Through the first 5 sessions, much time was spent exploring each member's values, expectations of the group, fears about being in the group, and significant interpersonal relationships outside the group. Ryan also discussed the risks of potential life changes that may occur because of the group experience and had begun to help members assess their readiness to face these possibilities.

It is now the 6th session, and 29-year-old Kevin, who has remained rather quiet and guarded to this point, becomes tearful. He states that he has begged Hannah, his live-in partner, to marry him, but she has refused. She has told him that she has already been through one painful divorce and will never make that mistake again. He discloses to the group that he suspects Hannah is cheating on him. He says he has some strong religious convictions that "people should not get angry, but rather forgive." He further explains that through individual therapy he has become aware of his own codependency issues and how he has difficulty standing up to Hannah and expressing his feelings. Hesitantly, he reveals that he feels guilty for having thoughts of cheating for revenge because such behavior would not be acceptable to his religious beliefs or his views on commitment to maintain a monogamous relationship.

While listening to Kevin talk, Ryan recalls how 35-year-old Lydia has talked for several weeks about her loneliness and not having had a date since she and her fiancé ended their relationship almost 3 years ago. He decides to use an innovative technique to help both Lydia and Kevin with their personal struggles. He creates a role-play with Kevin speaking directly to Lydia. Kevin is coached to tell Lydia how beautiful she is, his fantasies about her, and is encouraged to ask her out for a date. Ryan believes the role-play could help Kevin learn assertiveness skills for expressing his genuine feelings and covert thoughts and help him overcome his codependency issues with Hannah. Ryan is also considering Lydia's low self-esteem and how she might benefit by receiving positive strokes from a man complimenting her physical appearance. This might also help satisfy her previously expressed "yearning" to have a man look into her eyes and say "romantic words."

Immediately following the role-play, Ryan asks Kevin how it was to do the role-play. Kevin responds, "I really surprised myself. I was actually able to say what I felt inside, without holding back." Ryan then asks Kevin if he is willing to complete a homework assignment that could help him continue practicing his interpersonal skills outside the group. Kevin says he is willing to do the assignment, and Ryan instructs: "Your assignment, which is to be completed by next week's group session and reported back to the group, is to call Lydia, invite her to dinner, and then actually take her to dinner. This may also help you to get the courage to be more independent from Hannah because it appears that she's been unfaithful and is taking advantage of you."

Questions for Thought and Discussion

1. What distinctions do you see between therapeutic pressure and undue pressure in groups?
2. What do you think of the group leader's decision to ask the two group members to explore their feelings via the role-play?
3. If you had been Ryan's coleader in this group, might you have intervened? If so, at what point?

Analysis

The group leader's careful attention to ethical considerations in forming the group was commendable. His extensive screening procedures were well in compliance with the *Code of Ethics* (A.8.a.). He also appears to have provided prospective group members with information they needed in order to give informed consent to join, and he was conscientious in alerting them to the risks of potential life changes (A.2.b.).

Ryan's intervention during the 6th session, however, was ethically questionable in several respects. Given Kevin's expressed values and religious convictions, was it appropriate for Ryan to set up a role-play scenario encouraging Kevin to express romantic feelings and private fantasies to a woman other than his live-in partner? Was it appropriate to get Kevin's commitment to engage in behavior outside the group that conflicts with his values as part of the treatment plan? Counselors should not ask clients, individually or in a group setting, to change in directions they do not choose. Standard A.4.b. addresses the need for counselors to respect differences in values and beliefs and to avoid imposing their own values on clients. This case raises another issue related to counselor values: that of gender bias. Ryan's intervention seems to have been based on assumptions concerning the source of a female's self-esteem and the effect this intervention might have on Lydia. It is beneficial to process each person's experience immediately following a role-play enactment.

The role-play was an experiment that the group leader created spontaneously as he considered the revelations that members had made or were making. It was an experimental procedure, and Ryan should have considered Standard A.2.b. of the *Code of Ethics,* which deals with types of information needed pertaining to informed consent in the counseling relationship. Experimental treatment methods should be clearly indicated to group members *prior to* their involvement. The group leader also violated the spirit of informed consent when he asked Kevin to say whether he was willing to complete an outside homework assignment before knowing what the assignment might be. Kevin might well have felt severely conflicted over his homework assignment, wanting to please the counselor and group members by being assertive, yet not wanting to risk his relationship with Hannah or to act against his values and religious beliefs. When Ryan placed Kevin in this position, he violated his ethical obligation to protect clients in a group setting from psychological trauma (A.8.b.).

When working with groups, counselors are often confronted with multifaceted dilemmas in helping members work on their own personal issues. The competent group leader needs to assess each member's values and goals and intervene with techniques that do not impose the leader's values. The group leader also needs to be cognizant of how cathartic work for one group member may elicit extreme discomfort in another member and that each participant's role-play experience needs to be processed. The group leader's actions should convey respect to all group members by respecting diversity within the group.

Questions for Further Reflection

1. How can counselors guard against the possibility of imposing their own values on clients, either individually or in a group setting? Are there subtle ways this can happen outside the counselor's awareness?
2. What safeguards need to be put in place when counselors use intervention techniques that are potentially powerful?
3. How does a group leader differentiate between therapeutic pressure in groups and undue pressure or coercion? What determines whether a group leader is exerting undue influence?

Chapter 6

Counseling Minor Clients

Mark Salo

Counselors work with minor clients in a broad array of settings, including public and private schools, inpatient treatment facilities, private practice, community agencies, and youth law enforcement. They counsel children across a wide range of developmental stages and ages, from as young as 3 or 4 years old through the age of legal majority (18). Adding to this complexity is the fact that, except in very specific circumstances, minor clients have few legal rights apart from those of their parents or guardians. Counselors can feel pulled between their minor clients and the well-intentioned adults in children's lives such as parents, teachers, social workers, and grandparents. Relevant laws vary greatly from state to state, and in many situations statutes do not address specific circumstances. In addition, court rulings by judges can set precedent as laws are interpreted and reinterpreted in an ever-changing legal system. As a result, counselors who find themselves in confusing or "gray" situations often look to ethical standards for support and guidance. The case could be made that therapeutic work with minor clients is the counseling area in which ethical and legal issues are the most likely to arise.

Perhaps the primary ethical and legal issue arising from working with children is confidentiality. When, and with whom, is it appropriate to share information that has been revealed in a counseling relationship with a child? The laws vary greatly from state to state. For example, the California Education Code (Chap. 10, Sect. 49602) states the following: "Any information of a personal nature disclosed by a pupil 12 years of age or older in the process of receiving counseling from a school counselor is confidential." This statute recognizes the importance of counseling services being available for minor students as young as 12, and it acknowledges that confidentiality is crucial to the counseling process. There also has been continued legal support in many states to permit minors to seek medical advice and treatment for sexually transmitted diseases, birth control, and abortion without parental consent (Corey et al., 2007; Welfel, 2006). The reasoning behind these statutes is that if parental permission for services were required by law, some minors would choose not to seek treatment. Not surprisingly, this has led to legal conflicts between parents and the professionals involved in these medical matters.

Counselors of minor clients often straddle an ethical fence, caught between allegiance to their minor clients and the legal reality of parental rights. The *ACA Code of Ethics* requires counselors to act in the best interest of the client, but just who is the client when the parent is paying for services? What does a counselor say when asked by a parent or legal guardian for specific information about progress in the counseling process? Unfortunately, counselors may find themselves legally obligated to provide such information but ethically admonished against sharing this information.

The 2005 *ACA Code of Ethics* seeks to clarify counselors' ethical responsibilities when counseling minors. Standard B.5.a. states that "when counseling minor clients or adult clients who lack the capacity to give voluntary, informed consent, counselors protect the confidentiality of information received in the counseling relationship as specified by federal and state laws, written policies, and applicable ethical standards." This reference to laws and policies requires counselors to be current on applicable statutes and guidelines covering their location and practice.

Standard B.5.b. requires counselors to "inform parents and legal guardians about the role of counselors and the confidential nature of the counseling relationship." Counselors are further advised to be "sensitive to the cultural diversity of families and respect the inherent rights and responsibilities of parents/guardians over the welfare of their children" by virtue of their role and according to law. "Counselors work to establish, as appropriate, collaborative relationships with parents/guardians to best serve clients." This standard encourages counselors to take a proactive role with parents or guardians in establishing a clear understanding of the nature of the counseling relationship. Notice, however, that permission to work with children is not assumed; rather, the *Code* defers to state laws and other statutes regarding parental consent for counseling.

Standard B.5.c. addresses the release of confidential information. When counseling minor clients, "counselors seek permission from an appropriate third party to disclose information. In such circumstances, counselors inform clients consistent with their level of understanding and take culturally appropriate measures to safeguard client confidentiality." Whether these standards will clarify counselors' responsibilities in working with minor clients remains to be seen when they are tested in practice.

The work setting in which a counselor sees a minor client often will determine the types of ethical issues that are encountered. It is perhaps easiest to avoid ethical problems in private practice because parents typically have given legal consent for the counselor to work with the minor, and because the number of people involved in the counseling process is usually quite small—often just the counselor, the minor client, and the legal guardian(s). By addressing confidentiality issues at the outset, many problems can be avoided.

Children in an inpatient facility will almost certainly have been placed there by a parent or by Child Protective Services. These minors, no matter what their age, will be deemed largely incapable of making crucial decisions for themselves. The caregivers are assumed to be operating "in the child's best interest." Parents and other adults may be consulted over the course of treatment, often as part of a treatment team. It is important to clarify the roles of everyone involved at the beginning of treatment to avoid misunderstandings, especially with regard to sharing information.

School settings provide another arena in which questions of privacy in the counseling relationship are tested. Very often, state law does not require a school counselor to contact the parent for consent before counseling occurs, although some schools have adopted such a policy. The school counselor is usually regarded as being available to all students, much like the school nurse. This helps to minimize barriers to accessing counseling services.

Counselors need to be careful when pressed for information by the variety of adults in children's lives. Although school counselors can argue that information shared in a private counseling session should be kept confidential, school counselors interact with students outside their offices in less formal settings such as the playground, cafeteria, and hallways. Children may not understand that these informal conversations are not confidential.

Dual relationships in the schools are a real possibility, and counselors need to recognize them and remain vigilant to see that harm is not done inadvertently. Many times school counselors have multiple job responsibilities; for example, a counselor may also teach a class or coach a sport. Changing hats from counselor to teacher or coach can lead to confusion. Herlihy and Corey (2006) note that as the responsibilities and expectations of one role diverge from those of another role, the potential for harm increases. School counselors often encounter situations in which the expectations of their student clients, parents, teachers, and administrators all differ.

In summary, counseling minor clients can be ambiguous work (Salo & Shumate, 1993). Ethical standards cannot be written that cover all possible scenarios and situations. Similarly, the various laws that affect counseling minors vary widely across the country and may lack clarity. Ethical standards provide a solid basis for making sound professional decisions when treading on unfamiliar or nebulous territory. By following these standards, which represent best practices, counselors can minimize the risk of finding themselves in legal jeopardy.

Case Study 11

A School Counselor Is Caught in the Middle

Mark Salo

Susan works as a school counselor in a large middle school with students from sixth through eighth grade. Her primary duties include counseling individuals and small groups, teaching classroom guidance lessons, and consulting with parents, teachers, and administrators. Shortly after the beginning of the school year, a parent calls Susan and explains that her son, Nolan, a seventh grader, is experiencing difficulties in school where none had existed before. Susan invites the mother, Juanita, to her office to discuss specific concerns.

During this initial consultation, Juanita divulges that her husband has recently moved out of the house. Nolan, being the oldest of three siblings, is especially upset with the situation and has shown recent outbursts of anger both at home and at school. Teachers also have notified Juanita that Nolan's schoolwork is slipping badly. Juanita tearfully reveals that her husband had physically assaulted her and that, although he had never abused the children, they were certainly affected by the tensions at home.

Susan and Juanita decide that Nolan should begin to see Susan for counseling on a twice-weekly basis to help Nolan deal with his anger and failing grades. Susan counsels Nolan regularly for 6 weeks, and Nolan reveals a great deal to Susan about himself and his family. He also comes to realize that his angry outbursts and declining grades are related to the stress surrounding his family circumstances. At a follow-up meeting with Juanita, Susan is pleased to report that Nolan's grades and behavior have begun to improve.

An unexpected phone call from Nolan's father, Russell, alerts Susan to potential difficulties. Although Susan is cordial and professional during the phone conversation, she becomes increasingly uncomfortable with Russell's press for information about both Nolan and his mother. According to Russell, Juanita has filed divorce papers and is seeking full custody of the children. Russell becomes increasingly insistent in his demand to learn the content of all of Susan's sessions with both Nolan and Juanita. During the conversation, Russell alludes several times to his attorney's involvement and threatens to file a complaint with the ACA Ethics Committee if Susan fails to comply with his request. Although Susan closes the discussion by generally recounting Nolan's improved behavior and academic performance, she is concerned that Russell might continue to push her for information she feels is confidential. A follow-up phone call to Juanita confirms that legal papers have been filed. Juanita also tells the counselor that both she and Nolan want to keep the counseling records confidential and out of Russell's possession.

Questions for Thought and Discussion

1. If you were in the counselor's place, how do you believe you might react when pressed by Russell to reveal information about his son?
2. What do you think of the way Susan handled the situation? What, if anything, might you have done differently, and why?

Analysis

Susan's dilemma involved the confidentiality of information gained in counseling sessions and was compounded by the fact that Nolan is a minor. She feared that revealing information to Russell could be damaging to both Nolan and Juanita. Although Susan had no desire to get embroiled in a custody battle, she wanted to behave in an ethically responsible and legally sound manner.

Susan reviewed the *ACA Code of Ethics* for guidance and found Standard B.1.c. to be especially relevant. It states that "counselors do not share confidential information without client consent or without sound legal or ethical justification." Susan knew that it was going to be difficult to balance the confidentiality rights of all the parties involved. In addition, Susan knew that noncustodial parents do have access to school records as outlined by the Family Education Rights and Privacy Act (FERPA). However, the records in question were private counseling notes seen only by Susan and were stored in a locked file cabinet away from school records. Standard B.6.a. supported her records policy: "Counselors ensure that records are kept in a secure location and that only authorized persons have access to records."

Other portions of Section B provided Susan with direction in dealing with her dilemma. Standard B.5.a. spells out a counselor's responsibilities: "When counseling minor clients or adult clients who lack the capacity to give voluntary, informed consent, counselors protect the confidentiality of information received in the counseling relationship as specified by federal and state laws, written policies, and applicable ethical standards." After checking state laws, Susan confirmed that communications between school counselors and their student clients are not specifically protected by privileged communication statutes. She could not rely on client privilege in this case.

Standard B.5.b. noted that counselors inform parents about the role of counselors and the confidential nature of the counseling relationship, respect the inherent rights and responsibilities of parents over the welfare of their children by virtue of their role and according to law, and work to establish collaborative relationships with parents to best serve clients. Susan knew that she would need to explain to the father the counseling role and the necessity for privacy. It would be a tough sell, but a positive working relationship with Russell would ultimately benefit Nolan.

Standard B.5.c. states, "When counseling minor clients or adult clients who lack the capacity to give voluntary consent to release confidential information, counselors seek permission from an appropriate third party to disclose information. In such instances, counselors inform clients consistent with their level of understanding." Juanita had already indicated her desire not to have information released to Nolan's father. Susan knew that if she did disclose information she would need to inform Nolan and Juanita before the information was provided.

Susan understood that Russell could still be a legally recognized party, leaving a question that might require a judge's ruling. After consultation with her administrator and the school district's attorney, Susan decided that if the custody case went to court, they would let the court decide the issue as supported by Standard B.2.c. This standard advises counselors that, when they are subpoenaed to release confidential information without a client's permission, they "take steps to prohibit the disclosure or have it limited as narrowly as possible due to the potential harm to the client or counseling relationship." In the event that a judge ordered the record to be revealed, Standard B.2.d. would guide Susan's response. This standard states, "When circumstances require the disclosure of confidential information, only essential information is revealed." To the extent possible, clients should be informed before confidential information is disclosed and be involved in the disclosure decision-making process. Susan decided that she would reveal only essential information and would inform Juanita and Nolan before disclosing.

This case illustrates how Susan used the *Code of Ethics* to guide her decision-making process in an ethical dilemma. It is important to remember that the *Code of Ethics* is not a legal document and that federal, state, and local laws supersede its guidelines. If a judge orders Susan to release her records, she should do so after stating her objections. The ACA Ethics Committee would not find a counselor in violation of the standards for complying with a court order.

Questions for Further Reflection

1. Suppose a caring and concerned teacher approached you as a counselor and asked for information about a student's home situation to help her better understand the student's academic and behavior problems. What might you tell the teacher?
2. Would your responses to this scenario change if Nolan were 9 years old? 17 years old? How do ethical responsibilities regarding confidentiality change as a client matures?

Case Study 12

The Case of Jessica: A School Counselor's Dilemma

Gerra Wellman Perkins

Ann works as the only school counselor in a large school that serves children in prekindergarten through fifth grade. One Monday afternoon she was called to the office to see Jessica, a child with whom she had worked periodically over the past 3 years. Jessica, now a fifth grader, was crying and saying she wanted the secretary, a friend of the family, to call and have her neighbor come pick her up. Jessica revealed to the counselor that her dad, her primary caretaker, had "gone crazy" last night and was in the hospital.

Ann escorted Jessica to her counseling office to continue the conversation in private. Within the counseling session Jessica repeated the information and elaborated further. She had come home from school in the afternoon to find fire trucks and police cars at her house. Her dad had locked himself in the house and refused to let anyone else in, even her. Finally, the police had to break down the door. Her dad had taken a combination of drugs and alcohol and was rushed to the emergency room. Although his condition was stable, Jessica had been told that he would be spending the rest of the week in a rehabilitation center. Jessica would be staying with neighbors.

Understandably, Jessica had not completed her homework. She had not been able to retrieve any of her school materials from her house. Her bad night had now compounded into a bad school day because of confrontations with several teachers concerning her lack of preparedness. Jessica, no stranger to disciplinary action from teachers and administrators because of her attitude and defiance, had chosen to tell her teachers that she thought homework was stupid and had refused to complete it. After lunch Jessica had stormed out of the classroom shouting obscenities when her English teacher said it was her responsibility to come prepared with her book and notebook. The teacher was completing a discipline referral to the office.

After allowing Jessica to sob out her fears and frustrations, Ann requested that Jessica allow her to intervene and explain to the teachers and principal that Jessica would not have her proper materials for the rest of the week because of circumstances out of her control. Ann explained that she would tell them only what Jessica wanted them to know. Jessica refused, stating that she did not want Ann to even mention her name to them. Even though she had confided in the secretary, she was embarrassed by her family situation. Furthermore, none of the teachers had bothered to ask why she was not prepared, so now she definitely didn't want them to know.

Ann was in a dilemma. She felt it was important to respect Jessica's wish for confidentiality, yet she felt that problems at school would only compound Jessica's problems at home. She knew that if she did not intervene Jessica would be subject to disciplinary action that day, and probably for the rest of the week.

Questions for Thought and Discussion

1. Do you think the counselor should respect the child client's desire for complete confidentiality in this situation? Why or why not?
2. If you were the counselor in this scenario, what would you do? How would you explain the ethical reasoning that led to your decision?

Analysis

This counselor is confronting a difficult situation. Ann wants to respect her minor client's confidentiality and is supported in this desire by Standard B.5.a., which requires counselors to "protect the confidentiality of information received in the counseling relationship" when working with minor clients. If Ann were to inform the teachers and principal of Jessica's home situation without Jessica's permission, this action might preclude any possibility of continuing in a counseling relationship with a child who clearly could benefit from receiving counseling services.

Ann also wants to protect Jessica from the further harm that could result from the teachers' and principal's lack of awareness of Jessica's situation. Ann is rightly concerned that Jessica's problems could be compounded if she were disciplined by the principal and received more failing grades for her homework. Standard A.1.d. encourages counselors to enlist the support, understanding, and involvement of others (in this case, teachers and the principal) as positive resources, but this standard also states that such action should be taken only with client consent. Standard B.5.c. suggests that Ann could "seek permission from an appropriate third party to disclose information" about a minor client, but in this case, who would be an appropriate third party? Jessica's father is her primary caretaker and may be her legal guardian, but he is hospitalized at this time. The neighbors with whom Jessica is staying probably have no legal right to act on

Jessica's behalf. It is unclear whether Jessica's mother has any involvement in her daughter's life or whether she could be reached.

Ann may want to serve as an advocate for her minor client in this situation, a role which would be supported by Standard A.6.a., which states that counselors advocate to help clients deal with obstacles that inhibit their growth and development. However, Standard A.6.b. instructs Ann that she must obtain Jessica's consent before engaging in advocacy efforts, and Jessica has refused to allow Ann to talk to the principal or teachers.

After studying the *ACA Code of Ethics,* Ann might decide that the *Code* does not provide her with a clear answer to her dilemma. She will need to apply her ethical decision-making skills to the situation. Nonmaleficence (do no harm), fidelity (keep promises made), beneficence (do good or promote mental health), justice (be fair to all parties involved), and autonomy (respect client self-determination) all seem to have some relevance, and Ann will have to decide which principle takes precedence in the situation. She may decide that nonmaleficence supersedes fidelity—that it is more important to prevent further harm than it is to uphold her confidentiality pledge. If so, the course of action that seems indicated is to let the teachers know that Jessica is faced with circumstances beyond her control that prevent her from completing her homework or coming to class prepared, but without revealing the specific details of Jessica's home situation. This action would be in accordance with Standard B.2.d., which states, "When circumstances require the disclosure of confidential information, only essential information is revealed."

Perhaps Ann's best course of action at this time would be to agree, just for now, to Jessica's request to keep her revelations completely confidential but to continue to talk with Jessica. Her goals in continued counseling would be to defuse Jessica's agitation and anger and then, when Jessica is calmer, to help her examine the consequences of her choices. Ann's first inclination, to intervene with the principal and teachers by giving them a minimal explanation of Jessica's circumstances, was appropriately focused on her client's welfare. Perhaps after further discussion, this solution could be mutually agreed-upon. If Jessica remains adamant in her insistence that Ann not speak with school personnel, Ann would be well advised to consult with other school counselors about her dilemma. If she decides after consultation that she should speak to the principal and teachers, she should inform Jessica and explain her rationale.

Questions for Further Reflection

1. What are some ways ethical issues are more complicated when working with clients who are minors?
2. What resources, other than the *ACA Code of Ethics* and consultation with peers, can counselors use to resolve ethical dilemmas they encounter in their work with minors?

Chapter 7

Avoiding Detrimental Multiple Relationships

Harriet L. Glosoff, Gerald Corey, and Barbara Herlihy

Outside of counseling relationships, people naturally engage in multiple roles with others in a wide variety of settings, and they do so without much examination (Syme, 2003). Individuals who choose to go into the counseling profession are not expected to sacrifice their multiple roles or to restrain themselves from acting as neighbors, friends, employees, consultants, or relatives. However, whether it is ethical for counselors to assume any of these roles simultaneously with a *client*, or to participate in a dual or multiple relationship, has generated a great deal of controversy among helping professionals.

Counselors of various theoretical orientations have differing views of dual relationships or boundary issues. Traditional psychoanalysts believe it is necessary to maintain a detached and neutral stance with clients to best analyze and deal with transference (Lazarus & Zur, 2002). Counselors working from a humanistic, feminist, existential, or behavioral theoretical orientation will likely conceptualize boundaries in their relationships with clients in different ways. Depending on their theoretical orientation, counselors may consider interventions such as self-disclosure as either an important and effective part of a treatment plan or as a type of boundary violation.

The term *dual relationship* has become associated with harm done to clients by a mental health professional (Cottone, 2005). However, many professionals assert that not all multiple relationships can be avoided (Herlihy & Corey, 2006). This is particularly true in small, isolated communities: the smaller or more rural the community, the greater the likelihood that a counselor will be involved in some type of dual or multiple relationship (Sleek, 1994). Counselors who work in small communities face far greater challenges in dealing with multiple relationships than do practitioners who work in urban areas. They often have to blend several professional roles and functions. Campbell and Gordon (2003) address some of the unique aspects of rural practice and offer strategies for evaluating, preventing, and managing multiple relationships in rural practice. Counselors who live or work in the military face many of the same challenges as those who live in rural communities (Johnson, Ralph, & Johnson, 2005). The same is often true for counselors who live in urban areas and who are part of ethnic minority, feminist, deaf, gay, or religious communities.

Counselors must consider other factors when examining their relationships and interventions with clients from culturally diverse populations.

For example, in some cultures it would be unthinkable for individuals to talk about personal issues with someone they see as an outsider (Moleski & Kiselica, 2005), or to do so in the constraints of a formal office or a 50-minute session. In many cultural communities, giving a small token or gift is a common and important way to show gratitude and respect.

Lazarus and Zur (2002) have argued that some forms of multiple relationships are clearly beneficial. Haas and Malouf (1995) have questioned whether there is an ethical problem in accepting as a client a neighbor with whom one has little contact other than to wave hello or see occasionally at a local store. However, most professionals agree that mixing more significant roles, such as counselor and employee or counselor and lover, is clearly not appropriate. Whenever counselors play multiple roles, there is potential for a conflict of interest, loss of objectivity, damage to the counselor–client relationship, and exploitation of or harm to those persons who have sought help. Cottone (2005) encourages counselors to think in terms of detriment or harm to clients rather than focusing only on the possible exploitation of clients. He states that the term *exploitive* "implies malicious intent or malicious forethought" whereas the term *detrimental* speaks to outcome "regardless of intent" (p. 6). He notes that counselors need to be held accountable when clients are harmed by their actions or nonactions, regardless of intent.

It is not always possible for counselors to play a singular role in their work, nor is it always desirable. Counselors need to develop strategies for balancing multiple roles and responsibilities in their professional relationships (Herlihy & Corey, 2006). The *Code of Ethics* provides guidance on various issues pertaining to sexual and nonsexual dual relationships, and we recommend consulting it as you plan your own strategies to avoid detrimental dual relationships.

Sexual Dual Relationships

Sexual relationships with clients are among the most serious of all ethical violations. Research indicates that sexual contact between counselor and client has a high potential for severe harm (Knapp & VandeCreek, 2003). Sonne and Pope (1991) report that clients who had been sexually involved with their therapists often exhibit reactions similar to those of survivors of incest, such as role confusion, strong feelings of betrayed trust, and guilt. Virtually all codes of ethics categorically state that sexual relationships with clients are unethical, and licensure regulations and various state legislatures have added the force of law to ethical sanctions. At least 13 states have enacted laws that designate therapist–client sexual activity as a felony crime (Remley & Herlihy, 2005), as does the ACA Model Legislation for the Licensure of Professional Counselors (Glossoff, Benshoff, Hosie, & Maki, 1995). The *Code of Ethics* contains several standards that speak to sexual dual relationships with current and former clients. Counselors are prohibited from engaging in sexual or romantic interactions or relationships with current clients, their romantic partners, or their family members (A.5.a.), and this prohibition extends to former clients as well (A.5.b.).

Former Clients

The question of whether sexual intimacies with former clients are ever acceptable has been extensively debated. Mental health professionals agree that the fact that a counseling relationship has been terminated does not, in and of itself, present an adequate justification for changing a therapeutic relationship to a sexual one. Some professionals believe that the counselor–client relationship continues in perpetuity and that sexual relationships between counselors and former clients are *never* ethical. One rationale is that the seeds of the sexual attraction were planted during a therapeutic relationship in which information tends to flow one way, with clients being vulnerable and counselors disclosing little about themselves. Thus, there will continue to be an asymmetry of power that will not be healthy for most former clients.

Other professionals argue that we need to remain aware of the potential for harm that exists due to residual transference and the continuing power differential, but we also need to consider the wide range of circumstances that exist in the counseling field. They point to the real differences between long-term, intense personal counseling relationships and brief academic, career-oriented, or other types of counseling. Haas and Malouf (1995) note that prohibiting all future sexual contact with former clients, simply because they have been clients, speaks poorly of professionals' attitudes toward our clients' abilities to make their own informed decisions and could be viewed as a restriction of their autonomy. It could also be contended that it does not indicate great faith in the effectiveness of counseling.

When clients are involved in less intense types of counseling situations, one relevant issue is the length of time that needs to elapse before a counselor might justifiably enter into a sexual relationship with a former client. In the 1995 *ACA Code of Ethics,* the minimum time period before any sexual or romantic relationships were allowed was 2 years after termination. In the 2005 *Code,* counselors are prohibited from such relationships "for a period of 5 years following the last professional contact" (A.5.b.) The burden of demonstrating that there has been no exploitation clearly rests with counselors, who are required to "demonstrate forethought and document (in written form) whether the interactions or relationship can be viewed as exploitive in some way, and/or whether there is still potential to harm the former client" (A.5.b.). Factors that need to be considered include the amount of time that has passed since termination of therapy, the nature and duration of therapy, the circumstances surrounding termination of the professional relationship, the client's personal history, the client's competence and mental status, the foreseeable likelihood of harm to the client or others, and any statements or actions by the therapist suggesting a plan to initiate a sexual relationship with the client after termination. In cases where former clients could be exploited or harmed, counselors are expected to avoid entering into sexual relationships.

Relationships With Others Who Are Not Clients

Many counselors engage in professional relationships, other than the counselor–client relationship, where there is a power differential and thus a potential for exploiting those who are in a vulnerable, subordinate position. Counselors may serve as employer, superior in the workplace, supervisor, or professor. Several standards address the potential for exploitation in these relationships. Sexual harassment is defined and is prohibited (C.6.a.). There are separate sexual harassment standards pertaining to supervisors and supervisees (F.3.c.) and to counselor educators and students (F.10.b). Sexual or romantic interactions or relationships are prohibited with current supervisees (F.3.b.) and with current students (F.10.a.).

Nonsexual Relationships

Although most of our professional literature has focused on the harm that can result from sexual relationships with clients, nonsexual dual relationships (or nonprofessional relationships) can also pose a threat to the well-being of clients. Examples of possible nonsexual relationships with clients include combining the roles of teacher and counselor or supervisor and counselor; bartering for goods or services; lending money to a client; providing counseling to a friend, an employee, or a relative; becoming friends with clients or someone close to them; and going into a business venture with a client. The 2005 *ACA Code of Ethics* uses the phrase *nonprofessional interactions or relationships* to indicate relationships other than sexual or romantic interactions. Standard A.5.c. states that such "relationships with clients, former clients, their romantic partners, or their family members should be avoided, except when the interaction is potentially beneficial to the client." Potentially beneficial aspects of interactions with clients outside the counseling setting or relationship are a new addition to the *Code:*

> When a counselor–client nonprofessional interaction with a client or former client may be potentially beneficial to the client or former client, the counselor must document in case records, prior to the interaction (when feasible), the rationale for such an interaction, the potential benefit, and anticipated consequences for the client or former client and other individuals significantly involved with the client or former client. Such interactions should be initiated with appropriate client consent. Where unintentional harm occurs to the client or former client, or to an individual significantly involved with the client or former client, due to the nonprofessional interaction, the counselor must show evidence of an attempt to remedy such harm. Examples of potentially beneficial interactions include, but are not limited to, attending a formal ceremony (e.g., a wedding/commitment ceremony or graduation); purchasing a service or product provided by a client or former client (excepting unrestricted bartering); hospital visits to an ill family member; mutual membership in a professional association, organization, or community. (A.5.d.)

Note that counselors are still responsible for weighing the potential benefits to clients against the potential harm. Even in potentially beneficial interactions, counselors should consider the personal history and current mental status of the client, the nature of the counseling relationship, and possible effects on the client of attending or not attending an event or seeing the client outside the usual counseling setting (Syme, 2003).

Potentially Beneficial Relationships Between Counselors and Individuals Who Are Not Clients

Two new standards address the issue of nonprofessional relationships and potentially beneficial relationships with students and supervisees. Regarding nonprofessional relationships, "counselor educators avoid nonprofessional or ongoing professional relationships with students in which there is a risk of potential harm to the student or that may compromise the training experience or grades assigned" (F.10.d). With respect to potentially beneficial relationships, "counselor educators are aware of the power differential in the relationship between faculty and students. If they believe a nonprofessional relationship with a student may be potentially beneficial to the student, they take precautions similar to those taken by counselors when working with clients" (F.10.f). Additionally, "nonprofessional relationships with students should be time-limited and initiated with student consent" (F.10.f).

Many professionals consider mentoring counselor trainees or beginning counselors to be an integral part of their role. Mentors establish close working relationships, share research projects, coauthor articles, and engage their protégé in social or business networks. Although there are a number of clear benefits associated with mentoring relationships, the complexity and multidimensional nature of dual relationships should be carefully explored, and potential risks must be weighed against benefits. Potential ethical issues need to be discussed throughout the course of a mentoring relationship. Ethical problems are likely to arise if the mentor's role becomes blurred so that the mentor becomes more of a friend (Warren, 2005). The primary focus of mentoring needs to be kept on the protégé's professional development (Casto, Caldwell, & Salazar, 2005).

Friendships

Interpersonal boundaries are not static but undergo redefinition over time. Practitioners are presented with the challenge of managing boundary fluctuations and dealing effectively with overlapping roles. Given how closely counselors and clients work together, the idea of developing a friendship could be tempting. Similarly, most practitioners have been faced with close friends or relatives who have problems and who try (intentionally or not) to place the practitioner in the role of their therapist. The problem is that the underlying dynamics of friendships and therapeutic relationships are not the same. Friendships are built on mutual disclosure and support—on sharing joys and problems and being there for each other. Although therapeutic relationships are also based on trust, intimacy, and disclosure, they are not mutual (Haas & Malouf, 1995).

Counselors are obligated to avoid any relationship, such as a friendship, that might impair their professional judgment. The duality of the relationship might make it difficult for counselors to confront clients when it is clinically appropriate to do so. Counselors engaged in dual or nonprofessional relationships may lose sight of the true motives behind their clinical actions with clients. The same may be true of clients. Most clients occasionally are concerned that they may disclose something about themselves of which their counselor may disapprove. If their counselors are also their friends, clients may be even more reluctant to disclose for fear that they will lose both their friend and their counselor. They may decide to withhold information that is important to their progress or growth.

The risk of harm or exploitation increases proportionately with the discrepancy in power, whether it is actual or perceived. Several standards address relationship boundaries in teaching, training, and supervision and are discussed in Chapter 9. Three other types of situations related to multiple relationships are bartering, receiving gifts, and changing roles.

Bartering

There has been little agreement among counseling professionals about bartering. Counselors who engage in bartering, or trading goods or services in exchange for counseling services, are often motivated to do so for benevolent reasons, typically to help clients who cannot afford to pay for services. Even with these altruistic intentions, bartering carries the potential for conflicts. On one hand, bartering is an accepted practice in some communities and cultures. On the other hand, bartering may lead to resentment on the part of the client or the counselor. Services offered by clients often are not as monetarily valuable as counseling, and clients are at risk of becoming indentured servants as they fall further and further behind in the amount of time or money owed to the counselor (Kitchener & Harding, 1990). A client may also believe that counseling is not working and that, therefore, the counselor is not holding up his or her end of the bargain. Likewise, counselors may be dissatisfied with the timeliness or quality of goods or services delivered by clients and may feel that they are giving more to the exchange than they are receiving.

According to Standard A.10.d., "counselors may barter only if the relationship is not exploitive or harmful and does not place the counselor in an unfair advantage, if the client requests it, and if such arrangements are an accepted practice among professionals in the community." Before bartering is entered into, both parties should talk about the arrangement, gain a clear understanding of the exchange, and come to a written agreement. Cultural implications should be considered.

Receiving Gifts

A new standard in the 2005 *Code of Ethics* addresses the issue of receiving gifts. Standard A.10.e. reminds counselors that "in some cultures, small gifts are a token of respect and showing gratitude. When determining whether or not to accept a gift from clients, counselors take into account the therapeutic relationship, the monetary value of the gift, a client's motivation for giving the gift, and the counselor's motivation for wanting or declining the gift." Although counselors could take unfair advantage of the therapeutic relationship for personal gain by accepting gifts from clients, this is a matter that defies a rule-formulation approach.

Role Changes in Professional Relationships

Another new standard speaks to times when counselors change roles while staying within their professional relationship with clients. Examples of such role changes include

1. changing from individual to relationship or family counseling, or vice versa;
2. changing from an evaluative to a therapeutic role, or vice versa;
3. changing from a counselor to a researcher role (i.e., enlisting clients as research participants), or vice versa; and
4. changing from a counselor to a mediator role, or vice versa. (A.5.e.)

In these situations, counselors need to obtain informed consent from clients. Clients may refuse the services involved in the new role and must understand potential emotional, financial, legal, and therapeutic consequences of the role change.

Conclusions

There are few simple and absolute answers that neatly resolve dilemmas pertaining to multiple or nonprofessional relationships with clients, students, or supervisees. It is a somewhat daunting but necessary task for conscientious counselors to be familiar with the *Code of Ethics* and to keep current with the professional literature. Some multiple or nonprofessional relationships can be avoided if potential problems are foreseen, but others cannot. It is not always possible for counselors to play a singular role in their work, nor is it always desirable. It is likely that counselors will have to wrestle with balancing more than one role in their professional relationships. Thus, it is critical that counselors give careful thought to the potential complications of engaging in multiple relationships before they get entangled in ethically questionable relationships and that they take steps to safeguard clients by making use of informed consent, consultation, supervision, and documentation.

The two case studies in this chapter highlight potential pitfalls. The first case study deals with a sexual dual relationship between a student and a professor. The second case study illustrates how even a well-intentioned counselor can become enmeshed in problems when indirectly mixing friendship with counseling.

Case Study 13

Consenting Adults or an Abuse of Power?

Holly Forester-Miller

Maria is a graduate student who is pursuing her master's degree in counseling. She hopes to enter a doctoral program after she graduates. Last semester, she was enrolled in a course taught by Professor Perry. Throughout the semester, Dr. Perry went out of his way to encourage her and praise her work. After she completed the course, he asked her to serve as a teaching assistant under his supervision for the next term. Maria felt honored that he thought so highly of her abilities, and she accepted the position.

As a teaching assistant, Maria spent considerable time every week in the faculty office area and had frequent interactions with Dr. Perry regarding her work. Gradually, their conversations began to touch on personal issues. The personal interactions escalated to a point where Dr. Perry learned a great deal about Maria's private life and assisted her in making some important decisions, such as finding a new place to live.

Shortly after midterm, following a conversation in which Dr. Perry had emphasized to Maria that he thought her to be bright and competent, he made a sexual advance toward her. She was flattered that someone in his position could be interested in her. The next week, he asked her to come into the office on a Saturday to help him with some work, and she found herself alone with him. He told her that he found her beautiful and was very attracted to her. He began to kiss her. Maria felt complimented but a bit confused. She willingly entered into a sexual relationship with him.

They continued to work together regularly, with Dr. Perry supervising her work and constantly extolling her abilities. They began to have lunch together almost daily. About 6 weeks after the sexual relationship began, Maria started to question the relationship and her involvement with Dr. Perry. After considerable thought, she realized that she wasn't really attracted to him as a person, even though she admired his competencies as a professor and had enjoyed being so highly regarded by someone she admired professionally. She realized that her behavior was jeopardizing her relationship with her male friend who lived in another state and concluded that she didn't want to lose that relationship.

The next day she told Dr. Perry that she was no longer interested in having a personal relationship with him. He became upset and insisted that he was sure she would change her mind because he had been so good to her. No matter how hard she tried, the professor brushed aside her protestations. For the rest of the week, he continued to act as if nothing had changed. He was complimentary of her work, both in private and in front of others, and continued to behave flirtatiously when they were alone together.

Maria decided at this point to talk to a friend about the situation. She explained that she wants out of the sexual relationship but is afraid she will lose her assistantship, on which she is now financially dependent. She needs to continue to meet regularly with Dr. Perry as her supervisor, and she will need to take a course from him next semester. She just can't afford to have a bad relationship with him. Although she willingly agreed to this relationship in the beginning, she now feels trapped and manipulated.

Maria made her friend promise to keep their conversation in confidence, and she decided not to tell anyone else. Although her friend urged her to go to the department chair, Maria decided against doing this. She was embarrassed and felt foolish for getting herself into this situation to start with and was afraid that such an action could affect her assistantship and her recommendations for doctoral studies.

At this point, Maria is continuing to deal with Dr. Perry on her own. When he suggests lunch or going out for a drink after work, she tells him she is very busy. She avoids him whenever possible, but when she is with him she feels uncomfortable and pressured. She sees no way out of her situation and believes this is her only option until she graduates.

Questions for Thought and Discussion

1. If you were a fellow graduate student and Maria shared her dilemma with you, how might you respond?
2. If Maria asked for your advice, would you also urge her to talk with the department chair, suggest another course of action, or agree that her only viable option is to do nothing?
3. If Maria asked for help in reasoning through her dilemma, what factors might you want to raise for her to consider? What questions does this case raise for you?

Analysis

Standard F.6.a. states that counselor educators "are knowledgeable regarding the ethical, legal, and regulatory aspects of the profession, are skilled in applying that knowledge, and make students and supervisees aware of their responsibilities. Counselor educators conduct counselor education and training programs in an ethical manner and serve as role models for professional behavior." The professor in this case certainly did not serve as a role model for his student. He blatantly violated Standard F.10.a., which states that "sexual or romantic interactions or relationships with current students are prohibited." This professor violated Standard F.10.b., as well, which indicates that "counselor educators do not condone or subject students to sexual harassment." He had a sexual relationship with Maria, and then after being told she wanted to discontinue the relationship, he continued to respond to her sexually, ignoring her request.

Some professionals and graduate students have questioned why relationships like this are considered unethical. They might respond to a situation such as the one presented in this case by saying, "This is graduate school, and she is a consenting adult. She chose to be with him." A professor, whether male or female, is in a position of power over the student. This allows the professor to have undue influence over that student even though the student may not realize it. And, as is clearly an issue in this case, the student does not have equal power to decide to end the relationship. How can there be a mutual, consenting relationship when one of the individuals has the ability to decide the other's future through assigning grades, giving recommendations for future graduate study or employment, or other means of influence?

Because of the professor's leverage due to the uneven power base, the question isn't whether she chose to be with him but whether she will be able to keep her assistantship and receive favorable grades and recommendations for further study. This is not a choice students should be put in a position to have to make.

Questions for Further Reflection

1. Students often look up to their professors and seek their guidance. In what ways is the influence a professor has over a student similar to the influence a counselor has over a client?
2. If a faculty member did not have a particular student in class, and was not currently and would never be the student's supervisor, might it then be acceptable for that professor to date the student? to have a sexual relationship with the student?

Case Study 14

A Question of Boundaries

Harriet L. Glosoff

Teresa, a professional counselor, moved to a small town in Iowa with her 13-year-old son. She discovered that, except for a psychiatrist, the closest other mental health professional practices approximately 1½ hours away. Initially she felt isolated and found it emotionally and financially difficult to establish her private practice, adjust to small-town living, and develop a personal life.

After almost a year of struggle, her practice is fairly steady and her son is doing quite well in his new school. Teresa has become close friends with Evelyn, the principal at her son's school. In fact, her son and Evelyn's son have also become very close friends and spend a good deal of time together in each other's homes. Teresa and Evelyn discovered many commonalities, including that they are both divorced, receive little support from their ex-husbands, and are originally from large cities. They carpool, watch each other's children, socialize together, and have become strong social and emotional supports for each other.

Teresa and Evelyn spend a good bit of time commiserating on the joys and problems of being single parents and the difficulties of dealing with teenage sons. Evelyn confides that she is really concerned about her son, Chris, stating that he is having a lot of problems in school and that their relationship at home has become strained. According to Evelyn, Chris seems to be testing her authority and recently has been lashing out at her, especially in matters related to school. Evelyn tells Teresa that most of Chris's problems are caused by his inconsistent communication with his father and shares that she is at her wit's end. She thinks Chris needs counseling and asks Teresa to take him on as a client.

Teresa is initially reluctant and explains to Evelyn that she is concerned about how this might affect their friendship. They discuss the differences between friendships and professional relationships and how these differences might manifest themselves in their almost-daily contacts. Evelyn insists that she feels comfortable with the duality and that she doesn't see a necessity to make a 3-hour drive, round trip, when Teresa is well qualified to work with her son. Teresa is concerned that if she refuses Evelyn's request, it might damage their friendship. She is also fairly sure that she would do no harm in providing counseling to Chris and agrees to see him on a weekly basis in her office.

During their second session, Chris shares that he is uncomfortable talking about some of the things that are bothering him, particularly anything to do with his mother. Teresa discusses confidentiality issues, and eventually Chris seems to relax and open up. During the course of treatment, he divulges information about both of his parents that leads Teresa to believe that Chris is reacting to more than inconsistent communication with his father and that some of Evelyn's behaviors are contributing to her son's problems. One example Chris brings up in a counseling session is that his mom often complains to him about his father, and this upsets him. Teresa struggles with how to explore this with Evelyn. Discussing it in the office with both Evelyn and her son, as she might with other clients, seems too formal, given their friendship, but Teresa believes it would be unethical to discuss this with Evelyn over coffee without Chris. She decides to wait and see what else Chris might bring up in sessions.

Teresa also notices that when Chris is at her house with her own son, she feels uncomfortable. She realizes that she is shifting back and forth between the unconditional positive regard she tries to exhibit in her office and the realities of having to discipline two teenagers who sometimes get a bit out of hand. She brings this up with Chris during their next session, explaining that she is wearing different hats: in the office she is his counselor, and at home she is his best friend's mom. He seems to understand, but Teresa finds herself becoming increasingly uneasy as the weeks pass, especially after a few incidents at her home when Teresa finds the boys breaking "house rules" by smoking cigarettes and playing music much louder than allowed. When writing her case notes, Teresa realizes she is spending a good bit of time sorting through what she knows about Chris from his time in her home versus what he discloses in his counseling sessions. In addition, she becomes aware that she is measuring her words more carefully when she is with Evelyn, thinking about what she should and should not say to her friend in social situations. Teresa wonders how all of this might be influencing her effectiveness in her counseling with Chris. She is having trouble sorting through her current situation: what might be detrimental to Chris, to her friendship with Evelyn, and to herself. After the sixth counseling session with Chris, Teresa decides to consult by phone with a previous supervisor whom she trusts.

Questions for Thought and Discussion

1. Regardless of what Teresa's colleague may tell her, how ethical do you consider her behavior?
2. Compared to the great potential for harm that can exist in a sexual dual relationship, how dangerous does this situation seem?
3. Can Teresa remain objective in her work with Chris when she also sees him in nontherapeutic situations as well as through the eyes of his mother?
4. Do you believe that Teresa should continue to see Chris as a client? Why or why not?

Analysis

Standard A.5.c. mandates that counselors avoid "nonprofessional relationships with clients, former clients, their romantic partners, or their family members . . . except when the interaction is potentially beneficial to the client." Although it seems clear that Teresa does not intend to exploit Chris's trust or do him any harm, it is not clear that it is potentially beneficial to Chris to enter into a counseling relationship with Teresa.

It could be argued that there are no major power issues at play here. However, many contend that there is always a power differential between counselors and clients. A minor client might be even more subtly affected by this differential, especially when it is combined with Chris's perception of Teresa as his best friend's mother, a person who is very loving but has to discipline him when he stays over at her house.

What would Teresa need to do to demonstrate that she is not in violation of Standard A.5.c? First, she would need to demonstrate that she made a reasonable effort to avoid the dual relationship. Did she offer alternative providers? Does a 3-hour round trip to the next closest provider constitute a great enough hardship for Evelyn to warrant the risk in establishing a counseling relationship with Chris? Second, Teresa would have to show that accepting Chris as a client while maintaining the other nonprofessional relationships is potentially beneficial to Chris. Although it does not appear that Chris has suffered any harm at this point, Teresa has stated that her professional judgment might have been influenced at times by her struggles to wear different hats.

Another issue is that of informed consent. Teresa may think that she established informed consent regarding the potential risks in this situation. However, it must be noted that she initially reviewed the potential risks with Evelyn, not with Chris. Although many would argue the importance of securing informed consent from parents before counseling a client who is a minor, this does not by itself meet either the spirit or the letter of Standard A.2.d. At age 13, Chris is old enough to be included in the decision to enter into a counseling relationship with Teresa. Further, Standards A.2.a. and A.2.b. direct Teresa to provide the *client*, not just the parent, with all pertinent information when counseling is first initiated and throughout the counseling relationship. Finally, the emphasis of Teresa's conversation with Evelyn was on the risks to *their* friendship, not on any possible beneficial or negative ramifications for Chris as a client.

Three questions seem to be at the heart of the matter. First, "Did Teresa's own personal needs influence her work with Chris?" Standard A.4.a. cautions counselors to avoid harming their clients "or to remedy unavoidable or unanticipated harm." Teresa would need to demonstrate to an Ethics Committee, if she were charged with a violation, that her concern over maintaining her friendship with Evelyn did not influence her treatment of Chris.

Second, "How much are the multiple layers of relationships in this situation influencing Teresa's effectiveness as a counselor?" For example, does

Chris trust what Teresa will and will not tell his mother? Has Teresa shared with both Chris and Evelyn the bounds of confidentiality and defined her responsibilities to Chris (B.5.a.) and to Evelyn as his mother (B.5.b.)? Maybe more important, Teresa notes that her relationship with Evelyn may be influencing how she thinks about confidentiality as well as how this may be affecting her friendship with Evelyn.

Although the client in this situation does not appear to be harmed at this point, counselors need to go beyond avoiding harm and work to "promote the welfare of clients" (A.1.a.) and "continually monitor their effectiveness as professionals and take steps to improve when necessary" (C.2.d.). In addition, Standard C.2.d. states that "counselors in private practice take reasonable steps to seek peer supervision as needed to evaluate their efficacy as counselors." Teresa did think about her effectiveness, and she began to examine the potential for harm.

The third question is, "Can the potential for harm to Chris clearly be avoided or anticipated?" If so, what precautions did Teresa take to ensure Chris's well-being? Teresa's use of supervision or consultation with other appropriate professionals about the ethical issues involved would be an essential matter for the Ethics Committee to explore. Teresa sought consultation but did so only after her sixth session with Chris. It would have been preferable to consult with her previous supervisor before agreeing to see Chris professionally. This could have provided an opportunity for her to examine her own needs and weigh the potential risks to Chris. In fact, if she had done this, Teresa might have realized that she was initially focused more on the possibility of damaging her friendship with her one close friend in town than on the ramifications of her decision to counsel Chris. Her colleague might have helped her to anticipate problems likely to occur due to the divergent expectations involved in the dual roles she would be assuming. Ongoing supervision throughout the course of Chris's counseling seems warranted in this case.

Questions for Further Reflection

1. How do counselors determine whether nonprofessional relationships are avoidable or whether they may be potentially beneficial to clients?
2. If a nonprofessional relationship involving a client is unavoidable, what steps can a counselor take to safeguard client welfare?
3. What particular boundary issues do counselors need to consider when working with minor clients or adults who cannot give informed consent?

Chapter 8

Working With Clients Who May Harm Themselves

Adriane G. Bennett and James L. Werth Jr.

Clients who have the desire to harm themselves present special challenges that could have both professional and legal consequences. Clients who may be at risk for self-harm are often a source of anxiety and confusion for counselors. It is impossible to constantly monitor clients' actions, and there is significant pressure to make the "right" decision because the outcome of mismanagement can be devastating for all parties involved. In reality, clients could seriously harm themselves even under the best therapeutic conditions. However, the risk of a negative outcome can be significantly reduced if counselors practice in accordance with professional standards of care.

In working with clients who may harm themselves, counselors may have questions such as these: "What are my ethical responsibilities to the client? How will I know if the client is at an increased risk for self-harm? Should I break confidentiality to prevent self-harm, and if so when?" Fortunately, the *ACA Code of Ethics* (2005) provides guidance in the areas of informed consent, confidentiality, counselor competence, and consultation that can assist counselors in making decisions about the assessment and treatment of high-risk clients. The *Code* also addresses issues associated with terminally ill clients. This chapter highlights standards that can affect working with clients who are at risk for self-harm and clients who are making end-of-life decisions.

The *Code of Ethics* states that confidentiality "does not apply when disclosure is required to protect clients or identified others from serious and foreseeable harm" (B.2.a.). Counselors should be aware that a wide range of behaviors could be considered to place clients at risk of harm, including cutting, self-mutilation, and suicide. Although this discussion focuses on suicidal behavior—the most extreme form of self-harm—the ethical standards and techniques discussed can be generalized to other behaviors on the self-harm continuum.

Informed Consent

Counselors may be hesitant to discuss issues of self-harm with a client, especially if the client does not bring them up. Some counselors may fear that they will introduce the idea of self-harm or that the therapeutic relationship could be damaged if there is a serious concern and confidentiality needs to be broken. Counselors can ease the discomfort of addressing the issue of self-harm by discussing it within the context of informed consent. "Informed consent is an ongoing part of the counseling process, and counselors appropriately document discussions of informed consent throughout the counseling relationship" (A.2.a.).

The informed consent discussion is used to educate the client about the counseling process including agency policies, expectations about counseling, and confidentiality. Limitations of confidentiality need to be explained: "At initiation and throughout the counseling process, counselors inform clients of the limitations of confidentiality and seek to identify foreseeable situations in which confidentiality must be breached" (B.1.d.). It is important to clarify to clients that session material will be held confidential with some exceptions, including "when disclosure is required to protect clients or identified others from serious and foreseeable harm or when legal requirements demand that confidential information must be revealed" (B.2.a.). Explaining this exception provides counselors with a way to explore to what degree "serious and foreseeable harm" is present, which can aid in the decision about whether to break confidentiality. It also informs clients that, if there is concern about serious risk, confidentiality could be broken and further safety precautions, such as hospitalization, might be taken.

Counselors should also provide clients with information regarding treatment options because clients have a right to "refuse any services or modality change and to be advised of the consequences of such refusal" (A.2.b.). This does not mean that clients can override counselors' clinical judgment and refuse to go to the hospital when it appears that a suicide attempt is imminent. Rather, clients should be informed that involuntary hospitalization may be necessary if other crisis intervention strategies are not effective.

Assessment

If clients do not voluntarily self-disclose intentions to harm themselves, counselors may need to directly ask. Factors that could increase clients' risk for self-harm include severe mental illness, substance abuse, recent loss, and acute medical conditions (Bongar, 2002). The client may be experiencing high levels of negative thoughts and emotions such as feelings of shame, helplessness, hopelessness, or depression; have increased levels of self-hatred or loathing; and may have lost pleasure or interest in life. To gain a complete picture of the level of risk of self-harm, counselors need to assess the client's *ideation*, *plan*, and *means*.

When assessing for ideation, counselors want to learn about the content and frequency of thoughts about self-harm: "Have you felt bad enough that you have considered harming yourself?" If the client indicates this may be true, the counselor should determine *when* this occurred. If ideation existed in the past, the counselor should ask about that incident and its outcome. If the client indicates the thoughts are current, it is important to assess their *purpose*. For example, clients who cut themselves may not be suicidal because behaviors have different meanings for different clients.

Clients may want to cut to release anxiety or tension, to come out of a dissociative experience, to regain a sense of self-control, to manipulate attention from other people, or to indulge in self-hatred, vent anger, or alter sexual feelings. It is possible, however, that some individuals who cut themselves and who become demoralized over their inability to control these behaviors could be at increased risk of suicide (Favazza, 1999). Keep in mind that even if the client is participating *only* in self-cutting, it is still possible that the counselor would have to take additional steps to protect the client, depending on the severity of the behaviors.

If clients indicate that they do have suicidal ideation or other thoughts of harming themselves, counselors need to further explore to determine the level of risk: "Do you have a plan? Have you thought about how you would do it?" These are both good questions to determine how serious clients are about acting on their thoughts. If a client has a well-formulated plan, the level of risk may increase. In some situations, the client may have a plan, but the plan is not practical because there is no access to the *means* to carry it out. For example, if a client states she or he would only use a gun, the counselor needs to ask, "Do you have access to a gun?" If the client has ideation, a concrete plan, and easy access to the means by which to carry out the plan, there is a heightened risk of harm to self.

Counselors may also want to consider psychological factors such as the client's current sense of crisis, mental status, level of psychopathology, personality, and perception of the therapeutic relationship to determine the urgency of risk (Clark, 1998). Formal assessment tools may be helpful in collecting information about these intrapsychic factors and in monitoring the client's progress; however, the counselor must be trained in the proper use and interpretation of these instruments (E.2.a.).

Treatment Planning

Developing a good treatment plan can help counselors protect the client from "clear and imminent danger," and conducting a thorough assessment can help counselors decide if or when it would be necessary to break confidentiality. Disclosure may not be needed if crisis intervention is successful and the client is willing to work with the counselor to remain safe. Options for treatment could include increasing social support, individual or family therapy, substance abuse treatment, medication, access to the therapist or crisis hotline for times between sessions, and relapse prevention strategies (Slaby, 1998). Some writers recommend having the client sign a "no-harm contract;" however, it should be understood that this intervention does not provide counselors with any legal protection and may actually be used against them in court. We believe that using the informed consent framework to discuss treatment options, the choices clients could make regarding the course of treatment, and the consequences of those choices is a better option than relying on a contract. This framework allows the client to actively participate in treatment and does not provide the counselor with a false sense of security (Miller, 1999).

If the client does not respond to crisis intervention attempts and there is an imminent risk of harm to self, confidentiality may need to be broken (B.2.a.). In addition, "counselors consult with other professionals when in doubt as to the validity of an exception" to ensure that it would be appropriate and necessary to break confidentiality (B.2.a.). Before disclosure occurs, the counselor should make an effort to keep the client involved in the therapeutic process. Sometimes clients will agree to go to the hospital because the counselor would not be revealing the information to outside sources and thus clients could maintain some control over confidentiality of information. At other times, the counselor may decide to break confidentiality. "To the extent possible, clients are informed before confidential information is disclosed and are involved in the disclosure decision-making process. When circumstances require the disclosure of confidential information, only essential information is revealed" (B.2.d.). Informing clients before releasing information is not only ethically recommended but can help to keep them actively involved in treatment.

End-of-Life Decisions

The 2005 *ACA Code of Ethics* provides some guidance to mental health professionals in the controversial area of end-of-life decisions in a new section on End-of-Life Care for Terminally Ill Clients (A.9.). In addition, the standard on exceptions to confidentiality notes that "additional considerations apply when addressing end-of-life issues" (B.2.a.).

The 1995 version of the *Code* did not distinguish among the situations that may lead clients to have a desire for death (e.g., impulsive suicide or a well-considered decision to go off dialysis), making the *Code* inconsistent with statements made by ACA in a brief before the U.S. Supreme Court in which the organization endorsed the idea that different issues may be involved in end-of-life decision making (Herlihy & Watson, 2004; Werth, 1999a; Werth & Gordon, 2002).

The 2005 *Code* states that "counselors who provide services to terminally ill individuals who are considering hastening their own deaths have the option of breaking or not breaking confidentiality, depending on applicable laws and the specific circumstances of the situation and after seeking consultation or supervision from appropriate professional and legal parties" (A.9.c). Previously, a counselor may have been obligated to break confidentiality even with a terminally ill client who was considering going off a ventilator (because this could be construed as "imminent danger to the client"). Now, after receiving consultation or supervision, counselors may decide not to divulge such information to others. Although potentially controversial, the new standards on working with terminally ill clients provide counselors with more latitude when such clients have a desire for death.

Counselors may decide not to break confidentiality when a client is considering a legal act such as withholding or withdrawing treatment, and this decision may not raise concerns. However, the new standard would also allow counselors to not inform others even if a client is leaning toward having an assisted death (which is illegal in most states). There is considerable controversy associated with assisted death and mental health professionals' potential involvement in these situations. The *Code of Ethics* does not prohibit involvement in such discussions, and some have asserted that mental health professionals can play an important role when clients are considering end-of-life options that may include hastening death (e.g., Werth, 1999a, 2002).

The functions of the counselor in end-of-life situations, including those associated with assisted death, are to help clients get their needs met, maximize client self-determination, help clients engage in informed decision making, and conduct an evaluation or refer clients to receive a thorough assessment regarding their capacity to make end-of-life decisions. It should be emphasized that cultural issues may affect what "self-determination" and "informed decision making" mean for different individuals considering end-of-life decisions (Herlihy & Watson, 2004; Werth, Blevins, Toussaint, & Durham, 2002).

Counselors need to be able to conduct a thorough assessment, or refer a client to a competent provider, to comply with Standard A.9.a. The literature provides guidelines for competence in these situations (Werth, 1999b) as well as for what would be involved in a comprehensive evaluation (e.g., Werth, 1999a; Werth, Benjamin, & Farrenkopf, 2000; Werth & Rogers, 2005; Working Group, 2000). Standard A.9.a. does not state that such an assessment is necessary only when a terminally ill client is considering assisted death; it also applies to any dying person who is making end-of-life decisions. This is consistent with recent discussions that do not differentiate among various types of end-of-life decisions (e.g., Werth & Kleespies, 2006; Werth & Rogers, 2005).

It has been suggested that the same type of assessment could be conducted for people with suicidal ideation as for those who are making end-of-life decisions (Werth & Rogers, 2005). Some authors have asserted that the same issues may be involved when individuals want to kill themselves through a deliberate overdose, hanging, or using a gun as when someone wants to go off a ventilator, discontinue dialysis, or have a physician help the person die. In other words, just as clinical depression, hopelessness, and social isolation may contribute to a person's suicidality, these conditions might also be part of a terminally ill individual's end-of-life decision making.

Throughout the process of working with clients who are at risk for harm to self, including those making end-of-life decisions, counselors should take three additional steps. First, counselors should consult with other professionals: "Counselors take reasonable steps to consult with other counselors or related professionals when they have questions regarding their ethical obligations or professional practice" (C.2.e.). Consultation helps to ensure that counselors are practicing up to the standards of care, making informed decisions about the exceptions for confidentiality, and accessing all of the current treatment options. Second, counselors should determine whether they have the competency and training to work with such a client:

"Counselors practice only within the boundaries of their competence, based on their education, training, supervised experience, state and national professional credentials, and appropriate professional experience" (C.2.a.). Counselors who do not think they can work competently with a client should seek supervision from a professional who has these skills or make the appropriate referral. Finally, counselors need to appropriately document the assessment, consultation, and treatment planning that occurred. It is important to document the steps of the decision-making process, including which interventions were chosen, the rationale for the decision, and why certain treatment options were not chosen.

In summary, the 2005 *ACA Code of Ethics* addresses end-of-life decisions. Although it provides more substantive direction and allows for greater possibilities, it is also bound to be controversial. We believe, however, that the flexibility this standard offers counselors providing care to dying clients will enable counselors to direct their energy toward helping the client rather than being distracted by concerns about breaking confidentiality.

The first case study in this chapter illustrates how suicidality and end-of-life decisions can be interrelated and the important role of assessment in such situations. In the second case, a counselor works with a suicidal teenager.

Case Study 15

Suicide or a Well-Reasoned End-of-Life Decision?

Adriane G. Bennett and James L. Werth Jr.

Jason is a 38-year-old gay man with AIDS. In his counseling session, he presents with concerns about dealing with the progression of his illness and uncertainty about his future. He reports that he has struggled with depression and anxiety for much of his life and was suicidal during adolescence when he was coming to realize he was gay. He has been estranged from his family of origin (parents, older brother, and younger sister) since he came out to them when he was in his early 20s. He was also rejected by his church and believes that "God turned His back on me, so I turned my back on Him." He does have some friends in his local gay community and in the HIV support group he attends once a week, but he has not been able to maintain a significant relationship since learning of his HIV status.

Jason learned he was HIV positive 8 years ago, but based on how sick he was when he was tested, he reports that his physicians think he has been infected for at least 15 years. He started on medications immediately, but he has developed resistance to most of them because of an admitted lack of adherence to the sometimes complicated regimen. During a recent medical exam, Jason was told that the combination of medications he is now taking seems to be holding the HIV in check. But he does not appear to be getting any better, and there are no other options for him at this point. His physician told him that she could not predict how much longer these medications would continue working but that it could be years and that new types of drugs are coming out on a regular basis. Jason thinks his quality of life is poor right now because of the side effects of the medications and the advanced state of his HIV infection, with his daily symptoms including night sweats, nausea, diarrhea, fatigue, and numbness or pain in various extremities. He has been unable to work on a plant assembly line for the last 6 years because of the HIV and associated problems. Even if he could work, he doesn't think he would be able to find a job given his condition and the job market in the area.

Jason is not sure he wants to continue living this way, especially because he has seen several of his friends in the HIV support group and in the larger gay community die terrible deaths related to HIV disease. He adds that, because it looks like he is going to die anyway, he might as well have a good quality of life the last few months and has seriously considered stopping his medications so the side effects go away. When he mentioned to his physician the idea of a "drug holiday," which has been discussed in the HIV magazines he reads, his doctor said that if he stopped the medication he could expect to die within a few months and, at least right now, there would be no medications to start again if he changed his mind.

In addition to the HIV medication, Jason is taking two types of antidepressants, which help some with his anxiety. He has a prescription for an additional anxiolytic, which he reports taking more frequently recently because of his increased anxiety when he goes out in public. Jason thinks his HIV positive status is more apparent now and that people are staring at him and judging him. Jason also has a prescription for sleeping pills, a narcotic pain medication, and a prescription for the nerve condition he has developed. In addition, he is taking medications to counter the side effects of the other medicines, so he also has pills for nausea and diarrhea. As a result, Jason may take 30 or more pills a day, depending on how bad his symptoms are, and he is getting tired of having to do this day in and day out. Another side effect of all this medication is that he has little appetite and nothing tastes good. He smokes marijuana on a regular basis, both to increase his appetite as well as to help with the nausea. Although he admits that he used to drink every day, he stopped using alcohol and other recreational drugs (other than marijuana) when he began his HIV medications.

At the end of the session Jason says that he has appreciated talking and that it has helped him to look at everything he is facing in his life and what his future holds. He says that after listening to himself, he has decided that it makes the most sense to stop taking his HIV medication and enjoy the little time he has left by traveling. He wants to see parts of the country he has never explored instead of being stuck at home or at least close to a bathroom because of the side effects of the medications. He indicates that he may as well cash in his life insurance policy and pay for everything with his few remaining credit cards: it will not matter if he ruins his credit rating, and there is no one to whom he wants to leave his insurance money. Finally, he says that he does not think he needs another session because he will either be really sick or will be on the road in the next few weeks.

Questions for Thought and Discussion

1. If you were the counselor in this case, what components of informed consent would you want to review with Jason?
2. How could you determine if you are competent to treat Jason?
3. What decision-making process would you use for Jason's treatment planning? How could you keep Jason involved in this process?
4. What factors contribute to Jason's risk of harm to self? If you were Jason's counselor, under what conditions would you consider maintaining or breaking confidentiality?

Analysis

Depending on how the counselor interprets Jason's current situation and his past experiences, the counselor could consider him to be suicidal or to be making a well-reasoned end-of-life decision. Without further information that would be gathered during a thorough assessment, we believe the counselor could justify leaning either toward intervention or toward letting him leave. For the interventionist, Jason does have a history of depression and suicidal ideations, has few social supports, has no religious faith, is unemployed, is having health problems, has seen negative experiences in friends who had his illness, is using at least one illegal substance, and has medication on hand that could be used for suicide. For the noninterventionist, Jason is taking antidepressants, is in a support group, has considered his options, has consulted with his physicians, does have severe physical problems that do not appear ameliorable in the foreseeable future, does not appear to have loved ones who would be traumatized by his death, and does have a right to stop medical treatment.

Whatever decision the counselor makes should not come as a surprise to Jason. Counselors should have a thorough written and verbal informed consent policy and process that begins at the beginning of the counseling relationship and continues throughout the sessions. Counselors who work with people with terminal conditions need to be careful and specific about what they tell clients about intervening in the event that they consider harm to self to be a possibility. Clients deserve to know that it is safe to talk about something such as stopping medication and that such disclosures will not automatically be considered harm to self, initiating potentially forceful interventions. Counselors need to know their obligations under state law; unless there is a specific directive to intervene, they have options. The *Code of Ethics* does not *require* intervention when terminally ill clients are considering their end-of-life choices.

A thorough evaluation of Jason will help the counselor determine whether he has impaired judgment or whether any ameliorable conditions are negatively affecting his quality of life. A good assessment will help the counselor determine whether Jason's decision seems to be more similar to suicidality or to a considered end-of-life decision. In either case, we would recommend that the counselor review the literature, consult with others, and document what was done and not done, and why.

Questions for Further Reflection

1. If you were a consultant in this case, what advice would you give the counselor, and why?
2. How do cultural factors come into play in this case and in general when thinking about suicide and end-of-life decision making?
3. What would you do if you were in Jason's situation, and why? What would you want your counselor to do?

Case Study 16

A Suicidal Teenager

Robert E. Wubbolding

Frank, age 17, has been referred to a counselor in private practice because of recent changes in his behavior. He is withdrawn and is uncharacteristically irritable with his parents. He has been an average student, but his grades have fallen recently. He has also given away some of his prized possessions, including a baseball that was very valuable to him because he caught it in the stands at a major league game. Other gifts to friends have included a pair of boots, a school jacket, and a cherished set of baseball cards. His parents don't understand his behavior and are concerned about him, telling the counselor that Frank is given to expressions of hopelessness and anger. They connect these feelings with the fact that his girlfriend recently dropped him in favor of a more popular student at school.

During the first session, the counselor helps Frank describe why he has been sent. He freely describes his unhappiness at home and school, stating that he is fed up and very angry that his girlfriend dropped him. He says that she'll be sorry when it becomes impossible for her to get back with him, adding that soon he'll be free of all this agony. The counselor asks how he has handled disappointments in the past. Frank relates that he always gets upset when he can't get his way, and that if people don't like him he finds little ways to get even. He then feels overwhelmed with guilt over his reactions. The way he chooses to deal with the guilt, hurt, and ubiquitous pain is to get high with a few friends. He adds that his parents are unaware of his drug use, which he denies is a problem. Subsequent dialogue between the counselor and Frank goes like this:

Counselor: Frank, you said earlier that you had a solution to your problems.

Frank: Yeah, I guess so.

Counselor: Tell me more about your thoughts on ways you might best solve your problems.

Frank: Well, I've thought of things. . . . I just don't want to struggle so much anymore.

Counselor: Are you exhausted from the stress of struggling?

Frank: Yeah, sort of.

Counselor: Feeling down in the dumps?

Frank: That describes it.

Counselor: Maybe you've gone down as far as you're going? Do you want to come out of the dumps?

Frank: I sure would.

Counselor: I believe I can help you start to climb.

Frank: I've already found the best answer to my problems.

Counselor: I routinely ask people a simple question when they are upset about something. Are you thinking of killing yourself?

Frank: One of my classmates did that last year.

Counselor: Was this classmate a friend?

Frank: Yeah, kind of.

Counselor: Do you miss him?

Frank: I sure do.

Counselor: What are your thoughts about moving on and making other friends?

Frank: I don't want to be bothered.
Counselor: Have you thought about joining your friend?
Frank: I think it would be a good idea.
Counselor: Is that a "yes"?
Frank: Yes, I've thought a lot about it.
Counselor: Have you ever talked about this with anyone?
Frank: No. This is the first time I've said it out loud.
Counselor: Sometimes it helps just to talk about it. I've found that people feel better if they are willing to talk about what is on their minds. I'd like to ask you some more questions about your thoughts on dying. Is that okay?
Frank: Sure, it's okay.
Counselor: Have you tried to injure yourself or to commit suicide in the past?
Frank: One time about a year ago I took a razor and cut my arm. But I got scared when I saw the blood, and I stopped.
Counselor: Have there been any other times?
Frank: No, that's the only one.
Counselor: If you were to try to kill yourself again, how would you do it?
Frank: I was thinking I'd drive my car into a busy intersection at 4:00 p.m. on Route 12 when the 18-wheelers are out on the road. It would be quick and would look like an accident.
Counselor: I see. So you've thought about a plan and you have your own car?
Frank: Yes, I've had it for about a year.
Counselor: Frank, I believe I can help you feel better. I think I can offer you the possibility of getting past this misery. Would you be interested in thinking about some of these ideas before you make this final decision?
Frank: I might. . . .
Counselor: To put it another way, do you think you can do the work involved? It would be something you could handle.
Frank: I'd like to try.
Counselor: Good. First, I want to ask you if you can agree to make a firm commitment, not to me, but to yourself, to stay alive for a while?
Frank: Yeah, I think so. I haven't tried anything yet.
Counselor: For how long?
Frank: What do you mean?
Counselor: Can you agree to stay alive, not to kill yourself accidentally or intentionally, for a week? a month? or how long?
Frank: I can do it for a month. What did you mean by *accidentally?*
Counselor: Like driving recklessly or accidentally pulling out in front of an 18-wheeler.
Frank: I see what you mean. Yeah, I won't kill myself.
Counselor: Is there anyone around you with whom you could talk if you start to feel like killing yourself?
Frank: I have an uncle who might listen. I can't talk to my parents.
Counselor: Would you be willing to talk to him if you seriously start to want to kill yourself?
Frank: Yeah, that's okay.
Counselor: Frank, how do you feel right now, after you've talked about this for a few minutes?
Frank: I feel a little better.
Counselor: This shows that life can be better, that you are able to do some things, make plans, and take actions that result in feeling better. Would you be willing to work in that direction?
Frank: Yes, I'm willing. . . . Do you really think my life can be better?
Counselor: I really think so. I firmly believe that your life can take a turn-around.

Questions for Thought and Discussion

1. What components do you think are essential to include in a no-suicide agreement? Does it need to be in writing?
2. Should Frank be referred for a psychiatric assessment?
3. Do you believe that in Frank's case intervention other than counseling is necessary? Might it be necessary if Frank had refused to commit to a no-suicide agreement? If so, should the counselor then notify Frank's parents?
4. Frank has said that he can't talk to his parents. If the parents are brought in, what is the risk that Frank will feel angry and betrayed and that the counseling relationship will be destroyed?
5. What is your responsibility to the parents when counseling a 17-year-old student?

Analysis

Counselors recognize that the ultimate decision to intervene or not is subjective and often entails resolving the pull of apparently opposing responsibilities. Counselors who function at the highest level of ethical behavior ask specific questions of clients who express suicidal ideation. They know how to assess the lethality of the threat and determine the proximity of rescue. In assessing dangerous behavior on Frank's part, the counselor needs to determine the seriousness of the threat: Is there a plan? Has the person seriously thought about death? Does he have the means available to kill himself? Who could stop him? What kind of emotional support is available in the family, at home, or elsewhere? The counselor asks these questions calmly, clearly, and unambiguously after having established rapport with Frank. It is important for the counselor to express confidence that Frank will feel better, without minimizing the problems. The counselor tries to instill a sense of hope but avoids making a guarantee.

The counselor will want to consult with a colleague (B.2.a.) and to document the consultation. In documenting, quotes from the counselor and consultant are helpful in assuring that the assessment was both thorough and comprehensive.

Standard B.5.b. states that "counselors work to establish, as appropriate, collaborative relationships with parents/guardians to best serve clients." Frank's counselor is aware of the importance of proceeding with counseling related to other issues. After the crisis has passed, the counselor can begin to explore Frank's drug use, how he handles stress, the roots of his unhappiness, rational and irrational thinking, self-evaluation, effective fulfillment of needs, personal goals, interpersonal relationships, and myriad other issues. At some later point, the counselor may want to involve the parents in family counseling sessions if Frank is in accord with this decision.

In Frank's case, two sets of competing needs seem apparent: a responsibility to protect Frank from harm versus his right to privacy, and a possible need to intervene beyond providing counseling versus a need to keep the client engaged in the counseling process. The fact that Frank, at 17, is still legally a minor is a complicating factor. Confidentiality requirements do "not apply when disclosure is required to protect clients or identified others from serious and foreseeable harm or when legal requirements demand that confidential information must be revealed" (B.2.a.). In this case, after a careful assessment, Frank's counselor made the judgment that danger was not imminent. In addition, the counselor engaged Frank in the decision-making process: "When counseling minors or persons unable to give voluntary consent, counselors seek the assent of clients to services, and include them in decision making as appropriate" (A.2.d.).

As Corey, Corey, and Callanan (2007) have noted, the crux of the dilemma in dealing with suicidal clients is knowing when to take a client's hints or verbalizations seriously enough to report the condition. The burden of responsibility to make the right decision is high, and the ethically conscientious counselor will need to call upon a combination of skill and training, careful assessment of risk, consultation and documentation, and sound professional judgment.

Questions for Further Reflection

1. How well do you manage your own stress and deal with the awesome sense of responsibility that can attend working with clients who pose a danger to themselves or others?
2. Sometimes clients do commit suicide. When this happens, survivors may look for someone to blame and bring suit against the counselor for malpractice. What steps do counselors need to take, as they work with suicidal clients, to minimize the risk that such a suit could be successful?
3. What steps do counselors need to take to deal with feelings of loss and failure they may experience when a client commits suicide?

Chapter 9

Counselor Education and Supervision

Michael M. Kocet

Section F of the 2005 *ACA Code of Ethics* is devoted to issues in counselor education and supervision. Whereas other sections of the *Code* emphasize the counselor–client relationship, Section F focuses on the unique relationships between supervisor and supervisee and between counselor educator and student.

Supervision

In the past it was generally assumed that a good counselor would also be a good supervisor. As a result, most supervisors had little formal training to prepare them for the roles and responsibilities involved in clinical supervision. Today the need for specific preparation and competence in supervision is well recognized. Training in supervision can increase counselors' self-awareness, confidence, supervisory techniques and skills, and theoretical and conceptual knowledge (McMahon & Simons, 2004). Professionals who offer clinical supervision services need to have specific training in supervision methods, theories, and interventions (F.2.a.) and be sensitive to issues of multiculturalism and diversity and their impact in the supervisory relationship (F.2.b.). This includes doctoral students who are serving as supervisors to master's students as part of their doctoral training. Doctoral students must be supervised in their work by members of the faculty in their academic program.

A strong working alliance between supervisor and supervisee is essential for supervisee growth and development. The supervisory relationship can help counselors-in-training manage the emotions, challenges, and skill development that are inherent in becoming ethical and competent practitioners. Supervisors must create an environment in which there is an appropriate balance of challenge and support. Open and honest communication is necessary for the supervisee to grow and become a competent professional. Sometimes counselors-in-training are reluctant to openly discuss with their supervisors mistakes or errors they have made in their practicum or internship. However, it is critical for supervisees to talk directly with their supervisors about their missteps and their fears as counselors in order to correct mistakes and create new opportunities for growth. If this is to occur, supervisors must encourage their supervisees to be open about the concerns they are having in working with clients.

Just as securing informed consent is essential prior to initiating a counseling relationship, informed consent must be provided to supervisees and clients of supervisees. At the beginning of the supervisory relationship, supervisors need to address how to balance the rights and responsibilities of clients, the supervisee, and the supervisor. Holding such a discussion can empower supervisees to express their expectations and concerns, make decisions, and become active participants in the supervisory process (Corey, Corey, & Callanan, 2007). Supervisors need to ensure that supervisees are fully informed about the supervisory process, including ongoing evaluative processes (F.3.a., F.4.a., F.4.c., F.5.a). Clients who receive counseling services from a counselor-in-training have the right to know the status of the supervisee as a graduate student practicing under the supervision of a qualified site supervisor and academic program supervisor. They also need to understand the limits of confidentiality and the types of services the student counselor is qualified to render (F.6.h.).

Supervisors serve as gatekeepers to the profession and must monitor and evaluate supervisees' performance (Haynes, Corey, & Moulton, 2003). Supervisors must conduct explicit evaluations (both formal and informal) of their supervisees throughout the supervisory process. They document the ongoing performance appraisal of supervisees and share this information on a regular basis with supervisees (F.5.a.). Supervisees need to know that their knowledge and skills, clinical performance, and interpersonal behaviors will be evaluated at various points during the experience. Counseling programs should have written policies pertaining to supervisee evaluation.

Supervisors are expected to assist supervisees in seeking remedial assistance when supervisee limitations are impeding their performance as counselors (F.5.b.). Supervisees have the right to know when they are not meeting performance expectations, and their supervisors must allow them the opportunity to correct inadequacies by giving them specific information detailing the type of improvement required to be demonstrated to receive a satisfactory evaluation and to successfully complete their practicum, fieldwork, or internship experience (Cottone & Tarvydas, 2003; Remley & Herlihy, 2005). Supervisors must not endorse a student or supervisee who lacks the qualifications, competencies, and skills necessary to fulfill the role of a professional counselor (F.5.b., F.5.d.).

Within the supervisory relationship, it is critical to pay special attention to issues involving relationship boundaries and role changes. A role change that can be difficult to manage occurs when doctoral and master's students are enrolled as peers in the same counseling courses, and then later the relationship becomes one of doctoral-level supervisor and master's-level supervisee. The second case study in this chapter illustrates some of the ethical problems that can be encountered when students supervise students. Supervisors must exercise sound ethical judgment when establishing boundaries with supervisees within and outside of the supervisory relationship (F.3.). The role of the supervisor in the supervision relationship involves a careful blend of engaging supervisees in both personal self-reflection and clinical skill development. Supervisors must refer supervisees to appropriate outside resources when supervisees might benefit from receiving personal counseling to assist in working through interpersonal issues that may be impeding their effectiveness as counselors-in-training (F.5.c., F.7.b., F.9.c.).

Supervisors must be attuned to the importance of practicing ethically because they serve as role models for their supervisees. Supervision relationships change over time as supervisees gain competence and autonomy, and supervisors and their supervisees need to work jointly in appropriately bringing closure to the supervisory relationship (F.4.d.).

Counselor Education and Training

Counselor educators are individuals who typically have obtained an advanced degree (doctorate) in counselor education, counseling psychology, or a closely related field and have skills/competencies as both educators and practitioners (F.6.a.). Counselor educators are knowledgeable about the study of ethics and are aware of emerging ethical issues facing the profession. They must make students aware of the myriad potential ethical issues facing counselors, including culture and diversity, technology, and boundary issues as contextual factors that affect the resolution of ethical dilemmas. Students are obligated to understand and abide by the *ACA Code of Ethics* in the same way that professional counselors must.

Counselor educators take steps to actively infuse ethical standards and multicultural issues/diversity throughout the training program (F.6.a., F.6.b., F.6.d., F.11.c.). Some programs require students to take a separate course in ethics; others infuse ethics throughout the entire curriculum. In either case, counselor educators have an ethical mandate to impart the core ethical principles and values that play a central role in the counseling profession.

Part of the role of faculty members is to pass on the ethical legacy of the profession to its newer members. Counselor educators must teach students the core ethical principles and values that are the foundation for work with clients and others served by counselors (Jennings, Sovereign, Bottorff, Mussell, & Vye, 2005). Counselor educators have a responsibility to ensure that students become familiar with the ethical standards of the profession (F.8.a.), including the steps that need to be taken in the event that a counseling student is impaired or could potentially engage in behavior that is harmful to self, others, or potential clients (F.8.b.). In addition to teaching ethics, faculty must model how to integrate ethics into professional decision-making skills in a variety of contexts and settings. Ethical dilemmas are not always clear-cut, and it is important for counselors-in-training to become comfortable handling ethical situations that may have no clear "answers." Becoming ethically competent involves being open to complexity and ambiguity.

When designing curriculum, presenting innovative theories and techniques to students (F.6.f.), facilitating self-growth experiences (F.7.b.), and assessing the academic performance of students (F.9.a., F.9.b.), counselor educators must act ethically in training new professionals. When counselor educators introduce new approaches, techniques, or emerging theories, they have an obligation to state clearly that these innovations are "unfounded" or "developing" and to explain the benefits as well as the risks involved in engaging in techniques or procedures that lack a scientific and academic foundation (F.6.f.). Counselor educators must also present a balanced view of the range of theories, techniques, interventions, and clinical information available in the professional literature. Counselor educators are obligated to include a wide range of perspectives and positions on issues that affect the work of counselors.

The informed consent process in counselor education programs begins when prospective students receive application materials. Applicants must be provided with accurate and up-to-date information on current policies, practices, and expectations of the program. It is particularly important for candidates to be made aware of the fact that counseling involves a personal investment and that they will be doing far more than learning knowledge and acquiring skills. They need to know that they will be affected personally in many of their courses, that their program will be challenging to them both academically and emotionally, and that their participation in courses and fieldwork is not always likely to be a comfortable experience.

Admissions requirements typically involve both traditional and nontraditional criteria. Compared to other types of graduate programs that may only look at test scores, undergraduate GPA, and work experience, most counseling programs also examine applicants' ability to demonstrate self-awareness, emotional stability, and interpersonal skills (Remley & Herlihy, 2005). After being admitted to a program, students have a right to receive information about the structure of their academic program requirements, including the basis for assessment of students' academic work in both didactic and skill-based courses (F.9.a.), fieldwork and internship site requirements and expectations (F.6.g.), self-growth experiences (F.7.b.), and evaluation and dismissal policies and procedures (F.5.a., F.5.b.).

A critical component of most counseling training programs is an emphasis on students engaging in self-growth experiences that foster awareness of self and others. Students must be made aware of the ramifications of self-disclosing personal information in an academic setting (F.7.b.). Faculty members should not determine a student's grade or evaluation based on the student's level of self-disclosure and must, when requested, provide an appropriate alternative assignment that meets the student's academic and personal needs. As the first case study in this chapter demonstrates, counselor educators must anticipate potential problems when they use classroom exercises that require student self-disclosure.

Students look to faculty for guidance and support. Through formal and informal mentoring relationships, engaging in research projects, attendance at professional conferences, and day-to-day interactions, counselor educators have a tremendous impact on the lives of students. Counselor educators avoid engaging in abusive or coercive interactions with students and are mindful that they have the power to either positively or negatively influence the lives of students. Counselor educators do not engage in sexual or romantic relationships with current students (F.10.a., F.10.b.), and they foster open discussions with former students when considering any type of relationship outside of the faculty–student setting (F.10.c.). Counselor educators maintain appropriate boundaries in their professional relationships with students and discuss any concerns or issues that arise that may affect the academic preparation or well-being of students.

Case Study 17

The Guided Imagery Exercise

Michael M. Kocet

Dr. Weaver, an assistant professor of counselor education, is a new faculty member in her first semester of teaching. Dr. Weaver worked in a substance abuse treatment program for 2 years before she began her teaching career at the university. One of the courses she has been assigned to teach is Substance Abuse Counseling, which has 24 master's-level students. Most students taking the course are in their first year in the program. About midway through the semester, Dr. Weaver introduces the role that guided imagery can play in working with clients. She cites research from the counseling literature that addresses guided narratives and their effectiveness with clients who have substance abuse issues. She explains that she is going to take the class through a guided imagery and asks students to close their eyes as she begins the narration.

Dr. Weaver proceeds to read through the guided imagery, which involves students reflecting back to being 5 years old and living with their family of origin, which is affected by an alcoholic family member. The guided imagery asks participants to think about issues that occurred in their childhood and reconnect with those memories and experiences. One student in the class, Meredith, becomes tearful. Other students can hear her crying, and they become concerned. Dr. Weaver does not say anything but continues with the guided imagery. When Dr. Weaver begins describing very specific images related to growing up in an alcoholic home, Meredith becomes visibly upset. She is having difficulty remaining in class but is afraid that if she leaves she will get a lower class participation grade. Other students are deeply engaged in the guided imagery and find it to be a deeply powerful and meaningful experience.

Once the guided imagery is complete, Dr. Weaver announces to the class that there will be a 10-minute break and then the class will gather to have a process discussion about students' thoughts and feelings regarding the guided imagery. Students take their break, and Meredith is one of the first students to leave the class. Meredith immediately goes to the restroom to compose herself. Other students are out in the hallway waiting for class to reconvene. Some students talk with each other about how the exercise was helpful in their development as counselors. Meredith comes back into the hallway and tells some of her peers that she is upset and has to go home immediately. Meredith does not return to the classroom to tell Dr. Weaver that she is upset, nor does she stay for the remainder of the class.

The other students return to class after the break. Dr. Weaver devotes a significant amount of time to processing her students' reactions to the guided imagery exercise. She explains the importance of doing a proper assessment before engaging clients in such reflections. She further states that not all clients in counseling will want to do those kinds of exercises. Dr. Weaver notices that Meredith did not return to class and asks the students if anyone knows where she is. Jackie, another student in class, is unsure what to tell Dr. Weaver and simply replies that Meredith was "not feeling well and had to go home."

The next week Meredith is noticeably absent from class. Meredith feels that the guided imagery that Dr. Weaver used in class was harmful to her and brought up painful and difficult memories from her childhood. She felt violated because she lost her composure in front of her peers and did not have an opportunity to leave class. Meredith felt obligated to stay for the entire guided imagery so that she would not be penalized for not participating. Meredith feels so wronged by Dr. Weaver's actions that she contacts the ACA Ethics Committee and files a complaint.

Questions for Thought and Discussion

1. Do you believe Meredith has a valid complaint against Dr. Weaver? If so, what standards in the *Code of Ethics* were violated?
2. Was Dr. Weaver's guided imagery exercise appropriate for the class? If so, what steps might Dr. Weaver have taken prior to reading the guided imagery to prepare her students for the exercise?
3. What role should self-growth experiences (such as guided imagery) have in the training of counselors?

Analysis

Standard F.6. deals with the responsibilities of counselor educators; counseling faculty members must model ethical behavior and conduct training programs in an ethical manner (F.6.a.). As a new faculty member, Dr. Weaver might have considered consulting with her colleagues in the department before using this self-growth exercise in her classroom.

Standard F.7.a. states that counselor educators fully explain to students, in advance, the use of training components that encourage self-growth or self-disclosure as part of the training process. Counselor educators should provide students with information (in written and verbal form) that explains the use of class exercises or assignments that involve self-disclosure or self-growth. Dr. Weaver did not properly prepare her students for the guided imagery exercise. The students should have been made aware at the beginning of the course that experiential activities would be conducted, and this should have been noted in the course syllabus.

Standard F.7.b. addresses self-growth experiences. This standard states that "counselor educators use professional judgment when designing training experiences they conduct that require student and supervisee self-growth or self-disclosure." Dr. Weaver should have taken steps prior to reading the guided imagery to provide an alternative assignment for students who did not wish to participate in the exercise. Dr. Weaver failed to properly discuss with her students the risks and benefits of guided imagery and did not give students the option of participating in the exercise or doing an alternative assignment.

Meredith, as a counselor-in-training, has the same obligations to abide by the *ACA Code of Ethics* as do counseling professionals. Standard H.2.b. deals with the informal resolution of ethical violations. Meredith should have attempted to resolve the ethical dilemma informally by approaching Dr. Weaver to express her concerns about the guided imagery prior to filing a complaint with the ACA Ethics Committee. If Dr. Weaver was not open to hearing the feedback from Meredith, she might have talked with the department chair. If this failed to provide a resolution, she might have pursued her university's established grievance procedures. Although it would have been advisable for Meredith to take these steps, it is also important to keep in mind the power differential. Meredith may have felt intimidated by the thought of confronting those in power positions over her.

However, Meredith did file a formal ethics complaint with the ACA Ethics Committee. In this case, the committee would weigh all the evidence and information involved and would hear from both parties. The Ethics Committee probably would find Dr. Weaver in violation of Standards F.6.a., F.7.a, and F.7.b. She did not appropriately explain the parameters of self-growth experiences in class and potentially caused harm to at least one student in her class. Other students also may have been adversely affected by the guided imagery but may not have made this known. Dr. Weaver did take a considerable amount of time processing the students' thoughts and feelings about the guided imagery, but she did so only *after* the exercise.

Because of the power differential between counselor educators and students, it is sometimes difficult for students to feel empowered enough to confront their professors or to file a formal complaint with the ACA Ethics Committee. Counselors and counselors-in-training should know that the Ethics Committee serves as a sounding board for members and the public and provides guidance on how to proceed in an ethical manner. Students should consult with members of their faculty, their colleagues, and with the ACA Ethics Committee when faced with an ethical dilemma.

Questions for Further Reflection

1. What are your thoughts about including experiential activities aimed at fostering self-awareness in the counselor training curriculum?
2. What are some other ways Meredith might have dealt with the strong feelings the experiential activity aroused in her?

Case Study 18

A Resistant Supervisee

Zarus E. Watson

Phyllis is a 25-year-old single woman who was accepted into the Ph.D. program in counselor education immediately after she completed her master's degree in clinical counseling in the same department at a large urban university. During her first semester of enrollment in the doctoral program, she completed a course in supervision. Because the program has a supervisory emphasis, after completing the supervision course, all doctoral students are required to provide supervision to at least one master's-level student every semester. Doctoral students receive supervision of their supervision through weekly group meetings with a faculty member.

Phyllis has been assigned her first master's intern, Jena (age 38), who is just beginning her internship experience. Phyllis and Jena began the master's program at the same time several years ago and became good friends. However, Phyllis matriculated at a faster rate, and they grew apart when Jena was forced to take a leave of absence due to personal issues concerning her family (she is divorced with 2-year-old twin girls). Jena is overjoyed when she discovers that Phyllis will be her campus-based supervisor. Phyllis is also pleased and anticipates a rewarding supervisory relationship with Jena, much like their previous friendship and camaraderie.

During their initial supervisory meeting, Phyllis and Jena review the requirements for successful completion of Jena's 600-hour internship. Master's-level interns are expected to produce weekly audiotapes and monthly videotapes and to maintain a reflective journal. Doctoral supervisors are required to meet with their intern's on-site supervisor at least once during every semester.

Over the initial 5-week period of the supervisory relationship, things go smoothly. Jena brings both audio- and videotapes for review and seems receptive to Phyllis's feedback. Phyllis does note that Jena's counseling style is quite instinctive, and that she seems to have difficulty articulating a theoretical rationale for her interventions. However, Phyllis decides not to press this issue because most of the clients Jena has been assigned to counsel have career exploration or short-term counseling issues, and her clients seem to be doing well. Phyllis thinks Jena's case conceptualization skills probably will develop as she progresses through her internship experience.

When Phyllis and Jena meet during the 6th week of the semester, Jena announces that her site is so impressed with her skills that they are now referring more challenging cases to her, including clients with issues of clinical depression and substance abuse. When Phyllis asks whether Jena feels ready for the added responsibility, Jena replies rather sharply that she has as much "clinical" experience as Phyllis. Jena adds that she has relevant "life experiences" that Phyllis, being much younger, has yet to encounter. Phyllis, feeling somewhat uncomfortable, does not pursue the matter.

Jena begins counseling a female client who is experiencing severe depression and suicidal ideations. This client is a single female in her early 40s, with three small children, who is struggling with financial problems. After listening to several audiotapes, Phyllis has begun to feel that Jena is becoming somewhat enmeshed with the client. On the most recent tape, Phyllis heard Jena lead her client and give advice several times. When they meet for supervision, Phyllis asks Jena if she might be overidentifying with this client. Jena does not seem open to considering this possibility, and as they continue to review the taped session, Jena again states her belief that life experiences are at least as important, if not more important, than formal preparation for being an effective counselor. Phyllis makes a mental note to herself to ask her doctoral student supervision group for assistance on how to deal with supervisee resistance and to do some reading on the subject. At the end of the supervisory session, Phyllis reminds Jena about the requirement that they meet with Jena's on-site supervisor during the semester and asks Jena to set up the meeting. Jena says that she will schedule the meeting.

Over the next 3 weeks, Phyllis's concerns about Jena's lack of case conceptualization skills begin to grow. She is also troubled because Jena has not arranged the meeting with the on-site supervisor. At first Jena said that she forgot, and when Phyllis offered to call the on-site supervisor, Jena could not remember the supervisor's phone number. The next week Jena reported that the site supervisor was switching offices and her phone number was being changed.

At this point Phyllis has discussed strategies for dealing with supervisee resistance with her doctoral supervision group, without mentioning Jena's name, and she has done additional reading. Yet nothing she has tried seems to be working. She considered consulting with Dr. Walsh, the faculty member in charge of internships, but was afraid that if Jena were "red flagged" as having difficulties Jena's chances of being accepted into the doctoral program would be ruined. Jena had let her know that she intended to pursue her doctorate and, given her current home situation, she would not be able to apply to any other doctoral programs due to her lack of mobility. Also, Jena had once been her friend, for more than 2 years. Jena had juggled work, home, and school commitments in a way that had impressed Phyllis. In fact, Phyllis doubts that she could have done as well. If she gives Jena a little more time, Phyllis thinks Jena may become more accepting of her feedback.

Questions for Thought and Discussion

1. If you were the doctoral student supervisor in this case, what might you do at this point?
2. What are the possible sources for the difficulties in this supervisory relationship?

Analysis

Although Phyllis is a relative beginner as a doctoral student, she is qualified to serve as a supervisor to her master's-level intern. She has completed her course in supervision: "Prior to offering clinical supervision services, counselors are trained in supervision methods and techniques" (F.2.a.). When her supervisee appeared to become resistant to supervision, she attempted to resolve the problem by asking her supervision group for assistance and by consulting the literature for ideas.

Although Phyllis seems to be taking her supervision responsibilities seriously and is conscientiously searching for solutions to the problem, she might have avoided the problem altogether if she had consulted the *Code of Ethics* before she entered into the supervisory relationship with Jena. Standard F.3.d. states that supervisors "avoid accepting close relatives, romantic partners, or friends as supervisees." Realizing this, Phyllis could have approached Dr. Walsh, the faculty member in charge of internships, when she first learned that Jena had been assigned as her supervisee. Phyllis could have alerted Dr. Walsh to her previous friendship with Jena, and it seems likely that she could have been assigned a different supervisee.

If a change in assignment had not been possible for some reason, Phyllis should have considered the potential problems that could arise as a result of her previous friendship with Jena. During their initial supervisory meeting, a frank and open discussion of the potential difficulties that could occur as a result of their past relationship as friends and peers might have avoided some of the difficulties that developed.

It is not uncommon for students to have difficulty both supervising and being supervised by other students (Miller, 1996). Supervisory relationships can be challenging when they are tripartite in nature, involving a client, supervisee, and supervisor. When supervisory relationships are more complex—such as those that involve a client, a supervisee, a novice supervisor, peers of the supervisor who provide consultation and advice, the faculty member who supervises the supervisor, and the on-site supervisor—sorting out the roles and responsibilities can be a daunting task (Herlihy & Corey, 2006; Remley & Herlihy, 2005). It is essential to consider the needs and rights of all parties involved when students are placed in the position of providing supervision to, or receiving supervision from, other students (Miller, 1996).

Phyllis is in a difficult position. She wants to protect her supervisee from any possible repercussions of being identified as "resistant to supervision," yet she wants to find a way to break through the resistance so that Jena can benefit fully from the supervisory experience and learn and grow as a counselor. Phyllis may also be struggling with her own self-doubts as a novice supervisor.

Phyllis may need to set aside her reservations and contact Dr. Walsh. As the faculty member in charge of internships, Dr. Walsh has an ethical obligation to "ensure that the rights of peers are not compromised when students . . . provide clinical supervision" (F.6.e.). Dr. Walsh may be able to assist Phyllis in several ways. He might arrange for Jena to receive supervision from a different doctoral student supervisor, one who did not complete the master's program at the same university and who would not already know Jena. If it is not feasible to make a switch in supervisors at midsemester, Dr. Walsh might offer to provide Phyllis with individual supervision of her work with Jena. This could assist Phyllis in dealing with issues of supervisee resistance, her own self-doubts, and the boundary issues involved in the supervisory relationship.

Borders (2006) has pointed out that it is useful for doctoral students to encounter boundary and multiple role issues *before* they graduate. Recognizing and learning how to handle difficult situations can provide a valuable learning opportunity for student supervisors and may help them to recognize and effectively manage such situations in the future.

Questions for Further Reflection

1. How do you think you would react if you were in Phyllis's situation?
2. Do you think you might listen differently to supervision suggestions offered by a fellow student than you would to suggestions made by a faculty member? Explain.
3. Do you think students should be put in the position of supervising other students? What are the risks and benefits involved in this practice?

Chapter 10

The Relationship Between Law and Ethics

Mary A. Hermann

Counselors sometimes find it difficult to distinguish between legal and ethical issues. Law and ethics are two distinct concepts, but they overlap significantly. Although law and ethics are closely related to each other, there are some significant differences. According to Remley and Herlihy (2005), laws dictate the minimum standards of behavior that society will tolerate, whereas ethics represent the ideal standards expected by a professional group. Both the law and the *Code of Ethics* provide guidance for acceptable counseling practice.

As a general rule, the *Code of Ethics* advises adherence to the law. However, legal and ethical standards can create conflicting duties, such as balancing the ethical right of minor clients to confidentiality with the legal rights of parents. In such cases, fulfilling both legal and ethical obligations can be challenging.

Ethical standards are not legal mandates. Yet ethical standards could be used by a court of law as evidence of the "standard of care" in the counseling community. The standard of care is applied in lawsuits to determine whether an accused counselor may be guilty of malpractice. *Malpractice,* according to *Black's Law Dictionary* (Black, 1990), is a failure when rendering professional services "to exercise that degree of skill and learning commonly applied under all the circumstances in the community by the average prudent reputable member of the profession" (p. 959). Thus, in determining whether a counselor is guilty of malpractice in a particular situation, the question would be whether the counselor's actions (or failure to take action) were like the actions that other prudent and similarly trained mental health professionals practicing in the same community would have taken.

Legal Standards

Counselors' legal obligations emanate from state and federal constitutional and statutory law. Counselors are bound to follow federal laws as well as constitutional and statutory guidelines in the state in which they practice. Case law helps to define counselors' legal duties as well. Hudgins and Vacca (1999) explain that constitutional provisions and statutory law "lack practical meaning and remain legal abstractions until they are interpreted by a court of law" (p. 3). Federal district courts in each state and federal appeals courts in the various regions of the country interpret federal law. State courts interpret state law. Counselors' legal obligations are influenced by the interpretations of the law of the state in which they practice and the interpretations of federal law binding in their jurisdiction. Additionally, the case law of other state courts and federal courts in other jurisdictions can be persuasive to courts in the counselor's jurisdiction.

To practice counseling within the guidelines of the law, counselors need to be aware of the legal statutes and case law such as requirements to report suspected child abuse and counselors' duty to warn. Counselors can gain information on relevant legal issues through professional literature and continuing education programs. Furthermore, because the law is complex, counselors are also wise to consult an attorney on legal issues.

Failure to fulfill legal obligations can result in counselors violating criminal laws, civil laws, or both. Violations of criminal law are prosecuted by the government and can result in fines and imprisonment. Civil law actions are brought by individuals and can result in the counselor paying monetary damages to the aggrieved party.

Ethical Standards

The 2005 *Code of Ethics* is designed to provide the members of ACA and their clients with information on the nature of counselors' ethical responsibilities. Specifically, the *Code* establishes principles of ethical behavior and best practice, serves as an ethical guide, and is designed to be a basis for answering ethical inquiries and processing ethical complaints. All members of ACA are expected to adhere to the *Code*. Consequences for engaging in unethical behavior include suspending ACA membership or expelling the member who acted unethically. State licensure boards can also suspend or revoke a counselor's license to practice if the counselor engages in unethical behavior.

An addition to the 2005 *Code of Ethics* is the inclusion of aspirational introductions in each section, which set the tone for the section and provide an opportunity for reflection. The aspirational introductions represent ideal behaviors whereas the standards provide guidance regarding the standard of care in the counseling community. Thus, as courts are concerned with competent practice as opposed to ideal behaviors, counselors are not likely to be held to aspirational ideals in a court of law.

Avoiding Malpractice

Few events are more distressing for counselors than to learn that they are about to be sued or are being sued for malpractice. Perhaps the best defense against malpractice claims is to know the laws that apply to your practice and to practice at the highest level of aspirational ethics. Other risk management strategies that counselors can use include (1) consulting with colleagues when in doubt about an ethical or clinical issue, (2) consulting with an attorney when a legal issue arises in practice, (3) practicing only within the boundaries of your competence (see Chapter 4), (4) informing supervisors when situations arise that may have legal or ethical ramifications, (5) carrying professional liability insurance, and (6) keeping up to date with ethical and legal standards and developments.

Conclusion

Managing legal and ethical issues can be challenging, and knowledge of the *Code of Ethics* and the legal guidelines applicable to your practice is imperative. However, there is often no clear answer to a legal or ethical dilemma. When considering ethical issues, counselors aspire to act in the best interest of the client. When presented with an issue that could invoke legal liability, counselors are expected to act in a manner consistent with the standard of care in the community. Consulting with other counselors can help establish what is in the best interest of the client as well as the standard of care in the community. To ascertain the legal ramifications of their actions, counselors should consult with an attorney.

Case Study 19

Managing Ethical and Legal Obligations

Mary A. Hermann

Mark is a licensed professional counselor who has been counseling Paul, who is going through a divorce, for 3 months. Paul has been married for 9 years and has two young children: Monica, age 7, and Jeffrey, age 3. During his sessions with Mark, Paul discloses that, after he moved out of the family home 4 months ago, he had a brief extramarital affair. Paul also reveals that he has occasionally used marijuana, although he states that he has never used "hard drugs." He tells Mark that Debbie, his estranged wife, does not know about the affair or his occasional marijuana use.

During the counseling sessions, Paul expresses remorse over his extramarital affair and talks about how much he misses being with his children. Paul has been picking up the children once or twice a week after he gets off work and spending the evening with them, returning them home at their bedtime. He tells Mark that he is very concerned about his children's welfare because his daughter Monica has told him that "mommy has a boyfriend" and that he is "mean" to her and her brother. Although Paul doesn't suspect physical abuse, he thinks this man is being verbally abusive to the children. What Monica has told him has also led Paul to believe that his wife has been drinking alcohol to excess at times. Paul has tried to suggest to Debbie that she seek counseling for herself and the children, but she has told him, "*You're* the one who needs help!" Paul has decided to seek custody of his children.

Mark receives a subpoena from Debbie's attorney. The subpoena requests that Mark appear at a deposition with any and all records related to his client, Paul. Mark contacts Paul to discuss the subpoena. Paul states that he does not want Mark to disclose any information related to their counseling sessions, especially information related to Paul's extramarital affair and marijuana use.

Questions for Thought and Discussion

1. What are the legal issues involved in this case?
2. What are the ethical issues involved in this case?
3. If you were in Mark's position, what would you do?

Analysis

A subpoena is a legal document requesting testimony in a legal proceeding and/or documentation related to a legal cause of action. Whenever a counselor receives a subpoena, the counselor is wise to seek legal advice. Not all subpoenas are valid. The documents may look official, but sometimes subpoenas request information that is confidential or privileged.

Privileged communication is a legal term that refers to the admissibility in a court proceeding of information gained from a protected relationship. Under some privileged communication laws, clients can prevent counselors from disclosing information obtained in a counseling relationship. It is important to note that privilege belongs to the client, not the counselor. Accordingly, the client can waive privilege. Counselors are required to abide by privileged communication laws. Standard B.2.a. states that the general requirement to keep information confidential does not apply when legal requirements demand that it be shared. Thus, Mark should seek legal advice on how to respond to the subpoena.

Mark should let his attorney know that his client has requested that he not disclose the confidential information gained in the counseling sessions. He should inform his attorney that, according to his profession's *Code of Ethics,* if a court orders disclosure of confidential information and the client has not consented to such disclosure, he has an ethical duty to request that the disclosure not be required because of the potential for harm to the counseling relationship or to the client (B.2.c.). If the court mandates the disclosure in spite of such a request, counselors are ethically obligated to provide only essential information (B.2.d.).

Mark needs to consider whether exceptions to his ethical duty to maintain confidentiality apply in this case. If Mark believes that Paul is placing his children in clear and imminent danger, Mark would be ethically bound to report this information. Thus, Mark needs to ascertain whether Paul's use of marijuana is putting his children in danger. This could be the case if Mark is using the drug while he is spending time with the children or while driving them to and from their mother's home. If Mark determines that Paul's drug use is endangering his children, Mark would have to make a report to Child Protective Services in his jurisdiction.

Mark needs to be aware that reporting suspected child abuse is a legal as well as an ethical obligation. State laws describe the procedures involved in making these reports as well as the consequences of not reporting. Mark may be justified in being concerned about Debbie's boyfriend's behavior toward Paul's children, but he does not have direct knowledge of abuse. The question of possible abuse would best be addressed by Paul's divorce attorney.

It is important for Mark to remember that his role is that of a counselor and not a child custody evaluator. Mark has not even met Debbie and has no direct, unbiased information regarding her fitness as a parent. Debbie's behavior may or may not be putting the children at risk. Mark has worked as Paul's counselor and has not done a child custody evaluator's extensive investigation. Thus, Mark is not in a position to make a judgment about custody. Accordingly, when meeting with an attorney regarding the subpoena, Mark should clarify his role as Paul's counselor and not a child custody evaluator.

Counselors can be accused of violating a client's privacy if they give confidential information when a subpoena is invalid. However, failure to respond appropriately to a valid subpoena could result in being held in contempt of court and fined or jailed until compliance. An attorney who is aware of the intricacies of confidentiality and privileged communication in the state or federal court issuing the subpoena is in the best position to guide Mark's response to the subpoena.

Questions for Further Reflection

1. If you needed an attorney to assist you with a question about your counseling practice, how would you find one?
2. How will you gain the legal and ethical knowledge you need to practice in an ethical manner and minimize your legal liability?

Case Study 20

A Pregnant Teenager: A School Counselor's Quandary

Danielle Shareef

Michael works as a school counselor for alternative programs in a rural high school with a student population of 1,300. He is assigned to work with "at-risk" students whose home environments may be affected by poverty, absentee parents, drug exposure or use, or domestic violence. Michael conducts weekly group and individual counseling sessions with these students. As a married father of two adolescent girls, Michael often finds himself counseling students with issues he hopes his daughters will never encounter.

One morning Jenny, a 17-year-old sophomore, walks into Michael's office distraught. She explains that she requested to be excused from class to see a counselor because she was involved in a verbal altercation with another student and didn't want to get into a fight. Jenny says she gets into a lot of arguments lately at school. As Michael talks further with Jenny, he learns that she has been dealing with stress at home as a result of mistrust and disobedience issues between her and her mother. Jenny also reveals that she is approximately 6 weeks pregnant and that her aunt had taken her to the doctor for confirmation without her mother's knowledge.

Michael surmises that dealing with the pressure of concealing her pregnancy from her mother probably is contributing to the fact that Jenny is getting into arguments at school. After further discussion, Jenny says that she refuses to tell her mother because she is uncertain whether she wants to have the baby. If she chooses not to have it, then her mother will never know she was pregnant. If she tells her mother about her condition, Jenny believes her mother will not allow her to have an abortion. Jenny asks to end the session, stating that she has to go take an English test. Michael, aware that he is experiencing some strong emotional reactions as he talks with Jenny, agrees to her request and asks her to come back and talk with him some more at the end of the school day. Jenny agrees to do so.

After the session, Michael processes his feelings, values, and personal beliefs about teen pregnancy and abortion. He is not a staunch supporter of abortion, but he believes every adult woman has the right to choose whether she wants to give birth. However, he doesn't think this position applies to minors. He is totally against teen pregnancy and does not believe that young girls should be having and raising babies. He wants to strike a balance in his work with Jenny, providing her with support in her decision making without implying that Jenny should have an abortion. He is also concerned about whether he has a legal obligation to notify her parents.

Questions for Thought and Discussion

1. If you were the counselor in this case, how might you react to Jenny's revelation that she is pregnant?
2. Given Michael's values, what approach should he take to assist Jenny in her decision of whether to continue or terminate the pregnancy?
3. Do you think Michael should inform Jenny's parents about her condition? Why or why not?

Analysis

Counselors need to be aware of their personal biases and values in order to be nonjudgmental and convey unconditional positive regard in the counseling relationship. Michael is conscious of his personal beliefs regarding teen parenthood and abortion, yet he didn't anticipate the strong feelings that Jenny's disclosure would arouse in him. His concern is intensified by his uncertainty about whether Jenny's parents need to be notified. Because she is a minor, it may seem to Michael that her parents should be involved in such a critical decision, but he may not have ethical or legal justification to inform her parents.

Standard A.4.b. states that "counselors are aware of their own values, attitudes, beliefs, and behaviors and avoid imposing values." This standard also requires that counselors respect the diversity of clients. Michael knows that socioeconomic factors and cultural views of morality influence people's perspectives on teen parenthood and that, as a middle-class White male, his beliefs may differ from those of Jenny and her family. He is appropriately concerned that these differences and his values might affect his counseling interventions with Jenny.

Michael is uncertain whether he has either an ethical or a legal obligation (or both) to notify Jenny's parents. He looks to the *ACA Code of Ethics* and finds several standards that seem relevant to the situation. Standard B.1.c. informs him that "counselors do not share confidential information without client consent or without sound legal or ethical justification." Jenny has made it clear that she does not want her mother to be informed about her condition, and Michael is not sure just what would constitute "sound legal or ethical justification" to inform Jenny's mother against her wishes. He looks to the section of the *Code* that deals with exceptions to confidentiality and learns that "the general requirement that counselors keep information confidential does not apply when disclosure is required to protect clients or identified others from serious and foreseeable harm" (B.2.a.). It seems to him that Jenny, a healthy 17-year-old, is not placed in "serious" physical harm by her pregnancy. But, he wonders, what about harm to the fetus if she were to decide to have an abortion? Michael quickly realizes that this is a highly controversial and divisive issue in American society at large, and that he certainly does not have a definitive answer to that question.

Michael then searches through the *Code* for guidance on working with minor clients. He finds that he may enlist others, including family members, as positive resources when appropriate, with client consent (A.1.d.). But Jenny has not given her consent. He reads Standard B.5.b., which informs him that he should "respect the inherent rights and responsibilities of parents/guardians over the welfare of their children/charges according to law." This standard suggests to Michael that his quandary has both legal and ethical dimensions. What he knows about applicable law is that, in his state, parental consent is required to terminate a pregnancy of a minor under the age of 18. However, if a judge deems the minor to be mature enough and reasons are justifiable, a judge can grant permission to terminate a pregnancy without parental consent. Michael wonders whether it would be appropriate for him to share this information with Jenny. If he did so, would he be, in effect, giving legal advice?

Michael thinks the answer to his dilemma may be in his school district's policy manual. He peruses the manual to see whether the district has a policy regarding parental notification of student pregnancy. To his chagrin, he finds that his district does not have a written policy. He remains uncertain of what he should do in continuing to work with Jenny.

Michael's reflections have enabled him to identify a number of issues: the possibility that his personal values may interfere with his ability to counsel Jenny effectively; the ethical question of whether he should respect the confidentiality of Jenny's disclosure or inform her parents; and legal questions regarding the rights of minors and the rights of their parents. Before he meets with Jenny at the end of the school day, he would be wise to consult with a fellow school counselor whose judgment he trusts to address both his personal values issues and his ethical questions about the limitations of confidentiality. He should approach his principal and, without revealing Jenny's identity, ask the principal to get advice from the school district's attorney on his legal obligations in counseling a pregnant student. If Michael decides that his personal feelings may make it difficult to maintain his objectivity in counseling Jenny, he should be prepared to facilitate a referral to another counselor. If he decides to continue to counsel Jenny, his course of action will be affected by the legal opinion he receives. If he is required to notify Jenny's parents, he will need to inform Jenny before he does so. If he is not required to notify the parents, his task will be to assist her in considering her choices and to encourage her to inform her parents when and if she is ready to do so.

Questions for Further Reflection

1. What risks might Michael be taking if he continues to counsel Jenny and does not inform her parents of her pregnancy? What are the risks involved in telling them?
2. What are the potential benefits of involving the parents? What benefits might come from respecting Jenny's confidentiality?
3. What personal values and beliefs do you hold that could interfere with your ability to counsel a client effectively?

Part V

Highlights of Ethical Practice

In these concluding comments, we summarize much of the material in the casebook by putting into focus some principles that we believe are important for counselors to review throughout their professional lives. The emphasis is on considering the cultural context of ethical decision making. Because we work in a pluralistic society, it is essential that we increase our consciousness of ways to apply the ethical standards from a perspective that recognizes and respects diversity.

Ethics From a Multicultural Perspective

Issues of multiculturalism and diversity are addressed throughout the 2005 *ACA Code of Ethics*. Cultural considerations are specifically addressed in numerous standards including those that deal with the counseling relationship, informed consent, bartering, accepting gifts, confidentiality and privacy, professional responsibility, assessment and diagnosis, supervision, and education and training programs. Additional information on multicultural competencies can be found on the ACA Web site (www.counseling.org).

Respecting diversity means that you are committed to acquiring the knowledge, skills, personal awareness, and sensitivity that are essential to working effectively with diverse client populations. A new multicultural paradigm has emerged that considers diversity from a multifaceted perspective that is not focused exclusively on race and ethnicity (Lee & Ramsey, 2006). Rather, cultural diversity addresses broader issues including gender, sexual orientation, disability, and socioeconomic disadvantage. From this perspective, culturally responsive counselors need to possess the awareness, knowledge, and skills to effectively address the various aspects of cultural diversity that clients may present. Counselors who are not aware of cultural dynamics and who do not address the impact of culture on counseling practice risk engaging in unethical conduct. Counselors must address the challenges of diversity in a manner that is both culturally responsive and ethically responsible (Lee & Ramsey, 2006). Highlights of this perspective that we encourage you to reflect on as you examine the ethical standards and apply them to a range of different situations include the following:

- *Become aware of your own personal needs, values, and worldview.* It is your responsibility to consider any prejudices or biases you may have, even though many of them may be subtle. Cultural self-awareness includes counselors' awareness of their own assumptions, values, and biases (Roysircar, 2004). Self-exploration about one's own cultural heritage provides a pathway for understanding and appreciating differences in others. A counselor's cultural self-awareness is essential for effective and culturally relevant counseling.
- *Honestly examine your own assumptions, expectations, and attitudes about the counseling process.* To some extent, we all are culture-bound, and it takes a concerted effort for us to monitor our biases and beliefs so that they do not impede our work with a wide range of clients.
- *Acquire training in counseling persons from diverse backgrounds.* If you have not received adequate training in counseling persons from diverse backgrounds, realize that ethical practice demands that you find a way to acquire this competence. If you are not adequately prepared to work with diversity, it will not be ethical for you to provide direct counseling services to certain clients. Of course, this does not mean that you will need to have expertise in every culture or subculture, but it is important that you consider your limitations in working with diverse client groups and take steps to increase your competence as an effective multicultural counselor. The reality of working in a pluralistic society entails learning a variety of perspectives to meet the unique needs of clients.
- *Know when to make referrals.* When you do not have the competencies to work with a particular client, make referrals to appropriate resources. However, we hope that you would not be too quick to refer any client who might be challenging for you. Consider a referral only in those areas where you are not able to deliver competent service.
- *Seek consultation to expand your knowledge base.* Seeking consultation is an excellent way to develop increased knowledge and skills in multicultural counseling. You may need to acquire specialized training in working with persons from diverse cultural, ethnic, and racial backgrounds such as individuals from various socioeconomic groups, gay men or lesbians, or clients from different religious backgrounds. Understanding the role of gender socialization is also critical in the counseling process.
- *Participate in continuing education on diversity.* Continuing education is a pathway toward achieving competence in working with diversity. Professional development opportunities might include activities that examine cultural, social, psychological, political, economic, and historical dimensions.
- *Infuse counselor education programs with diversity training.* In the area of teaching, training, and supervision of counselors, it is essential that those responsible for counselor education programs infuse material

related to human diversity into all courses. This includes material related to cultural, ethnic, racial, gender, sexual orientation, and socioeconomic differences. The implications of these differences need to be explored as they pertain to counseling practice, research, and training. Ethical practice demands that counselor educators discuss the cultural limitations and biases associated with traditional counseling theories, techniques, and research findings.

As we mentioned in the Introduction, there is a difference between mandatory ethics and aspirational ethics. We hope you will strive for the highest level of ethical functioning and consider diversity in your practice of aspirational ethics. All of the standards in the *Code of Ethics* can be interpreted against a framework of diversity.

The Challenge of Developing Your Personal Ethics

As a professional counselor, you are expected to know the ethical standards of your professional organizations, and you are also expected to exercise good judgment in applying these principles to particular cases. You will find that interpreting the ethical standards and applying them to particular situations demand the utmost ethical sensitivity. Even responsible practitioners differ over how to apply established ethical principles to specific situations. You will be challenged to deal with questions that do not always have obvious answers. You will need to decide how to act in ways that will further the best interests of your clients.

Resolving the ethical dilemmas you will face requires a commitment to questioning your own behavior and motives. A sign of your good faith is the willingness to share your struggles openly with colleagues or fellow students. Such consultation can be of great help in clarifying issues by giving you other perspectives. It is essential that you keep yourself informed about laws affecting your practice, keep up to date in your specialty field, stay abreast of developments in ethical practice, reflect on the impact that your values have on your practice, and be willing to engage in honest self-examination.

It is our hope that you will think about the guidelines and principles explored in this casebook, apply them to yourself, and attempt to formulate your own views and positions on the topics we have raised. As you have seen, ethical thinking is not a simple matter of black-or-white categorization; there are gray areas in most of the ethical dilemmas you will face. The task of developing a sense of professional and ethical responsibility never really ends.

References

Allen, V. B. (1986). A historical perspective of the AACD Ethics Committee. *Journal of Counseling & Development, 64,* 293.

American Association for Marriage and Family Therapy. (2001). *AAMFT code of ethics.* Washington, DC: Author.

American Counseling Association. (1995). *Code of ethics and standards of practice.* Alexandria, VA: Author.

American Counseling Association. (2003). *Policies and procedures for processing complaints of ethical violations.* Alexandria, VA: Author.

American Counseling Association. (2005). *ACA code of ethics.* Alexandria, VA: Author.

Arredondo, P. (1991). Counseling Latinas. In C. C. Lee & B. L. Richardson (Eds.), *Multicultural issues in counseling: New approaches to diversity* (pp. 143–156). Alexandria, VA: American Counseling Association.

Association for Specialists in Group Work. (1998). Best practice guidelines. *Journal for Specialists in Group Work, 23*(3), 237–244.

Association for Specialists in Group Work. (1999). Principles for diversity-competent group workers. *Journal for Specialists in Group Work, 24*(1), 7–14.

Association for Specialists in Group Work. (2000). Professional standards for the training of group workers. *The Group Worker, 29*(3), 1–10.

Beauchamp, T. L., & Childress, J. F. (1994). *Principles of biomedical ethics* (5th ed.). Oxford, England: Oxford University Press.

Black, H. C. (1990). *Black's law dictionary* (6th ed.). St. Paul, MN: West.

Bongar, B. (2002). *The suicidal patient: Clinical and legal standards of care* (2nd ed.). Washington, DC: American Psychological Association.

Borders, L. D. (2006). Subtle boundary issues in supervision. In B. Herlihy & G. Corey, *Boundary issues in counseling: Multiple roles and relationships* (2nd ed.). Alexandria, VA: American Counseling Association.

Bureau of Labor Statistics, U.S. Department of Labor. (2004). *Working in the 21st century.* Retrieved June 10, 2004, from http://www.bls.gov/opub/working/home.htm

Campbell, C. D., & Gordon, M. C. (2003). Acknowledging the inevitable: Understanding multiple relationships in rural practice. *Professional Psychology: Research and Practice, 34*(4), 430–434.

Casto, C., Caldwell, C., & Salazar, C. F. (2005). Creating mentoring relationships between female faculty and students in counselor education: Guidelines for potential mentees and mentors. *Journal of Counseling & Development, 83,* 331–336.

Chauvin, J. C., & Remley, T. P. (1996). Responding to allegations of unethical conduct. *Journal of Counseling & Development, 74,* 563–568.

Clark, D. C. (1998). The evaluation and management of the suicidal patient. In P. M. Kleespies (Ed.), *Emergencies in mental health practice: Evaluation and management* (pp. 75–94). New York: Guilford.

Commission on Rehabilitation Counselor Certification. (2002). *Code of professional ethics for rehabilitation counselors.* Rolling Meadows, IL: Author.

Corey, G., Corey, M. S., & Callanan, P. (2007). *Issues and ethics in the helping professions* (7th ed.) Belmont, CA: Thomson Brooks/Cole .

Corey, M. S., & Corey, G. (2006). *Groups: Process and practice* (7th ed.). Belmont, CA: Thomson Brooks/Cole.

Cottone, R. R. (2001). A social constructivism model of ethical decision making in counseling. *Journal of Counseling & Development, 79,* 39–45.

Cottone, R. R. (2005). Detrimental therapist–client relationships—Beyond thinking of "dual" or "multiple" roles: Reflections on the 2001 *AAMFT Code of Ethics. American Journal of Family Therapy, 33,* 1–17.

Cottone, R. R., & Tarvydas, V. M. (2003). *Ethical and professional issues in counseling* (2nd ed.). Upper Saddle River, NJ: Merrill/Prentice-Hall.

Council for Accreditation of Counseling and Related Educational Programs. (2001). *CACREP: The 2001 standards* [Statement]. Alexandria, VA: Author.

Crawford, R. J. (1994). *Avoiding counselor malpractice.* Alexandria, VA: American Counseling Association.

Delgado-Romero, E. (2003). Ethics and multicultural competence. In D. B Pope-Davis, H. L. K. Coleman, W. M. Liu, & R. L. Toporek (Eds.), *Handbook of multicultural competencies in counseling and psychology* (pp. 313–329). Thousand Oaks, CA: Sage.

Durodoye, B. A. (2006). Ethical issues in multicultural counseling. In C. C. Lee (Ed.), *Multicultural issues in counseling: New approaches to diversity* (3rd ed., pp. 357–368). Alexandria, VA: American Counseling Association.

Favazza. R. K. (1999). Self-mutilation. In D. G. Jacobs (Ed.), *The Harvard Medical School guide to suicide assessment and intervention* (pp. 125–145). San Francisco: Jossey-Bass.

Forester-Miller, H., & Davis, T. E. (1996). *A practitioner's guide to ethical decision making.* Alexandria, VA: American Counseling Association.

Glosoff, H. L., Benshoff, J. M., Hosie, T., & Maki, D. R. (1995). The 1994 model legislation for licensed professional counselors. *Journal of Counseling & Development, 74*(2), 209–220.

Golden, L. (1992). Dual role relationships in private practice. In B. Herlihy & G. Corey, *Dual relationships in counseling* (pp. 130–133). Alexandria, VA: American Association for Counseling and Development.

Haas, L. J., & Malouf, J. L. (1995). *Keeping up the good work: A practitioner's guide to mental health ethics* (2nd ed.). Sarasota, FL: Professional Resource Press.

Haynes, R., Corey, G., & Moulton, P. (2003). *Clinical supervision in the helping professions: A practical guide.* Pacific Grove, CA: Brooks/Cole.

Herlihy, B., & Corey, G. (1994). Codes of ethics as catalysts for improving practice. *Ethical Issues in Professional Counseling, 2*(3), 2–12.

Herlihy, B., & Corey, G. (2006). *Boundary issues in counseling: Multiple roles and responsibilities* (2nd ed.). Alexandria, VA: American Counseling Association.

Herlihy, B., & Flowers, L. (2006.) Ethical and legal issues in group work. In D. Capuzzi, D. R. Gross, & M. D. Stauffer (Eds.), *Introduction to group work* (4th ed.). Denver, CO: Love.

Herlihy, B., & Remley, T. P., Jr. (1995). Unified ethical standards: A challenge for professionalism. *Journal of Counseling & Development, 74,* 130–133.

Herlihy, B. R., & Watson, Z. E. P. (2004). Assisted suicide: Ethical issues. In D. Capuzzi (Ed.), *Suicide across the life span: Implications for counselors* (pp. 163–184). Alexandria, VA: American Counseling Association.

Herlihy, B., & Watson, Z. E. (2006). Social justice and counseling ethics. In C. C. Lee (Ed.), *Counseling for social justice* (2nd ed.). Alexandria, VA: American Counseling Association.

Hudgins, H. C., Jr., & Vacca, R. S. (1999). *Law and education: Contemporary issues and court decisions* (5th ed.). New York: LEXIS Publishing.

International Association of Marriage and Family Counselors. (2002). Ethical code for International Association of Marriage and Family Counselors. *The Family Journal, 1,* 73–77.

Jennings, L., Sovereign, A., Bottorff, N., Mussell, M., & Vye, C. (2005). Nine ethical values of master therapists. *Journal of Mental Health Counseling, 27,* 32–47.

Johnson, W. B., Ralph, J., & Johnson, S. J. (2005). Managing multiple roles in embedded environments: The case of aircraft carrier psychology. *Professional Psychology: Research and Practice, 36,* 73–81.

Jordan, A. E., & Meara, N. M. (1991). The role of virtues and principle in moral collapse: A response to Miller. *Professional Psychology: Research and Practice, 22,* 107–109.

Kitchener, K. S., & Harding, S. S. (1990). Dual role relationships. In B. Herlihy & L. Golden (Eds.), *Ethical standards casebook* (4th ed., pp. 146–154). Alexandria, VA: American Association for Counseling and Development.

Knapp, S., & VandeCreek, L. (2003). *A guide to the 2002 revision of the American Psychological Association's ethics code.* Sarasota, FL: Professional Resource Press.

Koocher, G. P., & Keith-Spiegel, P. (1998). *Ethics in psychology: Professional standards and cases* (2nd ed.). New York: Oxford University Press.

LaFromboise, T. D., Foster, S., & James, A. (1996). Ethics in multicultural counseling. In P. B. Pedersen, J. G. Draguns, W. J. Lonner & J. E. Trimble (Eds.), *Counseling across cultures* (4th ed., pp. 47–72). Thousand Oaks, CA: Sage.

Lazarus, A. A., & Zur, O. (Eds.). (2002). *Dual relationships and psychotherapy.* New York: Springer.

Lee, C. C. (2006). Entering the cross-cultural zone: Meeting the challenges of culturally responsive counseling. In C. C. Lee (Ed.), *Multicultural issues in counseling: New approaches to diversity* (3rd ed., pp. 13–22). Alexandria, VA: American Counseling Association.

Lee, C. C., & Chuang, B. (2005). Counseling people of color. In D. Capuzzi & D. R. Gross (Eds.), *Introduction to the counseling profession* (4th ed.). New York: Pearson Allyn & Bacon.

Lee, C. C., & Kurilla, V. (1997). Ethics and multiculturalism: The challenge of diversity. In Hatherleigh Editorial Board (Ed.), *The Hatherleigh guide to ethics in therapy* (pp. 235–248). Long Island City, NY: Hatherleigh Press.

Lee, C. C., & Ramsey, C. J. (2006). Multicultural counseling: A new paradigm for a new century. In C. C. Lee (Ed.), *Multicultural issues in counseling: New approaches to diversity* (3rd ed., pp. 3–12). Alexandria, VA: American Counseling Association.

Lopez-Baez, S. I. (2006). Counseling Latinas: Culturally responsive interventions. In C. C. Lee (Ed.), *Multicultural issues in counseling: New approaches to diversity* (3rd ed., pp. 187–194). Alexandria, VA: American Counseling Association.

McMahon, M., & Simons, R. (2004). Supervision training for professional counselors: An exploratory study. *Counselor Education and Supervision, 43*(4), 301–309.

Meara, N. M., Schmidt, L. D., & Day, J. D. (1996). Principles and virtues: A foundation for ethical decisions, policies, and character. *The Counseling Psychologist, 24,* 4–77.

Miller, G. (1996). The supervision of students by students. In B. Herlihy & G. Corey, *ACA ethical standards casebook* (5th ed., pp. 281–284). Alexandria, VA: American Counseling Association.

Miller, M. C. (1999). Suicide-prevention contracts: Advantages, disadvantages, and an alternative approach. In D. G. Jacobs (Ed.), *The Harvard Medical School guide to suicide assessment and intervention* (pp. 463–481). San Francisco: Jossey-Bass.

Moleski, S. M., & Kiselica, M. S. (2005). Dual relationships: A continuum ranging from the destructive to the therapeutic. *Journal of Counseling & Development, 83,* 3–11.

National Center for Educational Statistics. (1997). *The social context of education.* Washington, DC: Author.

Pack-Brown, S. P., & Williams, C. B. (2003). *Ethics in a multicultural context.* Thousand Oaks, CA: Sage.

Pope, K. S., & Vasquez, M. J. T. (1998). *Ethics in psychotherapy and counseling* (2nd ed.). San Francisco: Jossey-Bass.

Rave, E. J., & Larsen, C. C. (1995). *Ethical decision making in therapy: Feminist perspectives.* New York: Guilford Press.

Remley, T. P., & Herlihy, B. (2005). *Ethical, legal, and professional issues in counseling* (2nd ed.). Upper Saddle River, NJ: Merrill/Prentice-Hall.

Ridley, C. R., Liddle, M. C., Hill, C. L., & Li, L. C. (2001). Ethical decision making in multicultural counseling. In J. G. Ponterotto, J. M. Casas, L. A. Suzuki, & C. M. Alexander (Eds.), *Handook of multicultural counseling* (2nd ed., pp. 165–188). Thousand Oaks, CA: Sage.

Roysircar, G. (2004). Cultural self-awareness assessment: Practice examples from psychology training. *Professional Psychology: Research and Practice, 35*(6), 658–666.

Salo, M. M., & Shumate, S. G. (1993). *Counseling minor clients.* Alexandria, VA: American Counseling Association.

Slaby, A. E. (1998). Outpatient management of suicidal patients. In B. Bongar, A. L. Berman, R. W. Maris, M. M. Silverman, E. A. Harris, & W. L. Packman (Eds.), *Risk management with suicidal patients* (pp. 34–64). New York: Guilford Press.

Sleek, S. (1994, December). Ethical dilemmas plague rural practice. *APA Monitor,* pp. 26–27.

Sonne, J. L., & Pope, K. S. (1991). Treating victims of therapist–patient sexual involvement. *Psychotherapy, 28,* 174–187.

Stadler, H. A. (1986). Making hard choices: Clarifying controversial ethical issues. *Journal of Counseling and Human Development, 19,* 1–10.

Sue, D. W. (1996). Ethical issues in multicultural counseling. In B. Herlihy & G. Corey, *ACA ethical standards casebook* (5th ed., pp. 193–197). Alexandria, VA: American Counseling Association.

Sue, D. W., & Sue, D. (2003). *Counseling the culturally diverse: Theory and practice* (4th ed.). Indianapolis, IN: Wiley.

Syme, G. (2003). *Dual relationships in counselling and psychotherapy.* London: Sage.

Tarasoff v. Regents of University of California, 13c.3D177, 529 p.2D553; 118 California Reporter, 129 (1974).

Tarvydas, V. M. (1998). Ethical decision-making processes. In R. R. Cottone & V. M. Tarvydas (Eds.), *Ethical and professional issues in counseling* (pp. 144–155). Upper Saddle River, NJ: Prentice-Hall.

U.S. Bureau of the Census. (2004). *U.S. interim projections by age, sex, race, and Hispanic origin.* Washington, DC: Author.

Vasquez, M. J. T. (1994). Latinas. In L. Comas-Diaz & B. Greene (Eds.), *Women of color* (pp. 135–162). New York: Guilford Press.

Walden, S. (1997). The counselor/client partnership in ethical practice. In B. Herlihy & G. Corey, *Boundary issues in counseling: Multiple roles and responsibilities* (pp. 61–72). Alexandria, VA: American Counseling Association.

Walden, S. (2006). Inclusion of the client's voice in ethical practice. In B. Herlihy & G. Corey, *Boundary issues in counseling: Multiple roles and responsibilities* (2nd ed.). Alexandria, VA: American Counseling Association.

Warren, E. S. (2005). Future colleague or convenient friend: The ethics of mentorship. *Counseling and Values, 49,* 141–146.

Watson, Z. E., Herlihy, B. R., & Pierce, L. A. (2006). Forging the link between multicultural competence and ethical counseling practice: A historical perspective. *Counseling & Values, 50,* 99–107.

Welfel, E. R. (2006). *Ethics in counseling and psychotherapy: Standards, research, and emerging issues* (3rd ed.). Belmont, CA: Thomson Brooks/Cole.

Werth, J. L., Jr. (1999a). Mental health professionals and assisted death: Perceived ethical obligations and proposed guidelines for practice. *Ethics and Behavior, 9,* 159–183.

Werth, J. L., Jr. (1999b). When is a mental health professional competent to assess a person's decision to hasten death? *Ethics and Behavior, 9,* 141–157.

Werth, J. L., Jr. (2002). Legal and ethical considerations for mental health professionals related to end-of-life care and decision making. *American Behavioral Scientist, 46,* 373–388.

Werth, J. L., Jr., Benjamin, G. A. H., & Farrenkopf, T. (2000). Requests for physician assisted death: Guidelines for assessing mental capacity and impaired judgment. *Psychology, Public Policy, and Law, 6,* 348–372.

Werth, J. L., Jr., Blevins, D., Toussaint, K., & Durham, M. R. (2002). The influence of cultural diversity on end-of-life care and decisions. *American Behavioral Scientist, 46,* 204–219.

Werth, J. L., Jr., & Gordon, J. R. (2002). *Amicus curiae* brief for the United States Supreme Court on mental health issues associated with "physician-assisted suicide." *Journal of Counseling & Development, 80,* 160–172.

Werth, J. L., Jr., & Kleespies, P. M. (2006). Ethical considerations in providing psychological services in end-of-life care. In J. L. Werth Jr. & D. Blevins (Eds.), *Psychosocial issues near the end of life: A resource for professional care providers* (pp. 57–87). Washington, DC: American Psychological Association.

Werth, J. L., Jr., & Rogers, J. R. (2005). Assessing for impaired judgment as a means of meeting the "duty to protect" when a client is a potential harm-to-self: Implications for clients making end-of-life decisions. *Mortality, 10,* 7–21.

Working Group on Assisted Suicide and End-of-Life Decisions. (2000). *Report to the Board of Directors.* Washington, DC: American Psychological Association. Retrieved February 22, 2005, from http://www.apa.org/pi/aseolf.html

Yalom, I. D., with Leszcz, M. (2005). *The theory and practice of group psychotherapy* (5th ed.). New York: Basic Books.